My Soul brother.

I look forward to spending time with you.

Love is the remedy! Spread the word!

More to come.

Love,

John

BORN TO HEAL

HEAL YOURSELF
HEAL THE WORLD

Luke Adler

HEALER PRESS

Born to Heal: Heal Yourself, Heal the World
© 2016 Luke Adler

Case Studies reflect actual patient experiences. Names and pertinent details have been changed to protect the identity of individuals.

Printed in the United States of America

Cover Photo: Sean Desmond
Cover Design: Claire Flint Last

Healer Press
1633 Willamette St.
Eugene, OR 97403

LCCN: 2016935748
ISBN: 978-0-692665-0-77

Dedicated to the Light in You

You are Beautiful. You are Exquisite. The most sublime, wonderful, blissful experience you've ever had times one thousand does not come close to how Incredible you are. You are more brilliant than ten thousand suns and ten thousand moons. You are the perfect reflection of the Highest Himalayan peaks in still, glacial-fed, high mountain lakes. You are the Purest Light. Your Effulgence is more magnificent than the Milky Way and Andromeda. You are the Dream of all Dreams come true.

You are every auspicious wish and hope. You are Pure. You are Powerful. Your Beauty is unmatched and adored by all beings seen and unseen. Mother Nature bows at your feet with great reverence and adulation. You are the most Excellent, the Highest. You are Supreme. You are the embodiment of unadulterated Love and Joy. You are the most Beautiful Light I have ever seen. You are Divine.

Your purpose is to Love yourself and everything you see into wholeness. As you trust the Divinity within to guide your life and show you how to heal, the outer world heals as well. As you realize your supreme Beauty, the darkness and dysfunction of the external world submits to the powerful, shining, brilliance of your Supreme Heart. Brighter than that brightest sun in the cosmos, your destiny is to shine your Light upon this planet and make Earth the paradise it is meant to be. You are Divine and your purpose is to Love yourself and everything you see into wholeness.

When in doubt, choose Love. You can't go wrong.

CONTENTS

The Tools

Namaste

CONTENTS

About This Book

Born to Heal is based on the belief that disease originates when we are disconnected from the heart. Just like other seekers, I discovered this truth through my journey of self-exploration, a journey that we each make, individually and together. This truth always exists and only awaits our realization.

When I was thirteen, I discovered God inside my heart and inside everything that exists. Through meditation and the practice of eastern yoga I found a method to know God. After my initial taste of the Divine, I was hooked. As a teenager, I became fervently devoted to meditation and chanting, eagerly striving for enlightenment. In time, I came to realize enlightenment was not a far-off destination, but a natural evolution of doing one's spiritual work.

I am enlightened and so are you. Every day the Universe gives us an opportunity to become, feel, and grow our "Light". And every day I am grateful for that gift and re-commit to that choice to nurture a relationship with Spirit. My mission is to help grow the Light and support others to do the same.

I am a mystic and a healer. I am compelled by this inner force to make an offering of my innermost Heart, in hopes that it may be supportive and add light to the already increasing pool of Love in the Universe. I was born to heal and so were you. Our destinies are to make this beautiful planet reflect the inherent dignity and wholeness that never changes and is the very core of our being. You and each of us have a mystical core that connects you to God. I can help you know that mysterious place and bring it out and into your life.

From the outside I look like any other person. But on the inside is a deep connection with the Divine, a connection that continues to grow and blossom. I've tried to do and be other things in my life, but nothing satisfies my soul more than dipping into the awareness of Universal Love and sharing this experience with others. There is not even a close second.

As I embarked on my studies of eastern mysticism, Chinese medicine, and meditation, many universal truths became apparent to me. One of them is that the body offers feedback—a yardstick, if you like—for how to navigate your life lessons. The Universe uses the process of disease to get your attention. Before communication from the Universe reaches your physical body, it first occurs in your heart. The body provides numerous cues as to what areas of spiritual growth you most need to work with and heal to further evolve. There are no accidents. The Universe uses everything, down to the minutest detail to help each one of us grow towards love. *Born to Heal* teaches a way to hear universal messages to help guide you towards your most optimal life path.

The material ahead is informative, poetic, gritty, and at times challenging. Go as deep as you can. You can revisit this material throughout your life and find new insights and breakthroughs each time you do. Mixed with personal reflections, case studies, and teachings from the ancient traditions of Chinese Medicine and the yogic traditions of India, *Born to Heal* is my attempt to be completely transparent, honest, and vulnerable about the healing journey, both my own and the journeys of people who have blessed me with the opportunity to serve them. I hope that you'll be inspired to create a stronger connection with the Universe, and discover and deepen your ability to take a more active role in your own healing.

As you read this book, you may feel like you're waiting for me to offer some technique or teaching that will *fix* you. I'm not here to fix you. For one thing, I do not see you as broken. You may hold a radically different point of view from mine, or occasionally think that what I'm saying is crazy. No matter. I invite you to take full ownership of your thoughts, feelings, and reactions. The more this material provokes you, the more there is to look at and ask, *What is really triggering my reaction?*

I'm not interested in being placed on a pedestal. If you put me above you, at some point you will have to chop me down to claim your divine Nature, and I don't want that.

Meet me as a friend, a guide, a facilitator, and a companion on the path. Allow me to point out easeful ways to grow. I have my shortcomings and I've learned to love them. I can teach you to do the same. Loving the parts of yourself that you don't love is the key to healing and enlightenment. I offer you the possibility of finding a satisfaction in life that will allow you to freely and purposefully live from your heart.

I do not believe progress in life is accidental or up to chance. If you want to grow, heal and evolve, choose to do that now. Open yourself up to Universal Support to show the Universe that you want to move forward. And then apply the effort required of you. I invite all of you to come forward and take up this work in the deepest possible way right now.

If you accept my invitation, take a deep breath in and say out loud,

I am open to Universal Support. I'm ready to move forward in my life in the highest possible way.

Throughout *Born to Heal* I use the word *Universe* and occasionally interchange it with *God, Spirit, Nature, Divine, Love* and *Grace*. At times I draw distinctions between these concepts. The word *Healing* can be interchanged with *Growth, Maturation, Enlightenment* and *Evolution*. For some, the word healing implies something broken that needs to be fixed. On that note, let me say this, there is nothing wrong with you or your body. There is nothing to fix or mend. There are only places you have yet to know, explore, and love. On a practical level, medical intervention may be necessary for your improved health. Alone, they will not heal you. Healing happens inside your heart.

I invite you to use the practice of self-inquiry as a pathway to spiritual growth and physical health. Like riding a bike, once you see your blind spots, they'll never blind you again. Most healing occurs simply by witnessing the once unconscious parts of your self. When you see it, you can free it. You can make a new choice empowered by your deepest wishes for well being.

Healing is not black and white. It is an exploration of contradictions that requires steadiness, openness, and self-love. It necessitates asking questions, listening to answers, and sometimes embracing uncomfortable truths.

Steadfast dedication is required to persist in the face of life's challenges. The great meditation master, Maharishi Mahesh Yogi says, you can dig a shallow well over and over, but to find the thirst-quenching water that you seek, you must dig deeply in one spot. Some eclectic seekers pick and choose parts and pieces of ritual and philosophy from this or that tradition. That may be fine at the outset of the path, but I have observed that this smorgasbord approach to spiritual growth becomes an excuse to avoid commitment and going deep. If you are not committed on your spiritual journey, you may not be committed in other places in your life.

My grandfather said, "There are many roads to the top of the mountain. Choose one." The higher you climb, the better your vantage point of the world before you. As your view becomes more expansive, you make connections about where you've come from and how you've arrived. No matter how high you reach on your journey, you'll only see the entire view when you reach the top. Keep striving! Don't give up! If you want to have a breakthrough, get committed and get invested. Go!

No matter what religious background or spiritual inclination resonates with you, the information here is universal. Though I lean to mystical paths of the East, this book is not a recruitment tool for my personal traditions. The path offered here will make you a better and healthier Catholic, Lutheran, Muslim, Hindu, Buddhist, Jew, Pagan, Jain, Seventh Day Adventist, Mormon, Republican, Democrat, or Independent. The right to know your true Nature is yours. Only you can find and know your divinity. *Born to Heal* can help you know the truth that can only be accessed by your own heart. To face the great unknown of the Universe and know it directly for yourself is the greatest adventure to be had. I wholeheartedly encourage you to begin, explore, refine, and enjoy.

Born to Heal exposes how our culture and current health care model reflect the fear of feeling emotion and listening to your own innate wisdom. As a healer, fifteen times a day I walk into small private treatment rooms and listen to individuals share health issues, secrets, fears, and insecurities. I comfort them when they cry, hold space for them to break through their perceptions and encourage them to heal.

I have the same conversations with everyone. People are afraid of the same things: to open up to their boss, spouse, kids, friends - and ultimately, self—about something that is true and meaningful. And most people are not aware that their neighbor is struggling with the same core issues. Part of the intention of *Born to Heal* is to engage in a powerful conversation about health, happiness, and fulfillment, and make it more public, normal and accepted; to change culturally how we view disease and health; and to have society reflect that underneath every complaint, is a desire for more love, intimacy, and connection to yourself and others. Together we can heal this world and ourselves!

We are here to heal, evolve, cultivate compassion and respect, and, over time, awaken to our Divine Nature. We have work to do on this planet. *Born to Heal* is part autobiography and part guidebook—a set of tools for the trade of life. In your hands is a tool to more intimately know yourself as human and divine. Read it in order, or start with the sections that call to you the most. Browse the table of contents, and pick a topic that appeals to you.

Some people have wanted to know how I became a healer, so I've included the story of my own journey. You can read how I discovered spirituality, and of the tenacious work of self-love that has been essential for my own healing. Chapter 1, "Wisdom From the Ancients," sets up the core ideas of the book. If you want to dive right into the crux of the work, start with the Heart chapter.

In each chapter of the Crux Section, I've included some Chinese medicine theory to show the interrelationship of emotion and physiology. I've presented the material for you to grasp the interplay between your intuition-emotions-behavior and symptoms. If at first things do not come together, stay with it. Some of these concepts need to germinate in your awareness before they reveal themselves. As you gain insight into what makes you sick, you also gain insight into what makes you feel connected, healthy, and whole. You will increase the power to create new patterns of health and vitality. The genius of Chinese medicine is that its core philosophy makes sense of the interplay between every aspect of your life in relation to your health.

Born to Heal has seventy-four exercises to help you uncover your unconscious beliefs and assumptions that keep you stuck in life. Some of these exercises will feel like soulful prayer, while others may feel like deep psychotherapy. The purpose of the exercises is to move the stagnant energy through your body. If an exercise triggers old emotions or memories, use the breathwork practice to clear the energy out of your body, taught in the tools section or found on my website on the product page (download the Heart Cleanse). Avoid getting bogged down in the need to understand your past. If you need to understand some aspect of your past in order to move on, your mind will persistently bring the issue to the surface for you to process. If you don't need to understand the issue, leave it alone. Trust the intelligence of your body, mind, and spirit to guide you.

Draw this material towards you. Grab a fresh journal and dive in. Underline, highlight, and write in the margins to reinforce your insights. This book is vibrating with life. Add your energy to it. Take my insights further by bringing them inside you to allow your Light to see beyond the words that convey this information. Leave this book in tatters. May it be a reliable companion for your journey and spur you forward to support the journey of others.

Further into the Light we go!

All Love, All Ways ... Luke

P.S. Can't wait to hear how it goes for you!

My Healing Journey

Today I have the privilege to do what I love. I create environments for people to experience their true Self. It may sound strange to say I give people an experience of the Ineffable, but it's true. How I do that is embedded in my own healing journey and the rest of this book.

Evolution is not about the survival of the fittest. It is about love. Those who choose love evolve. That's true not just during the good times, but even more so when you choose love during periods of turmoil and discomfort. Those who choose to contract and resist the Universe, only make their suffering worse.

Love is a winner. The part of you that resists and blames others is very small. The part of you that is made of love is enormous. Try as you might to resist, your ship has set sail. When you chose to incarnate, to come here and learn, the momentum of the deepest desire for freedom has set your course. Your destination is a continuous unraveling of a Love so expansive it will overwhelm you at times. It probable already has. That's partly what drew you to this book.

I didn't come to this awareness all at once. It happened over time with effort and a lot of grace. The same process is happening to you, whether you are aware of it or not.

My life did not always seem destined for such fulfillment. I was raised in Banning, California, a small, impoverished town in the middle of the desert between San Bernardino and Palm Springs. Although my family was comfortable compared to our neighbors, I witnessed the pain of my community.

My parents operated a factory that made fashion belts. They employed gang members from notorious street gangs like the

Crips and Hells Angels. I remember my dad being called to the hospital after a lead worker was stabbed in a gang fight. Even as a child I could sense that life was neither safe nor predictable.

One day, a third-grade classmate came to school with swastikas sketched all over his high-tops. I thought the symbol was cool, so I drew it on my shoulder that night before bed. During a Saturday morning cuddle session, my dad, who is Jewish, noticed the magenta swastika on my shoulder. He was infuriated, and yelled, "Wash that off right now!" I was shocked and confused. I had no clue what it meant and was stunned when he explained. Why would anyone proclaim hatred to others, let alone to a third grader? I'm saddened to think of the environment that surrounded my classmate. Hate is learned. It is not a natural state.

Another classmate, Paco, had an older brother in the infamous Crips gang. Paco recounted horrible and frightening events he witnessed and participated in afterschool and on weekends. Other friends and neighbors battled with cocaine and alcohol addiction. I witnessed many violent exchanges between parents and children during my early youth in Banning.

Life at home with my mom and dad starkly contrasted with life at school and visits to the homes of my friends who lived in poverty. My parents allowed me to roam freely in the San Jacinto Mountains and explore canyons and arroyos as I pretended to be a warrior. Though my own home life was wonderful, I remember thinking clearly even as a seven year old that I had to leave this town or my life would be destined for a miserable existence.

When I turned eight, we moved to Upland, California: the heart of the Inland Empire, forty-five minutes east of downtown Los Angeles, a vast improvement from Banning. I remember the foggy, misty mornings in the foothills, which laid flat at the base of ten-thousand foot Mount Baldy. Something about that fog felt like home. Perhaps it was a precursor to my future life in Oregon.

This was a classic coming of age time. My friendships felt deeply connected. I had five buddies. We were like brothers and spent everyday together in and after school until my freshman year of high school.

In late junior high and early high school we explored marijuana, cigarettes, and beer. Fortunately or not, drugs and alcohol were very hard to come by for kids our age. Usually we ended up smoking paper filled with oregano to see if we could get high. It didn't work, but it satisfied my rebellious side.

My friends in Upland were bright, athletic, and kind. However, the environment that awaited them in and after high school had a dark shadow. Two of my closest buddies were jailed for drug dealing and eventually served time in the state penal system. The others made it without such reprimands, but not without scars that diminished the bright innocence we had shared with one another.

Initial Awakening

Life closer to Los Angeles offered more diverse spiritual opportunities. After our exposure to Christianity, the faith tradition my mom was raised in, my dad wanted us to participate in Judaism. After elementary school let out, I attended two hours of Hebrew school. I learned the Aleph-Bet in preparation for my Bar Mitzvah, but preferred playing soccer to studying an ancient language. My parents honored my wish, so after two years, I quit Hebrew School to pursue soccer instead. Both Church and Temple were fine. But neither captivated my interest. Instead they both felt like a chore.

In the fall of 1993, when I was 13 years old, my mom met a woman at a PTA meeting. That encounter changed the course of my life. The woman asked my mom over for tea. Mom recognized a photo on her new friend's wall of a renowned meditation master. My mom Sandy, and dad, Will, had been teachers of Transcendental Meditation in the late '70 and early '80s. In the summer of 1980, their teacher, Maharishi Mahesh Yogi, had instructed all of his meditation teachers to visit a revered meditation master who had just arrived in Santa Monica to launch his world tour. At six months old, my parents brought me to a program to meet the revered saint. At the end of the program my parents stood in line for Darshan, a practice to offer gratitude to and receive blessings from the teacher. As an experienced meditator and teacher of meditation, my mom knew the powers of a Sanskrit mantra, and asked the teacher to give me a spiritual name.

Mom's new friend Maria had prayed before the PTA gathering to meet someone spiritual in this middle-class suburban community. When my Mom exclaimed, "Oh I've met him," Maria burst into tears before confiding her own amazing spiritual odyssey to my mother. In her early twenties, during a trip to Mexico, federales pulled her bus over. She was arrested for trespassing on a private beach. Incarcerated for weeks in a Mexican jail, Maria became desperate for help. She prayed to God, all the Catholic saints, and to some great being for help. Days later, a man came to her in a vision and assured her everything would be fine. A peace and ease washed over Maria; hours later, she was released from jail and on her way home to Southern California. Years later, she recognized this man from the vision in a framed picture at her cousin's house: It was the same meditation master my parents went to see with me as an infant in Santa Monica.

On a crisp fall day, a few weeks after meeting Maria, my family caravanned with Maria's big, beautiful, Italian household, to the Meditation Center in Los Angeles for a program. The celebratory tune of the harmonium and the Indian drum captivated me as we chanted exuberantly with a hundred other people in the mediation hall. I didn't know what the words meant, but chanting the words made me feel happy and alive. I delighted in watching my younger siblings laugh and dance in the back of the hall during the chant. Their favorite part of the evening was the fresh chocolate cake, cookies, and sweet chai tea after the program.

The center was an hour drive from Upland. We managed to attend program twice a month. I learned to chant Sanskrit mantras and meditate. After chanting for a half hour in the center, sitting for meditation came easy. My meditation practice at home was another story. The turbulent thoughts of my mind would not let up. It was challenging to find the stillness. I noticed even though my meditations were filled with thoughts, I began to feel better about myself.

A turning point in my meditation practice came a few months later. My mom drove my siblings and me to San Francisco for our first weekend meditation retreat with the head of the meditation lineage. As a thousand others and I entered the downtown hall, I felt a palpable, scintillating energy. The air had a silky and light texture. I'd never experienced anything like it before.

The first day, during a round of chanting, the teacher gracefully walked in and took her seat. She was the most beautiful being I had ever seen. She embodied grace and radiated Divine Love. She floated across the room like an angel. I felt a tingly sensation around my heart as she sat. The room was alive with electricity. The harmonium player began a chant to invoke grace. The refrain, I learned later, asks the teacher to "Light my heart with the light from your heart." Whenever I had chanted this song in the Los Angeles meditation center I felt so happy and joyful. This particular instance changed my understanding of life completely.

While singing the second verse, a sensation from the very bottom of my spine pulsated and then whipped quickly back and forth through my lower vertebrae like a snake. It felt pleasant. I continued to chant, not knowing what was happening to me. The strong energy moved decisively as it rose through the middle of my back. I felt a surging force move through my heart that caused my neck to snap upright as the energy pierced the top of my head. My body shook wildly in wave-like motions. Near the end of the chant, my body relaxed. I felt like I was a baby in my mother's arms and began to cry. A space in the center of my chest opened up like a blooming rose and filled with a very warm liquid. My heart erupted with a powerful feeling of love. A profound sense of coming home moved through me. I felt more loved, safe, and understood than at any other moment in my life.

As my sense of homecoming deepened, I had the most distinct awareness that I had been searching for this sense of home for lifetimes and had now, finally, deeply, and completely found it. I wept with gratitude, so thankful for this sense of arrival and the astonishing energy and peace that came with it.

In a flash, questions I'd wondered about were answered: Who am I? Why am I here? What is my purpose? I suddenly felt suffused with clarity: I am Divine. I'm here to share Love and help others along the path. A wonderful sense of contentment washed over me. I was home, inside my Heart, connected to my Divine Source.

Later, I learned that the spiritual energy known as Kundalini Shakti had awoken within me. As I shared my experience with other meditators, many said they'd had similar experiences. One of the meditation monks explained to me that the Shakti lays dormant at the base of one's spine, until the time has come for it to be awakened, usually through the grace of a meditation master. The Shakti is supremely intelligent. It purifies the mind and body as it guides the spiritual aspirant along the path of liberation.

I didn't fully understand the experience, but my life at home began to dramatically improve.

Prior to the program, I'd look in the mirror and think, *You're ugly and stupid, and nobody likes you.* These searing thoughts and feelings diminished noticeably after my first meditation retreat. The pressure to look cool, be liked, and act tough were replaced with ease and a feeling of gratitude to be alive. I felt comfortable in my skin for the first time in my life. I was so relieved to look in the mirror and smile at my reflection. I loved myself and it felt amazing. The summer of 1994, less than nine months after my first visit to the Meditation Center, I became very involved in my new spiritual path. I continued to go to programs in Los Angeles with my family, and continued to meditate for twenty minutes in the morning.

Prior to my awakening, I was dreadfully shy, easily embarrassed, painfully sensitive and insecure. I was a dork, a nerdy, gangly boy who earned slightly above average grades. After my awakening, the fear, shame, shyness, and embarrassment that had been my constant companions fell away. In the space that opened, the natural light of my heart expressed confidence, friendliness, humor, and love. The angst-ridden teenage boy turned into a kind, open-hearted, lover of life.

For the first time, I could comprehend what I was reading. I could focus for much longer periods of time. My grades improved. Girls began to look at me differently. It wasn't because my appearance had changed. My classmates were attracted to the divine energy glowing in me. I so badly wished that they could experience the Truth inside themselves. I introduced a few of my buddies to chanting and meditation. After soccer practice we chanted, danced, and talked about the nature of reality.

In the winter of my freshman year, my family and I moved to Eugene, Oregon. I blossomed. It was as if a genie appeared and granted me all my wishes. Instant popularity, great friends, awesome teachers and classes, varsity and club soccer, adventure, the outdoors, all with a pristine sense of innocence and purity that I hadn't felt in Southern California. I knew the results of the drastic changes in my life were to a large extent due to my meditation practice and encounter with the striking female Guru.

Ironically, as my desires for popularity and admiration were fulfilled, I lost interest in them and became aware how they left me unfulfilled. Exploring alcohol and marijuana with my friends made me notice their dulling impact. They compared poorly to the intoxication of meditation and chanting. As I tasted the inner fulfillment that came with meditation, I saw my true path clearly.

I immersed myself in meditation, Vedic chanting, and the teachings of the lineage of my Indian meditation master. I wanted only one thing, to become fully enlightened. I delved deeper in exploration of myself. I read books about the teachings of meditation and autobiographies of spiritual masters. I dedicated myself to the path with tremendous fervor and longing to fully know my Divine Nature. I wrote my senior thesis on a venerated Hindu text, Narada's Bhakti Sutras on Divine Love and tried to apply the master's ancient teachings to my modern-day high school life.

The Revelation

I first visited my Guru's Meditation Ashram on the East Coast in the summer of 1995. I was fifteen. The two weeks I spent there rocked my world.

For months, I'd eagerly anticipated visiting the epicenter of this great meditation tradition. As my mom, brother and I drove closer to the ashram, I felt a tingling sensation wash over my entire body. With my first step across the threshold of the ashram grounds, I felt as if someone had lifted a fifty-pound weight off my shoulders. That evening I fell asleep at 7 p.m. I awoke the next day at 5 p.m. I'd slept for nearly twenty-four hours. I felt refreshed, alert, and rejuvenated like I'd never felt in my life.

I was lucky to spend several months at the ashram over the next five summers. There, I had frequent powerful visions and experiences that awakened me to the Divine. I experienced states of consciousness that I later read about in the autobiographies of various meditation masters. During my second summer, I took a meditation course about the first guru of the meditation lineage. I had an experience that defined the course of my life and is at the heart of my healing work.

I sat deep in meditation. The hall was completely silent, with the faint glow of blue LED lights lining the periphery of the room. In the dim light, I could make out the silhouettes of other meditators absorbed in the palpable meditation energy of the course. Suddenly from a silent and serene place in my consciousness, awareness of my body vanished. My sense of self merged with endless space. Out of the dark, borderless void, a leaf made of scintillating gold drifted high above me. From a perch above my body, I watched the leaf shift as it descended with a luminous glow, back and forth through the darkness. The leaf settled on top of my head and melted into my body. The imprint of the leaf on top of my head felt instantly warm and soothing as my skull filled with a liquid of golden honey that penetrated downwards into my spine. When the energy arrived at my heart, a pleasant sensation like a rose blooming spread through the middle of my upper chest. Tears poured from my eyes like a waterfall as my heart melted open, vulnerable and safe. Warmth moved through the chambers of my heart and surged through my body. The darkness of meditation instantly transformed into a blanket of white and golden light. An overpowering sense of love, fulfillment, and safety came over me. Then a powerful recognition arose as my body began to tremble with increasing intensity. I cried uncontrollable tears, feeling ecstatic bliss roll through my body. I cried tears filled with gratitude for life. I cried for a love that I had unknowingly longed for, which now felt deeper than I could have imagined. I knew then what the ancient sages meant when they spoke of bliss. The liquid golden honey energy poured wave after wave of bliss through my body. Tears of joy flowed down my face. I was in disbelief as my experience increased in ecstasy.

After a half-hour of this captivating experience, my eyes gently opened. Hungry, I made my way down a silent path through birch and maple forest towards the dining hall. My inner bliss increased, along with the tears. Even with my eyes open, bliss and love continued to build inside of me. My love for life and for people grew and grew. I wanted to grab people by the shoulders and tell them, "You are soooo beautiful."

I could see with utter clarity the precious and sacred nature of life. The profound knowing of all life as sacred moved deeper in my heart. I trembled with gratitude. Out of this sweet experience of bliss, the thought rang through my mind:

Do people know how beautiful they are?

The thought continued to reverberate through my being. Love moved through my heart with more power and force: Do people know how beautiful they are?

The thought played over and over through my consciousness. I could think of nothing else. Do people know how beautiful they are? Again and again, the thought persisted. Do people know that inside them is everything they are searching for on the outside?

I knew I was experiencing a shift in the trajectory of my life. I became aware that my calling was to help others experience, know, and trust their divine beauty and to live a life that reflects that understanding. I did not know how I was going to accomplish this. I trusted that the path would reveal itself to me.

While at the ashram, I learned a story about the life of one of the meditation masters of this lineage. He was known to have miraculous healing abilities. People came from all of India to the great master to ask for healings. As a young man, after hearing their petitions, he was known to climb trees with medicinal qualities. After he reached a certain height he plucked several leaves and floated them down to the grateful people below, and then advised them how to take the medicine.

I realized that I had been the recipient of one of the master's medicinal leaves. His medicine healed any inner doubt of my Divine Nature and the Divine Nature of all beings. The experience marked in me a burning desire to pursue my spiritual path to its completion and to provide others a space to heal to whatever extent they are ready.

Over the next six months, I had more similar spontaneous experiences. I became increasingly anchored in an expanded awareness. From the first program in Los Angeles to my three-month pilgrimage after graduate school to the Mother Ashram in India, my relationship to the Divine has fueled every aspect of my life. The grace of my spiritual path shifted the trajectory of my life from one rooted in insecurity and a trajectory of possible substance abuse to a life of tremendous blessings and abundance.

The grace and teachings of the meditation masters of this path healed deep inner feelings that I was unworthy of love and happiness. The early years of my spiritual path directed my life towards fulfillment and healing. My path was clear. Each experience made me hungrier for liberation. While I may have looked like any other surfer or soccer dude, I knew I was a mystic, utterly devoted to the path of enlightenment.

Meditation was not a cure-all for my problems. It gave me the clarity to see that I had a choice. I could choose to see the lesson or choose to point blame. Overtime, I gained the courage to see that my unworthiness and insecurity were begging to be healed, not concealed. I learned to direct tenderness towards my reluctance to let love into these vulnerable parts of my life. Insecurity and unworthiness became new pathways for love to flow. With every opportunity to choose love over unworthiness, my confidence in the Universe and myself grew. Eventually, I came to fully know that the Universe pushes fear, hatred, and darkness to the surface of life for healing, not suffering. My purpose was clear: be steadfast with my spiritual practices and create an environment for people to experience the Divine.

Through meditation, acupuncture, and a desire to heal, I've witnessed transformations in clients from every walk of life: elementary school teachers, insurance agents, interior designers, college students, carpenters and entrepreneurs. Everyday, I witness people discover experiences of inner peace and joy and begin to drop many of their negative habits. Loving your life is not just possible. It's highly probable. Choose to believe in love. You'll surprise yourself with how wonderful you are.

RENUNCIATION AND HEALING

I searched and worked hard to find a career path that would integrate my spiritual development. At first, the two didn't mix well.

In my 20s, an intense desire within me longed to embrace renunciation and live in an ashram. I saw a future self with a shaved head, prayer beads, and the orange robes of a monk. While I was at the ashram, my predominant state was joy, peace, and quietude, with my awareness anchored firmly on the inner Light. I wanted to remain in the Ashram and continue to pursue my spiritual practices. However, my meditation master was no longer initiating new monks. She encouraged young people to be in the world while maintaining their spiritual practices. Despite my deep inner longing to renounce, I listened to her instruction. Years later, I realized her message was simple. Do spiritual practices. Be responsible. Make a difference. The next ten years, I learned how to do that.

My dad established the spirit of entrepreneurship for the family and me. He created a business for my brother and me called The Belt Boys. As kids we sold belts and wallets at street fairs, flea markets, craft fairs, and rodeos in California and Oregon. My dad made sure I had the skills to make a living; he kept me engaged in the world as I struggled with the desire to cloister myself.

In June 2001, I graduated from the University of Oregon with a major in International Studies and a minor in Spanish. Simultaneously the relationship with my college sweetheart ended. I could not reconcile a deeper commitment to a woman with such intense feelings for God. I was distraught and lacked clear direction. I began to think seriously about my vocation. The desire to share the inner experience of love and freedom with others grew stronger. I felt that the only way for the world to change was for people to know their divine beauty. I did not understand how to live in the world with an awakened state; I struggled not to feel dissociated from the world and people, and worked to develop an ability to engage in relationships, in part to find a job. I also realized the robes of a monk would limit my exposure only to a narrow range of people.

My experience of the Divine was not about Hindu mysticism or any other single tradition. Divine beauty transcended all surface categorization. Divine beauty is the True Nature of all beings. I needed a more universal approach to share my truth.

I asked myself, *How can I create an environment for people to discover their True Nature?* The desire to study and practice medicine resurfaced. As I explored my healing journey, I noticed how illness does not discriminate based on religious, political, or social customs. Medicine became my doorway to serve others, which led eventually to the rich tradition of Chinese medicine. It captivated my attention because it views all illness as an imbalance of one's spirit. I'd found my vehicle to express my heart and live in the world. A decade later, I realized the external choice to become a monk or a healer did not change my longing and dedication to the spiritual path. It only changed the way I share the path with others.

PEACE WITH MOM AND DAD

As a new father I can already see some of my willfulness in my baby girl. I can picture my dad holding me thinking, *This kid is cute, but can someone make him stop screaming?* Recently, I learned that my dad used to love the smell of my breath when he held me. The image of that brings a smile to my face and warms my heart. Parenting is a deeply rewarding challenge and a great teacher.

Two significant relationships that reflect the majority of life lessons are those with Mom and Dad. Parents are our first teachers. Classically for men, the relationship with their fathers will be more challenging and for women, the relationship with their mothers. As a healer who specializes in the mind/body/spirit connection, I have worked with thousands of people around relationship with their parents. I have found it to be essential to heal one's relationships with parents in order to heal physical and emotional pain.

We're all hardwired to desire love and attention from our parents. And yet our parents have to prepare us to live in the world. This can create friction and difficulty around loving and feeling loved. Often we project the parts of our relationship with our parents that feel incomplete onto our relationships with significant others. We tend to attract romantic partners, bosses, or close friends who will allow us to work through the issues with our parents. One example is having a needy parent and unconsciously looking for a needy partner, or a parent who is harsh and withholds love, and then looking for a partner who is unavailable or a bad communicator. You might have a smothering parent and choose a bad boy/girl partner who is rebellious. Most people look for a partner very like or just the opposite of a parent.

Classical Chinese medicine declares that the mother's job is to nurture and nourish the child's emotional and physical development. Note that masculine and feminine in Chinese medicine is *yang* and *yin*, which is not determined by gender. Thus, a mother can often play the yang/masculine role and vice versa. The father's job is to nurture the child's potential and prepare him/her for "the real world." When a father is absent in a child's life, the child can have trouble grasping the present moment and difficulty expressing himself or herself freely. In a child whose father is missing, the lungs are particularly impacted. The mother's role is to connect the child with his/her emotions and inner life. With a missing or unhappy mother, the child may have trouble bonding, and once bonded, may experience separation anxiety.

When I was a kid, my parents feverishly operated their business. My father often traveled weeks at a time to maintain sales and put food on the table. I missed him. I have a distinct memory of playing soccer as a kid and suddenly gasping for air. I panicked for what seemed like minutes until a normal breathing rhythm came over me. From the Chinese medicine perspective, my breathing issues were related to the lack of my father's presence at the time. As business became more stable, Dad was around more and my breathing issues settled down.

As my spirituality developed, I became very comfortable and confident with the feminine side of my being. My dad noticed this. He often told me, "Get out of your head, and get into the real world!" I was always annoyed when he said that. Plus, I didn't really know what he meant. To relate to me, he recounted a story of his acting teacher Milton Katseles.

Before my parents married, Dad returned from a six month meditation training in Mallorca, Spain with his meditation teacher Maharishi Mahesh Yogi. When he returned to acting class, his teacher Milton noticed that my dad wasn't emoting with as much intensity and ferocity as he had before his trip to Spain. Milton told him to stop meditating. My dad took Milton's instruction to mean that meditation kept him from being as emotional and expressive as he could be.

My own experiences of meditation and yoga were expansive and powerful. The intensity and fervor for my longing to know God was insatiable. The inner fire to know the Divine was so hot, nothing could put it out. No one and nothing could have convinced me that there was anything more important than my own spiritual growth and to share spirituality with the others. So my dad's opinion of meditation put me in direct conflict with him.

Now, as a father, I can see and appreciate the immense challenge of simultaneously providing for my family and nurturing my spirituality. It takes effort to care for my wellbeing and make quality family time. I have also noticed a random streak of anger and irritability arise during the months of sleepless nights sitting with my newborn daughter. I'm so thankful for the life my dad provided for me. He gave me an incredible start both as a child and a young adult, even as he faced professional challenges in my early years.

After I graduated college, I worked for Dad's company. The fashion industry proved intense. Deadlines, stress, and pressure were my first exposure to the work place. After a Las Vegas trade show, I felt a serious constriction around my chest and a twenty-pound weight pressing my shoulders down. That's when I thought about Dad's "real world."

Dad encouraged me to volunteer. During cold winter evenings, I passed out food and clothes to homeless youth living on the streets. These hours of service kept me connected to the spirit of giving. I felt renewed and purposeful after volunteering. I also realized how fortunate I was to have a father who cared about me. My interest in healing came knocking again.

I visited medical schools and shadowed physicians in Seattle and Eugene. One doctor suggested I visit Bastyr University in Seattle. When I arrived at Bastyr, a few Chinese medicine classes were about to begin. I sat in to observe. Quickly, I recognized that Chinese medicine was a great fit for me. I researched schools and found the website for Emperors College of Traditional Chinese Medicine. It called to my soul. The founder, Bong Dal, says, "The effectiveness of a Superior Physician depends upon his or her ability to be a clear conduit through which energy can flow. Beyond wisdom and intellect, this requires an open heart." I visited the campus in Santa Monica and applied for admission a few weeks later. At Emperor's I was able to integrate my spiritual, intellectual, and entrepreneurial selves. It was a magical, arduous, and deeply rewarding education with the great luxury of being surrounded by like-minded and like-hearted professors and colleagues.

Shrimp Shack

The most challenging relationship of my youth was with Dad. The difficult lessons I learned with him were sometimes suffused with anger and yelling matches. Beneath any anger, I felt a love so intense that I was afraid to express it by really being myself and standing up for it whether he liked it or not. A series of confrontations with him finally led us to speaking instead of yelling, and hugging instead of walking out and slamming doors. The confrontations taught me how to release and express the love inside me and prepared me to bring my gifts to the world.

The father has a tough role, because the world is tough. At some point the father negotiates how to fashion his children into people who can succeed when he is no longer present to protect them. One of the most defining moments with my father that helped me step into my role as a man occurred during a lunch on Kauai. The "shrimp shack incident" was this kind of growing event.

The Christmas before I graduated from Emperor's College, I went on a family vacation to Hawaii. Dad was irritable and edgy. He always needed a few days to de-stress from entrepreneurial mode; this trip was no exception.

The shrimp shack chef served up plates of fresh-grilled coconut shrimp and steamed rice. We dove into the island treat with tremendous delight. Midway through our meal, my dad asked about the ten-day healing retreats I'd recently led in Oaxaca, Mexico. "What did you do at your retreats?" he inquired. I shared about the spiritual work and shamanic rituals my business partner and I led. He replied curtly, "Get into the real world." Rather than swallow his criticism like I had in the past, I faced the anger that rose up within me.

"What's your problem?" I said.

"Your yoga, spiritual bullshit!" said Dad.

At this point, my mom, brother, and sister coughed up their shrimp and backed away from the table as the two bulls (we share the star sign of Taurus) began to stomp their feet, ready to attack. I grabbed the lunch table, lifted it overhead and threw it at the shrimp shack. Then I marched across the street towards our car.

"Just gonna walk away?" Dad said.

I turned around and looked at him straight in the eye,

"Do you have a problem with me?" he shouted.

"Yeah I do." I yelled back "You think you can just pick on people. You think you can treat them like shit and they're gonna do what you want?"

At that point, as the scene escalated closer to physical violence,

Mom told us to get in the car. We started to drive away, but Mom noticed we'd destroyed picnic tables and chairs. She said, "Someone go clean that up." I jumped out and told the guy in the shrimp truck, "Sorry for making a scene," as I put his furniture back in order. "It's okay," he said. "I've had my share of confrontations with my father. Have a nice day."

Strangely, I was comforted by his aloha spirit. *I guess we all have shit to work out with our parents*, I thought.

When I got back in the car my heart cracked open as tears of sadness and relief soaked my T-shirt. I had never spoke to my father like that. We arrived at a beach on east side of Poipu. I laced my running shoes and jogged down a sugar cane road. I felt overwhelmed by ancient sadness. The sadness was connected to lifetimes of confrontation with authority. I felt a sense of freedom and strength grow inside of me. A resounding thought played over in my mind, "Dad, I love you and I'm not afraid you." I realized I was OK being myself, with or without my father's approval. I felt good. I ran faster and faster and I cried harder.

As my feet pounded the red earth, I felt more love for my father and for myself. I was angry that we'd spoken so harshly to one another. I didn't like that we were so ferocious with our words. But the interaction healed tremendous pain and fear inside me. I'd claimed an aspect of my manhood and gained freedom from feeling diminished by authority. My dad's criticism presented me with a choice. I became clear about expressing the importance of spirituality in my life, whether my dad agreed with me or not. With reflection, I saw confrontations with my father as opportunities for me to build confidence, rather than to feel oppressed or just cave in to his perspective. I learned that the people with whom we have the most difficulty can evoke a hidden reservoir of love in us, if we're willing to see our reflection in them.

- *Have I experienced a Shrimp Shack moment in my life?*

- *How did I choose to act in the heat of it?*

- *Did I speak my truth?*

- *How did I feel afterwards?*

- *Is there someone in my life that I feel suppressed by?*

- *What keeps me from speaking up? (Notice the commentary your mind comes up with, and the fear or other emotions underneath it all.)*

If you have developed the habit of suppressing your truth, you allow people into your life who are oppressive to you. Until you learn to speak your truth, you will attract people to help you learn this lesson. This exercise is an energetic primer to help you get ready to go deep into how suppression works through you. In the coming sections of *Born to Heal*, you will dive into the nature of suppression, how it affects your health, and what you can do to shift this insidious driver of dis-ease. Good job! Stay with it!

STANDING ON MOM AND DAD'S SHOULDERS

After the shrimp shack event, I had more conviction about my purpose, more able to assert myself, and more ready to take my place in the world.

One afternoon, in a discussion with a business coach, I shared my concerns that my dad worked too hard and my fears over his health. Her reply took me aback: "Have you told him that?"

I coughed up a feeble, "No." Her next question, of course, was "When are you going to tell him?" *Damn,* I thought to myself.

The next day I began to tremble inside when I called my dad and said, "Dad, I want to share something with you. I worry about your health, with how hard you work. I wanted you to know." When he answered, "Thank you for telling me. To tell you the truth, I didn't know that you cared so much." An upwelling of tears surged from the depth of my stomach up to my heart and throat. As I cried, I said, "Dad, I do care so much, and I love you." He asked, "Is this why you're so hesitant around me?" "Yes," I blurted.

I'll never forget the calm and clear tone in his voice when he said, "I want you to know that I love what I do. I love every minute of it. I am having so much fun, and you stand on the shoulders of your mother and me. I love you," he said. "I'm proud of you. I release you. Go forward and make a difference in the world." As he said this, a flutter of energy from my toes through my gut released. I felt as if wings spontaneously grew out of my shoulder blades. For the first time in years I actually said in a volume that was audible: "I love you Dad." Then we chatted and said good-bye. After I hung up I began to vomit copious amounts of phlegm and saliva. I purged myself from the weight of withholding my love and concern for my dad. As the phlegm dissolved a great heat released throughout my body.

I knew that I loved my dad. He hadn't known that. When I communicated my love to him, I was also able to receive his love, empowerment, and charge to be someone who takes advantage of the gifts he has been given from his parents and make a difference in the world. I didn't know that withholding love could make you sick until I went through this experience. I was possessed by the fear to share my concern. When I released that fear, an old place of hurt filled with a new power to love.

The great adventure I'm having with my father is still unfolding. After I graduated from Emperor's College, passed my boards, and returned from a pilgrimage to India, I was nearly $100,000 in debt and had no idea where I was going to practice. My dad's encouragement and guidance gave me the confidence to go into business for myself right after school, something all medical providers agree is the hardest way to break into the profession. I decided to start my practice in Eugene because I had the most support there, and because Eugene is a place I love. I had the naive notion that people were going to show up and fill my practice because I had a degree, and because I'm a good healer and a compassionate, likeable person. This is where I learned about the "real world" that Dad had so often reminded me of while growing up.

HEALER, THE FIRST DAYS

I chose to study Chinese medicine because, of the major forms of health care in America, it is the only one that acknowledges that the health of someone's spirit is related and vital to the overall health of the body.

Chinese medicine has the means to heal the spirit. This guiding principle is the cornerstone of my healing practice and all other dimensions of my life.

When I graduated, I was determined to start a practice that exemplified the mind-body-spirit connection I had studied for four plus years. I was full of idealism. I leased a space, remodeled it, and hung up an Open for Business sign. I thought the world was going to open up for me and all I had to do was show up. The rude awakening didn't take long.

My first patients were my mom, my brother, some high school buddies, and their moms. You get the idea. I was not emotionally prepared to take full responsibility for someone else's health care. In the past there had always been a supervising clinician. But now, I was on my own to help my patients get better. For the first time, I felt the energetic weight of full responsibility for someone's health.

An old saying goes, "All is well when mother is home. When mother leaves, the children quickly feel insecure." Insecurity and anxiety gripped me, even though I'd been a hotshot intern at my various clinical internships, applying my spirituality and new-found knowledge freely and with confidence. The first six months on my own, responsible to help alleviate my patients' major physical and emotional symptoms, I trembled daily. Fortunately, my training kicked in and over-rode my freshman jitters.

I was overwhelmed financially, from school debt and start up costs for the clinic. News of my classmates experiencing the same dreary prospects elsewhere didn't make it any better. I barely made ends meet, lived at my parents' place, and wore my dad's over-sized hand-me-down business attire to work. Noticing my meager plight, Dad bought me a suit, and some dress shirts and ties. His incessant drive to "get the customer," as he called it, served me tremendously. I was finally receptive and eager for his coaching.

I had only one option: to put one foot in front of the other, open my mouth, and start sharing about healing with anyone who would listen. The magic word that I dreaded hearing tumbled from his lips and those of fellow entrepreneurs: networking. I became a regular at Chamber of Commerce meetings, business networking meetings, booster associations, wellness guilds, and wellness and business fairs at local businesses and the community college. I joined the ranks of plumbers, lawyers, insurance salesmen, network marketers, doctors, journeymen, all selling themselves.

If there was an invitation to meet people, my answer was "Yes!" I got over my snobbery and got with the program. I practiced my thirty-second elevator speech at 6 a.m. and stood up in front of up to two hundred people and started sharing, four days a week.

Hi, my name is Luke Adler. I practice Chinese medicine and acupuncture. I specialize in the treatment of orthopedic pain, in-

somnia, and depression. Right now, I'm offering a promotion for a free initial consultation. If you have any health concerns, I'd be happy to discuss them with you.

At first I was mortally embarrassed, viewing jail as preferable to such vulnerability. *I'm a healer, not a car salesman,* I told myself. Then I realized that we are all salesmen, even those who are a teacher, lawyer, doctor, or mom. We're selling what we know how to do to others who need our expertise. My hubris and entitlement dissolved through the salesmanship initiation. As I became a better salesman, I felt less corny and more authentic. I started to really understand that my opinion of myself only got in the way of helping people. So I stopped worrying about me and started to focus on people and their needs.

I believed in my product and began to speak more freely about Chinese Medicine and myself. I committed to morning networking meetings and walked the streets of Eugene handing out flyers and business cards. I hosted open houses and invited people. At one, my dad showed up and declared to fifty strangers "Luke is the best healer in the world!" *Good Lord,* I thought. *How could he say such an ostentatious thing?* I was completely embarrassed. I learned that my embarrassment didn't matter one bit. It worked; my dad brought me new business. I got over my shyness and started to step into being the healer he saw and that I wanted to be.

The more I embraced this idea, the faster my practice grew. People didn't care if I was embarrassed. They wanted to know if I could help their kid get over croup, or alleviate menopausal hot-flashes, insomnia, depression, or fatigue from the side effects of chemotherapy drugs. I could help those conditions improve and that's what mattered. Looking good and being liked in the process was only useful if it accompanied making chronic lower back pain diminish, even if by only thirty percent.

A month in, a woman named Juliette Mulgrew (who has since

become a naturopathic doctor) walked into my clinic looking for a job. She volunteered to help build the practice. Within a month, I was able to pay her, and the rent, and the utilities. I believe Juliette is an angel sent to help me help others. Even the networking meetings and promotional events became fun with her as my sidekick.

I learned how to build a practice, help people, and make a living. I could feel myself becoming emotionally and intellectually stronger. As a healer, I'd had a notion that patients would just flow towards me. But the business world doesn't work like that. A river needs a source. I learned that if I wanted more patients, I had to ask for them. As I continued to reach out to new patients, my dad asked, "What happened to the people who stopped coming in for treatment?" "I don't know." I replied, dumbfounded. He said, "Call them and find out." *Shit!* Again he saw the chink in my armor. My dad could smell fear.

The philosophy he taught me was simple: wherever you find fear, move towards it and you'll find expansion. This lesson was painful for me. I felt embarrassed and ashamed, afraid and unworthy, to ask people to try me out and even more afraid to call on patients who had fallen off the schedule to find out why. Hiding my fears did not help me grow; so I dialed. Often, the reasons were arbitrary ones, like scheduling. Nothing had gone wrong with their treatment. But I hadn't given them clear direction, and life had moved them elsewhere. More lessons learned.

Dad taught me to take charge of my life. His instructions were simple. "Pick up the phone, and call people," he would say. "Ask them to come in for a treatment and then, let them choose, yes or no. Then help them arrange their life to make time to take care of themselves by coming in for treatment." I learned how to share my gifts with people who could benefit from them. All of the awkward emotions eventually fell away as I realized that my healing gifts were valuable, and that there were people who could benefit from them that didn't yet know me. I became more courageous. People felt my good intentions and authentic wish for their healing. I learned how to merge entrepreneurship and spirituality gracefully. I am so grateful that I let my dad teach me how to share my heart with the world.

Something incredible began to happen. I could see the Universe respond to my efforts and my faith in the Universe grew. My practice expanded rapidly as if out of nowhere. Six months after opening my doors, I treated eighty patients a week. I began to pay back my student loans. I bought a new car. The practice overflowed with energy and abundance. It was more than I could handle. I had a very good problem and I loved it.

Until this point, I'd never fully supported myself. My parents and Uncle Sam had picked up the slack. I was now part of working America, and I experienced the "daily grind" of work. At the end of the week, I was exhausted. My patients were professors, janitors, students, servers, stay-at-home parents, business owners, receptionists, lawyers, construction workers, and accountants. They all worked hard, were worn down, stressed out, and in search of relief. I witnessed the heart that's required to show up every day and work for a living. Most patients had families, bills, ambitions, and dreams. They gave life a serious effort.

The balance of personal well-being, family, work, spirituality, and fun is a complex workload that requires support. I learned to respect and have compassion for my patients and myself as I witnessed the steadiness required to sustain so many responsibilities. And I began to see that my healing was interlinked with their healing. If I felt resistant to a patient, I knew there was something unconscious for me to heal in order to hold a loving space for them. We all need support. In this way our destinies are interlinked. When I heal, you heal. As you grow, you pave a path for me to follow. We are connected. With great gentleness and courage, we can heal anything together.

The Mission

Universal Love is a seed that can be nourished to become a forest of the tallest Redwoods and the thickest Sequoias. I see myself as a gardener who nurtures seeds and allows nature to take its course. There is much about the world in general that can erode the seed of Light within your heart. It is human nature to crave expansion and freedom. Nothing in the external world—drugs, alcohol, sex, sports, fame, or power—will satisfy the inner longing for freedom other than freedom itself. You can gain access to your inner Light if you nurture it regularly. I feel strongly about the importance of meditation and other methods that expand and stabilize the connection to the Eternal Heart. My mission is to support the growth of Universal Love.

If you are intrigued by what I've shared thus far, then let's spend some time together. The next part of the book outlines a sequence that depicts the physical and emotional cues that your body uses when your attention is misaligned with your heart.

The ancient Taoists believed the thinking part of brain was closely linked to digestion. They also believed that the true sense of knowing originates in the heart. Knowledge that arises from the heart is not always based in logic or reason. The heart, out of its own autonomy and freedom, reveals the truth for each of us. Inner guidance can be as simple as knowing who's calling without caller ID or as serious as the selection of a career path or life partner. Simply said, the heart knows. You can learn to tap into the heart's unlimited resource of knowledge without exhausting yourself physically and emotionally. You don't have to prove anything to your parents, boss, children, or yourself to obtain access to the wisdom of the Heart. You don't have to climb Mount Everest, starve yourself, run a hundred miles, or isolate yourself from the chaos of the "real world." You can go to extremes to find inner peace, but extreme actions are not a prerequisite to know your inner divinity.

Learn to listen to the voice of truth within you. Learning to listen is equally available to all people regardless of background. Love is where we start. Love is where we end. In the middle we learn what love is, what love is not and how to bring more love into the world.

Section One

THE CRUX

MY MESSAGE

Until you discover the wellspring of love within, you will endlessly seek love from the outside world. Deep inside, most people experience a degree of feeling empty and not good enough. When you look solely to the external world to fill you up, you will remain unfulfilled. At some point, you can or will experience your Divine essence deeply and thoroughly enough that you can relinquish your search for fulfillment externally.

To quench the thirst of your soul, go within! Learn to meditate and do breathwork. Inside your heart is the doorway to the entire Universe. It is a vast chamber of Love that can flow through you towards the external world. You can become a tributary that channels love to help others know that same source within themselves.

Practice radical self love no matter what's going on outside you. It's easy to love yourself when your expectations are being met. Try loving yourself when you're in the doldrums. Try loving yourself when you lose your keys, cell phone, job, spouse, or sense of self. You gain affinity for grace when you choose to love yourself in the midst of a challenge. To bring light to the challenges we face externally, we must shine it upon the darkness within. When you show love, generosity and compassion to yourself, you can show love to anyone.

My approach to healing is threefold. Self-inquiry, self-love and spiritual practice. Summon the courage to look at your unconsciousness. Love and accept what you discover. Practice meditation, breathwork, or other methods that increase your capacity to hold Universal Love. These three methods synergistically work to accelerate healing, love, and enlightenment. If you're ready to move past the beginning stages of healing and spirituality and get invested in the evolution of your soul, keep reading.

Mark this day in your calendar. Today we are changing the culture of how love flows. This is a self-love campaign designed to change our world. Beneath the perceived scarcity or crises of oil, water, coal, foodstuffs, healthcare, human rights, and environmental protection, lies the fundamental lynchpin that keeps all other crises spinning in chaos. I'm talking about the crisis of no self-love. Today we are shifting the values of our culture. We are shifting the way we relate to ourselves so as to shift the way we relate to one another and the planet. I am starting with me.

The exercise below is my answer to the question, *What are ten things you love about you?* Grab your journal and write your own list of ten (or twenty) things. Keep adding to the list as you work with this book. You'll keep discovering and creating more things about yourself to love.

TEN THINGS I LOVE ABOUT ME EXERCISE

- *I love my sense of humor.*
- *I love being goofy and singing out loud when I get home from work.*
- *I love my good heart.*
- *I love that I'm learning to take care of myself and be gentle.*
- *I love that I show up to work, even when I want to stay in bed.*
- *I love that I know when to change my diet when my body shows signs of weariness.*
- *I love that I love my wife, daughter, family, and friends.*

- *I love that right now my heart is swelling and aching as I share what I love about me.*

- *I love being creative and innovative about business, healing, and spirituality.*

- *I love being courageous and sensitive in challenging situations.*

- *I love myself deeply.*

I think that was eleven, but you get the idea. Now it's your turn. When you write these down, take a few deep inhalations and exhalations to root the self-love into your being. Then say them out loud and breathe them in even deeper. Every time I do this, my body begins to tingle and heat up

If you are having trouble with this exercise, then you've found the first roadblock to your healing. Breathe into any discomfort and soften your body. Keep working on this exercise until it becomes easy. For some of you, this may take some practice. We are social beings, and we create reality by sharing our lives with each other. So in order to spread the *Self-Love Revolution*, I request that you share 10 things you love about you with me and everyone you can think of and that you ask people, "What do you love about you?" Let's hear it.

Wisdom from the Ancients

The state of consciousness that brought on the disease cannot be the same state that heals the disease. Don't change who you are and the disease has no other option but to stay.

—Dr. Jeffrey Yuen

You were born to heal. Every role you play, everything you do, is part of your life to help you learn a life lesson that your soul needs to evolve. The issues that bother you the most, that make you feel out of control with emotion, are the things you were born to heal.

BORN TO HEAL EXERCISE

- *What is my biggest life lesson?*
- *What obstacles am I currently facing?*
- *Am I making progress?*
- *What's stopping me from advancing on my path?*
- *Am I having any fun?*

Disease is born when you ignore the voice of your heart. Doubting your intuition is the root of all disease. Whenever you shun the voice of the Heart, you cut off your ability to receive universal guidance. The more you listen and honor the voice of the heart, the clearer it gets. When you cooperate with the voice of your heart, you build confidence in the heart's guidance. The voices of admonishment, conformity, and mediocrity become dimmed, as new streams of love begin to flow in their place.

Intuition is a way of listening to the subtle communication system of your body. You can learn to recognize the refined signs and signals the body emits before they become loud symptoms. The tradition of Chinese medicine recognizes that the key to a healthy, joyful life is linked to the smooth flow of emotion and a strong sense of life purpose.

Chinese medicine reveals the subtle energetic communication of the body through a refined paradigm called "five-element theory". In Chinese medicine, physical symptoms signal a misstep or wrong turn on life's path. The five-element theory depicts the physiology, emotion, and spirit of a human being through the lens of Mother Nature. The bedrock of Chinese medicine views the origin of disease as rooted in an imbalance of the heart.

Inherent to the five-element theory is the view that the body is an extension of Nature's creation. Just as trees, rivers, animals, flowers, and bodies of water are subject to daily, seasonal, and yearly cycles, so too is the human body. The body, like nature, can be strengthened with proper care and attention and be weakened from neglect. Through care and attention, the body maintains strength, along with an efficient metabolism, and a robust immune response. All of this contributes to a state of increased happiness and longevity. Neglect of the body attracts mold, fungus, virus, bacteria, yeast, and diseases that encrust and penetrate the system. These pathogens enshroud the luminous expression of the Spirit, until the very light that maintains life retracts itself completely.

Something Happens

The inception of disease occurs in a moment. Life moves along smoothly, and then suddenly, in a flash, something happens that triggers a feeling of diminishment. A simple, seemingly insignificant, event can initiate a silent progression of physical illness. The decline may happen slowly or rapidly, or even remain latent until a future event. But the affliction has laid roots, and its momentum will build over time if left unchecked.

Disease never comes randomly. Disease grows like a seed until the right moment comes along for it to sprout. The seeds of disease come from many sources, even from what may seem like a momentary slight. That's especially true when your sense of innocence and purity feels diminished. This slight of self creates separation from your sense of wholeness and your connection with Universal Love.

An unconscious moment of emotional pain first affects the heart energetically as a heavy contracting sensation in the chest area.

ENERGETIC COACHING

Whenever you see italics, read what follows, and then put down the book.

Breathe in long through your nose and exhale gently through your mouth.

Pay attention to the thoughts that show up, especially those that knock loudly, as well as the ones your more conscious mind will conjure. Sense in your body where it is you feel ill at ease, be it a tightness, or any place that seems out of sync with how you prefer to feel. Do this each time you read, and you will start to work with your healing on a deeper, more energetic level. You are engaging your right brain, your unconscious, and your healing guides when you do this. The synergy will facilitate your healing.

Recall a moment when you heard surprising or shocking news. Remember how it caused your breath to gasp and chest to tighten.

The physical response occurs quickly, as the lungs constrict and the breath becomes shallow. If the event is extremely traumatic, the breath can even stop altogether. Maybe someone said something that hurt your feelings: you may have felt a stabbing or heavy sensation in the chest, followed by a skip in the breath. Perhaps you then felt angry, got quiet, pulled in your energy, and began to shut down. If the issue is not resolved, physical symptoms can arise. Feeling unsafe in your body can turn into a feeling of insecurity that drains your system of vitality. It lays the seedbed for future ailments to flourish.

Greg, the Emotional Warrior

Greg, a major in the army who had served in Iraq and Afghanistan, came to see me for breathwork and acupuncture. As a private, he'd been in battle many times in his career. Now a high-ranking officer, he primarily oversees missions from the base. In the treatment room, Greg related stories of horrific atrocities. He talked about locking the pain of war deep inside. He came to me because he was having trouble with intimacy; he felt unable to fully connect with his wife emotionally. She said that he is distant. Greg cried in my office, and said, "I can't trust myself like

I used to before war." Battle has left a psychic scar on Greg. Using breathwork and his deep desire to heal, he has made terrific progress. Greg feels his emotions more as he continues to do the breathwork I taught him on a regular basis. In addition to his workouts and training regime, he now actively makes time for his Spirit. Before his most recent deployment, he spoke with more ease and freedom about his heart and dreams with his family. As long as he keeps doing the work, I'm confident Greg will heal the wounds inflicted by war.

Feeling diminished has a physical impact. If you feel unsafe, you're storing trauma from the past in your body. This tension creates a ripe environment for disease. One by one, each organ system absorbs the strain of the original stressful event. It multiplies beyond the original wounding and makes one less responsive to the present moment. If unresolved the issue moves into latency, and will erupt into disease in the future. In the meantime, it saps your vitality by using your vital energy to store the stress in your body instead of keeping it available for daily life, let alone for joy and creativity.

As you habituate yourself to feeling worse and ignore stressors, latency becomes an unconscious process. You stop recognizing your stressors and begin to automatically suppress your intuition. In this way, you further ingrain and physically encapsulate the original event that caused you pain.

The insidious progression of disease is avoidable. You may try to ignore life until you can no longer ignore life, until the pain becomes so great and so frequent–even constant—that it demands your attention. Through cultivating an awareness of how you react to the challenges in your life, you can recognize how your unconscious reaction to them is expressed. Only then can you choose a new path.

Luke Adler

Underneath every reaction is a deeper reaction. Most upsets are really about something unresolved from the past.

🪷 HOW TO LOOK DEEPER EXERCISE

- *When my stress level gets high and my old patterns of reactivity show up, what am I mad, sad or upset about?*

- *Is it truly the circumstance in front of me? (It's likely deeper.)*

- *If not, what is it really about?*

- *What fear is underneath my reaction?*

- *How is this current fear a projection of an old fear or event from the past? Does it have anything to do with the present circumstance?*

Practice holding the energy of love along with the energies of anger, sadness, fear, and worry. You'll begin to be present to the circumstance in front of you and not react from a place of any one emotion that is devoid of love. When you're crystal clear that all you want to grow is love, then no matter what emotion or challenge arises, the greatest amount of healing will always come through.

Look closely at any upset in your life and you will find some unresolved issue from the past projected onto the present circumstance. Feel into your upset and be willing to admit to yourself (and others, if necessary) what's really going on. Don't be shy about taking time away from daily life to work on this. Journal about it, or talk it over with a trusted friend or practitioner. You'll need a dose of generosity to forgive yourself and others. Then you'll be able to move on with a renewed commitment to love and be loved.

HEALING CRISIS

The body's ability to hold a disease in check is so great that major diseases can lie dormant even as you seem to be in relatively good health. Every once in a while, a patient comes into my clinic and opens with, "I'm really in pretty great health." After I look at the seven western drugs he's on, study his hyper-acidic diet, and run through my diagnostics, I have to break the news to him, "Things could be a whole lot better."

The body encapsulates disease in an inactive state to preserve the health of the internal organs. As it loses the capacity to hold the disease dormant, the body releases the disease from a stored state. You'll notice this if you find yourself increasingly reliant on substances like caffeine or sugar to boost your flagging energy, or if you just don't have the oomph that you remember you had, and that at least part of you still aspires to. These symptoms tend to accelerate, especially under stress.

A healing crisis can bring this process to an abrupt and unavoidable moment of change. Sometimes when the body senses an opportunity to heal—like when you finally allow yourself to relax into the deep rest of a long vacation—the latent pathology releases. A healing crisis can occur when you experience the same symptoms of the original illness just as it is being cleared from the body: The illness that had been willfully suppressed into latency roars back, your capacity to hold the pathology at bay is lost, and the disease process ensues, sometimes slowly, though sometimes in an acute and frightening way.

Lost in the Woods

On a beautiful late winter Sunday, Javier, one of my patients, took a mountain bike ride in the high Cascades with a friend for what was supposed to be a few hours. Two hours into the trip, after gaining three thousand feet of elevation and covering fifteen miles, he took a wrong turn on the trail and ended up twenty miles from the car and three thousand feet down on the opposite canyon. When they recognized their error, Javier recounted, "The sense of doom compounded with the realization of also being out of water and food was overwhelming." To stave off dehydration they drank unfiltered water from a creek. An hour later Javier's stomach began to cramp. "I knew we had another three thousand feet of elevation to climb and twenty miles to go," he related. " Getting sick was not an option. So I commanded myself to keep it together, and for the next six hours of hiking and biking I didn't get sick. It was a sheer act of will. I think even if I had collapsed with the runs, I would have gotten back on my bike afterwards."

Just as the sun fell below the horizon, they made it back to the car. Three weeks later Javier went on vacation. Within the first twenty for hours of unwinding, he got the stomach flu and purged from both ends. While he was sick for three days he also purged the feelings of helplessness and doom that he had experienced a few weeks earlier in the woods.

The body always gets the last word. Latency is the physical impact of consciously suppressing the thing you want to forget. When you suppress something long enough, it becomes repressed or unconscious. Latency occurs when you declare mentally or out loud, "I don't have time for this," or "I don't have time for you right now. I don't want to deal with this. No, not now." You ignore the situation at hand. You pretend it's not there and in so doing, push the resistance to feeling that experience into some part of your body. This is mediated by the energy of your immune system, your digestion and your constitutional vital energy reserves. If these systems are strong, you will have more capacity to put a stressor or pathogen into latency to be dealt with another day. If not, you are much more likely to experience the discomfort right then and there.

When you choose not to deal with life in the moment, the body stores stress in the lymph, liver, fat cells, and major articulations of the body. This stored stress creates stagnation in fluids like lymph and blood, which circulate through your entire body. This creates an environment of inflammation ripe for virus, bacteria, fungus, yeast, and the like. As a result of the loss of capacity to hold a pathogen in latency, the body creates heat or inflammation, which manifests as arthritis, tumors, autoimmune disorders, and diseases that eat away at the body's vital resources and tissues. The epidemic of cancer and autoimmune diseases is not only caused by exposure to environmental toxins in our water, air, and soil; the compounding trigger that ignites free radicals into a state of oxidative stress is suppression. It fools the immune response and jumps past our body's now diminished defenses. We have become prey to our own failure to deal with trauma in a healthy way.

Pushing a pathogenic factor into latency merely defers health problems. It does not make them go away. Latency allows you to survive as well as to respond with some degree of fight or flight. The pathogens you put into latency are only waiting for their chance to express themselves in the future. They are encapsulated moments in time that await expression. Eventually the annoyances, frustrations, pains, and wounds of your past will surface. When they do, they will express themselves as diseases that consume your body's resources.

It's fine to move some stress into latency. The body is built to store disease. But the body has a limit of how much pathology it can maintain in latency. As you become aware of the people, places, and things that you don't have time for, you will see the patterns of unconsciousness that cause disharmony and disease in your life.

🪷 DECLARE MY HEALING EXERCISE

In the same way that you push a pathogen into latency, you can free a pathogen.

Simply declare, "I am ready to heal. I am ready to examine the parts of my life that speak to me in forms of pain in my body. I am healing now. I choose to surround this ailment with love and vitality."

Take a moment to think about a life trauma. Not necessarily a giant life crisis, but something smaller that you can practice this technique with.

Say the healing affirmations as you think about and begin to heal this incident. Feel where in your body the stress has been stored, and pay attention to where you sense a shift.

THE SEQUENCE OF SEPARATION

Emotion is a compass that points to your heart. Your heart connects you to the Universe. Suppressed emotions result in feeling separate from Universal Love. Separation from your heart is perpetuated by suppression of your emotions. Suppression perpetuates the myth that you are separate from the Universe. It's hard to remember that you are part of the One, when you feel angry, lonely, afraid, sad, bored, jealous, or _____(insert your most habituated reactive emotional response here).

Suppression impacts your health, and if left unchecked, impacts organ function. I call this progression the "Sequence of Separation" because the act of suppression separates you from the insight of your heart. The Sequence of Separation is based on an ancient Chinese medicine theory of disease. It is a long lineage that transcends history and geography. In a way, the sequence is a barometer for how well we navigate our life lessons.

Suppression is defined as a conscious intentional exclusion from consciousness of a thought or feeling. Repression is a mental process by which distressing thoughts, memories, or impulses that may give rise to anxiety are excluded from consciousness and are left to operate in the unconscious.

Suppression requires a conscious moment of acknowledgment to make something become unconscious. In order to suppress something in a wakeful moment, you dismiss it from your awareness. To take suppression a step further—to go unconscious—you have to create a reason, a belief, or make up a story to convince yourself to suppress your truth. The big problem is this: if the thing you want to suppress is something that the Universe wants you to face and heal, you're paddling against the current. Eventually you will have to return to this scene and act with awareness. Everything you do to suppress your truth is only a temporary warding off; you're building a wall you will need to take apart later, stone by stone.

Universal Love only wants your freedom. It will not stop for the preferences of your small self. So be careful about being too picky with how and when you're willing to learn your life lessons. God takes custom orders for spiritual growth, but you don't always get exactly what you want: You get what you need in order to grow, whether you think you are ready or not. Grace fills in the gaps. Or as my wife Emily says, "You get what you get and you don't throw a fit."

Suppression says to the Universe, "I'm gonna put off learning this particular life lesson. I'll deal with this issue someday if I have to, but for now, I'll put it on the back burner." One of my mentors shared with me that people build their lives around avoiding three things: loss, anxiety, and death. The only problem is that loss, anxiety, and death are the three things you are guaranteed to face in life. Loss, anxiety, and death will imprint a pattern of anxiety and distress upon your body and mind if you have not cultivated the capacity to be present when these experiences arise.

Suppression is built into the fabric of society. For most people, in order to start a business, get an education, or buy a house, you have to take on some debt, in the form of a loan or a credit card. If you're not crystal clear about the interest rates and the time it may to take to repay the loan given current and future employment, you are completely suppressed around money and the exchange between what you want and what it really costs you. If you are super aware of what you're getting into financially, then kudos to you. I didn't have a clue about debt when I was twenty-three and started graduate school. I thought, "Free money. Cool!" Years later, as I applied my education professionally, and understood the nature of variable and fixed interest rates, I felt good about paying back student loans.

Not dealing with your lessons works the same way, except the interest you're going to pay will come out of your body, not your bank account.

Another area of collective suppression is food consumption. Food is a major hot button issue of suppression. Sugar, alcohol, bread, dairy, chips, and dips are the engines of suppression. How do you get rid of your guilt, shame and blame? You eat. Eat. Eat. Eat. Eat until you're full, and then you eat some more. You stuff yourself full, so you don't have to feel. Some of us love chocolate, others salt. But it's rare to find the person who turns to salad when they've been told something they didn't want to hear, gets turned down for a promotion, or goes through a break-up. When I have a rough day at work, I get home and pound the corn chips. Crunch. Crunch. Crunch. Without stopping to take a breath unless my wife catches me and slows me down. Thank God for her.

Ancient Taoist healers from China discerned the Sequence of Separation from observing the patterns of nature thousands of years ago. They perceived how suppressed emotions affect the body physically as disease progresses from one organ system to the next. Though the Universe uses emotions to physically grab your attention, emotions are not the root of disease. The root of illness is the *way* you suppress them.

Universal Love operates out of its own infinite intelligence. Our job is to learn to trust the Universe's communication. My intention is that you will become more aware of how the Sequence of Separation works in you. The only person who can really know the unique beauty and gifts that the Universe has for you is you. If I've done my job, by the end of this book, you will have a clearer sense of where you can be more responsible for your wellbeing and teach others to do the same.

SEQUENCE OF SEPARATION UNRAVELED

For a long time, I viewed emotion as random, volatile, and unpredictable. Then I noticed a sequence to emotion rooted in physiology. As I peered more deeply into the pattern, I realized what my predecessors had discerned thousands of years ago, that suppressed emotion affects organ function in a sequence. That sequence follows the principles of the five-element theory. As I worked with emotionally courageous people in the treatment room or at my workshops and retreats, their breakthroughs followed a consistent sequence of release that had an effect on their physical health.

When I encourage patients or retreat participants to feel with their heart in the middle of a healing session, tears of sadness flow. For those more resistant, anger or passive aggression might come up first, and later, when the patient feels safe, tears follow. For others, to avoid feeling anger and resentment, they become philosophical, their eyes dart up and out of any window in the room to avoid their feelings. For the most part people offer me good reasons to suppress intense feelings of fear. The fear of feeling out of control is a big motivator to keep the lid on emotion. It is easier to think your way through life, rather than feel. When I work with intellectual people who would rather understand than feel, I ask them to feel with their heart and let go of their need to understand. At first they display a look of confusion, then they often turn beet red as anger surges forth. If they feel free from judgment (their own or that of others), they might reach sadness and begin to hear their intuition.

Only when people feel safe to feel, can they own their suppression and grant themselves forgiveness and love.

Authoritative clinician and scholar of Chinese medicine Giovanni Maciocia says about emotion:

66 *Emotions are a natural part of human existence and no human being escapes ever being sad, angry or worried sometimes. The emotions only become causes of disease when they are particularly intense, and most of all, when they are prolonged over a long period of time, especially when they are not expressed or acknowledged...The emotions can not only cause a disharmony, but they can also be caused by it.* 99

Ann Cecil-Sterman renowned teacher of Classical Chinese Medicine declares:

> *Pathological emotion is one which can be expressed yet lingers and is undesired. The patient suppressed the emotion. A pathological constitutionally derived emotion is a repressed feeling the patient often denies having but is observed...by the practitioner... [P]athological emotions...are preventing the fullest expression of life in the patient.*

The first emotion people instinctually suppress is sadness, which impacts the lungs. If sadness is not felt and released, the liver responds with anger. Anger is one of the more uncomfortable emotions to feel. So people substitute worry, which is governed by the spleen. As worry wears down the digestive tract, the kidneys release fear, stimulating cortisol levels and the fight or flight part of the nervous system. Worry is the emotion people are most comfortable expressing, because society deems it an appropriate emotion. Excessive worry over a short period of time drains the adrenal and thyroid glands and wreaks havoc on the digestive process. When fear drives actions, many people become emotionally numb. The chapters ahead will take us much deeper into the specific inner mechanics of the Sequence of Separation.

EMOTIONS AND THE BODY

According to Chinese medicine, different emotions reside in different organs. Each of these organ systems contains emotional and spiritual functions as well as specific physical functions. When the sequence of separation is activated, that is, whenever you suppress your emotions, the organs pick up the physiological slack for one another. Rather than easefully flowing into each other, in the sequence, the organs stress one another. None is functioning optimally, and they compete for your reduced energy and vitality. It is a complex way of getting your attention, trying to buy time to help the heart restore receptivity to the Universe. Often it ends in disease, because we are so busy responding to symptoms and repressing them, that we do not address the original source of suppression. The longer we avoid doing so, the more we make the problem bigger and more difficult to heal.

If you can learn these next diagrams, you will be able to quickly correlate each organ system with its emotion:

Here is the Sequence of Separation with emotion highlighted:

Elementally, the Sequence of Separation is as follows:

Use these diagrams to gain a deeper understanding of how emotions move throughout the body and identify those triggers that cause you to suppress specific emotions.

Take a moment for this next meditation. In fact, it's a good idea to read over the exercise, and then take a walk to really think about it and note how you feel. Write your insights in a journal.

They'll arise both now and later. This is your heart speaking to you, telling you how to heal.

🪷 SUPPRESSION EXERCISE

- *In which organ system do I currently and in the past most often experience symptoms?*

- Lungs – *sinus, cold and flu, cough, sneezing, asthma, breathing issues, thyroid.*

- Spleen – *digestion, energy level, bowel movements, musculoskeletal issues.*

- Liver – *headaches, menstrual cramps, irritability, flank pain, left sided symptoms.*

- Kidneys – *urogenital issues, sexual function, adrenal issues, low back and knee pain.*

- Heart – *sleep issues, memory issues, language articulation issues.*

Now that you've identified an organ system related to your symptoms, look at the emotion related to your symptoms:

- Lungs - *sadness.*

- Spleen - *worry.*

- Liver - *anger.*

- Kidneys - *fear.*

- Heart - *anxiety.*

Do you feel surprised or validated?

Now move your awareness to the areas of your body

where you experience these symptoms, whether you feel them there right now or in the past. That area may or may not be the same place in your body as the named organ. Place your hands over that part of your body and breathe for a few minutes. Pay particular attention to any subtle sensations in your body. When you become aware of a feeling or sensation ask, "What is this?"

As you do this and any other future exercises, just be with your body. There is no need to conjure up anything or force yourself to feel a specific emotion. Be attentive and loving with your body, and be open to what arises. Something will come up for you, if not now, then within the next few days.

Stay aware of the insights that will arise. When the insights come, you may feel lighter, your vision may get clearer, or you'll get goose bumps or some other sign. I want you to recognize more clearly how the Universe speaks to you through your body. As you do this, the signals of Universe will become stronger and more pleasant and very likely occur more frequently. When you ignore the Universe, She gets your attention in often more unpleasant ways. The goal here is to enjoy life more by going *with* the flow, rather than against it.

The sequence of emotions almost always begins with sadness. Sadness resides in the lungs. If the lungs cannot process the trauma at hand, the liver jumps in to help. It responds with anger and its many forms. If the liver does not create a smooth resolution to the situation, disharmony progresses to the spleen, and triggers worry, which is a form of over-thinking. When we try to mask our worry to others, we may say we are "ruminating," a fancy word for worrying. Excess worry stresses the spleen. The kidneys are the last organ system called to work through the fear. You may be wondering about the heart. If the kidneys do not contain the stressor, the body begins to fail, sometimes quickly, but most of the time slowly. When the kidneys cannot retain a connection with the heart, severe impairment to the body results. I'll touch on this in depth in the spleen and kidney chapters.

The Sequence of Separation can be difficult to recognize because it becomes activated during a moment of unconsciousness. If not addressed, the suppressed moment slowly and gradually sucks away vitality and causes people to rely heavily on stimulants and sedatives like caffeine, alcohol, drugs, and sugar to regulate energy and mood. Often people come in to my clinic describing one set of symptoms, but their diagnostic pulses reveal what is going on at a far deeper level.

The body is designed to minimize stresses to the heart. The heart is protected from the full impact of suppression. Yet it experiences some impact of suppression from impaired function to the other organ systems. This manifests as a sense of dullness in your awareness, along with diminished energy level and connection to a sense of fulfillment. Any act of suppression big or small constricts the heart's capacity to receive Universal Love. Below is a chart that depicts the impact of suppression on the organ systems beginning with an emotion. I've included the paired organ systems and the elements for those who like more information.

Emotion	Organ Systems	Element
1st Sadness/Grief	Lung/Large Intestines	Metal
2nd Anger/Resentment	Liver/Gallbladder	Wood
3rd Worry/Rumination	Spleen/Stomach	Earth
4th Fear	Kidney/Urinary Bladder	Water
5th Anxiety	Heart/Small Intestine	Fire

FEEL YOUR FEELINGS

Most people hate feeling vulnerable. Many people are more afraid of public speaking than death. For the most part, society teaches us to dismiss, ignore—or worse, suppress—the lesser feelings of loss in life. To feel grief and weep like a baby is something reserved for funerals and the loss of major life achievements. Loss, diminishment, and contraction of a sense of self occur all the time, but society doesn't encourage, let alone permit us to express grief over little things. Just suck it up, right? When you disallow yourself from crying or feeling your grief about anything big or small, you block the reception of Universal Love, which results in compromised physiological health.

Suppressed emotion is the root of all forms of stress. Stress exacerbates every other physiological issue in your body. That's true from the moment it occurs until it erupts into a life-threatening situation however many years down the line. Dr. Jeffrey Yuen goes into how exactly suppressed emotions affects the body:

> " They (emotions) relate to how one interprets and negotiates reality. Emotions may be expressed, over expressed, or suppressed. To understand emotions is to navigate emotions. They are currents. They have vectors or an axis of Qi. For example, if anger is suppressed it might show up in the legs. Expressed emotions go up and out. Suppressed emotions go down and in. Emotions may be positive or negative, but when one is wise, one develops temperance. Emotions are only truly negative when there is intemperance: unexpressed or over expressed emotions. "

He continues extolling their nuances with:

66 *Anxiety scatters the Qi. Constant need for excitement can cause tremors, palpitations, and arrhythmia. Being stuck and allowing others to make decisions for you is pensiveness and can cause constipation, sciatica, and stagnation. Sadness moves energy down. Fear puts things in suspension. Shock causes the system to shut down.* *99*

If suppression persists over time, a chronic state of impaired physical health results. Suppressed emotion goes hand-in-hand with a decrease in happiness and satisfaction. The aftermath of long-term suppression can be utter ruin, a complete relinquishment of Universal Love from your heart, leaving a profound vacancy in the body. Suppression of the heart causes the beautiful Spirit that expresses through the body to draw away almost completely. It eventually leaves the body and its faculties vacant for what the Buddhist tradition calls *Rakshasic* entities, or foreign energies that are distinct from the individual soul.

I've worked with it. The poor souls overcome by possession are filled with negative emotion and attract similar energies. A person in this state can appear like the walking dead, a zombie that allows other people (or even other entities) to dominate the body and its faculties.

Initially, the best way to help someone entrenched this deeply in the metaphysical darkness is with authentic prayer and offering conscious blessings. A full possession stage of suppression is shrouded in confusion and apathy, which makes face-to-face interactions very challenging. I'll get into this more in the chapter dedicated to the kidneys.

POPULAR SOCIETY PROMOTES SUPPRESSION

Particularly pernicious examples of societal suppression are learned behaviors reinforced by family, schools, and religious institutions. These impact how we conduct ourselves through different genders, ages, and in a variety of social and professional contexts.

Who has never heard any of these? *Boys have to be tough and strong. Girls have to be sweet and kind. Children should be seen and not heard. You should never challenge authority. It's better not to speak up if it makes other people uncomfortable. Don't rock the boat.*

Agreement with society's truth over Universal Truth is almost always harmful to one's health. It's the one instance where being true to your heart can cause confusion. Society may say one thing and your heart another. Listening to your heart above all other voices is a major part of growing up and becoming a spiritually responsible adult where you and you alone are accountable for your spiritual progress.

When you agree with someone's definition of truth, and that truth does not feel right in your heart, you suppress your Essence. This is an act of self-deception that appears differently for a given constitutional type. Strive to hear what your own heart is telling you, and to listen to it above and beyond the voices of others. Authenticity is good for your physical health, even if being authentic upsets others.

The idea of deception points to the unique way you suppress yourself, and how suppression shows up as a pattern of disease in your body. Suppression is a form of self-deception. By deception, I mean the stories you tell yourself (and likely share with others) to build a case that your point of view is right with regard to a particular issue. If the story you create to justify yourself suppresses your truth, it will never lead to Love. If you're looking for a cue that you're doing this, listen when you feel compelled to tell a story over and over to anyone who will listen. Pay particular attention to any sense of urgency in you and any sense of validation you feel when people agree with you.

You have the freewill to create any story you want. Most of the time you don't get to have love and also be right about your made-up story as though it were Absolute Truth. Almost all the time you'll have to choose between no love plus self-righteousness or Universal Love. The bottom line with any upset in life, whether it is romantic, professional, or in relationships with family and friends, is that if you are committed to love and true intimacy you'll give up needing to be validated for your point of view and choose love instead.

Any story you create is only your perception or perspective on a given event. It will feel completely true. But your story may be one of several or hundreds of interpretations of what is actually true. That's not to say that you're intentionally lying to yourself and/or others. You feel hurt, so you create a story to make sense of the pain. Those kinds of stories usually involve blaming someone (who could even be yourself) or something for why you feel hurt.

To be fully responsible for your life, you must see all sides of the picture. You have to really try to feel what it would be like to live in someone else's shoes. Easier said than done. If you can bring yourself to see something the way even an enemy might see it, you will begin to see how your own point of view is limited. If you keep probing and doing your work, you will likely encounter and identify the deeper fear that prevents you from taking ownership over your circumstance.

To take responsibility always entails some degree of emotional pain and some degree of letting go. You are defensive and reactive because you unconsciously sense sadness, anger, worry, and fear buried beneath the story. In order to survive, you create an energetic shield (the story) to justify not feeling your emotions.

Fear triggers a survival reaction, rather than a response of openness and understanding. The story begins from a pattern rooted in your body. Perhaps anytime you spoke up at the dinner table, your dad told you to be quiet. So you've become quiet around anyone who reminds you of your dad. Maybe your teacher pulled you off a project and didn't tell you why. So you quit and won't try anything new because you're afraid to fail.

An unpleasant anxious physical sensation arises when the fear beneath the story activates. Fear feels uncomfortable. You want it to go away. You're pretty good at taking care of yourself, you think, so you've developed a way to do that. Sadly those self-protective mechanisms are inherently restricting to your Heart and your sense of personal truth.

Here's an example of me working with the fear of facing my truth as an adolescent.

Facing Suppression as an Adolescent

The first time I consciously faced the fear of feeling my emotions, I was 12. I felt like I was going to die by feeling the mix of emotions in my body. I'd been sitting on the bench of my soccer club for an entire season, while my coach brought in a bunch of superstar players from the surrounding area. It was fun to win all our games, but riding the bench sucked. I remember this one cold and dry night so clearly. We just lost a semi-final game of the Thanksgiving shoot-out tournament in Anaheim. I had decided days before that I was done. When the final whistle blew, I stoically walked up to my coach, looked him in the eye and said, "Len, I quit." I cried on the drive home. With that statement, I gave up my dream of being a professional soccer player like Pele. I was devastated to not see my soccer buddies after school and on the weekends. My story became that I was not good enough to play, that I sucked; that my coach was an asshole for not letting me play. I wanted to run away. I felt embarrassed and ashamed that I sat on the bench. I was angry with my coach and devastated that I gave up my dream.

This is where I learned my first great life lesson. Because I was so distraught about the whole mess, my dad intervened. He instructed me to call my friends and tell them why I had quit and thank them for their friendship. I thought my dad was crazy. It made me so nervous inside to even think of doing such a thing. He wanted me to open my heart and reveal my innermost feelings to my friends, by whom I was so desperate to be liked. I was petrified. I wanted to suppress my feelings, but I knew the moment my dad suggested calling my friends that I had to do it. I couldn't live with all of those feelings buried inside.

The first phone call, I cried like a baby, barely able to blurt a word out between sobs. I called my friend Josh first, because he was very mellow and would be the most sensitive. I choked on my emotion, weeping, as I thanked him for the fun car rides across Southern California. I explained why I'd quit and he said he was thinking of doing the same because he wasn't playing much either. I parted by wishing him the best with the team, and thanked him for the laughs. During the phone call I felt like my heart was being ripped apart, but by the end I felt warm inside. My heart felt full, and I felt strong. The next call was almost as painful, but by the last one I had a little grace in my cadence and I felt composed inside. My dad navigated me through this first experience to share my truth and I felt powerful, full of hope and purpose.

This was the first of many experiences where I took a risk to open and share my soul. I can say now, after two decades of practice, that I'm getting better at it. I'm still making friends and I'm living in my heart. I feel secure inside. I feel steady in my heart. Now, when my heart has something to say, I don't argue that much. I listen and take action. I'm done with needing the Universe to kick my butt to learn the lesson. I'd rather have fun with the brief time we have.

HOW YOU DECEIVE YOURSELF

Our organ systems allow Nature to work through each one of us in a myriad of ways. Just to make it more complicated, each of us has lessons to learn rooted in the organ systems. Everyone also has a single organ system or two where most pathology and deceptive behaviors stem from. Which organ is your particular locus for such behavior is about both your personal history and how your body processes the learning of your life lessons.

Remember, suppression is a conscious act. When you engage in suppression, there is a distinct way you trick yourself to think and feel that your choices are for the best. This form of trickery feels utterly normal to you because you have done it your whole life. Therefore it may be hard to see objectively.

You may not be a specialist. You may even be adept at the various forms of self-deception below. But as you read the list, pay attention to what resonates in your body, and to what questions trigger a *Yes, that's me!*

❀ SELF-DECEPTION BY ORGAN SELF EVALUATION

- *In general, do I see the negative side of things more than the positive?* (Lungs)

- *Do I justify my actions by saying and thinking that I have-to, got-to, should, or must do something a certain way?* (Liver)

- *Do I ingratiate myself to others, putting my personal or essential needs on hold just to please someone else at my own expense? (Spleen)*

- *Do I withhold information or omit pertinent information from others? (Kidneys)*

- *Do I often lie to people to control my world? (Heart)*

Which question(s) did I resonate with the most, or which bothered me the most?

The question that triggered the most sensation in my body or resistance in my mind indicates the organ system that is the root of illness for me.

- *What behaviors and habits do I engage in to cover up my tendency to deceive myself and others? For example: food, television, sex, drugs, alcohol, sugar, video games…*

- *What is the effect on my wellbeing?*

- *What is the effect on others?*

This is a quick check-in about how self-deception works through your belief system and your daily actions. Most people find a primary organ and a secondary organ through this first self-test. Once you have a sense of your organ system, pay attention to that area of your body and related signs and symptoms.

When you engage in one of these forms of self-deception, a feeling of constriction shows up in your throat, chest, gut, or pelvis depending on which organ system is affected. Your body gives you immediate feedback that what you just said or did was not authentic to what your heart wanted you to say or do and now you are feeling the result of suppressing your truth. It doesn't feel good. When you speak and act from your truth, the anticipation sometimes feels scary. But once you trust and take action, the heart takes over, and the Universe fills in the details.

Begin a deeper inquiry into how and why you deceive yourself. Feel how deceptive energy moves in and conceals itself in your body. Only in knowing lies the freedom to transform disease into vitality.

Your emotions point towards your intuitive truth. By listening to your emotions you will hear your intuition more clearly. When you choose to suppress something, your intuition becomes less clear. This lack of clarity leads to confusion around trusting your intuition. It's a downward spiral.

Suppression is the mechanism that buries intuitive truth in to your body, thereby depriving your organ systems of the energy needed to function. It remains buried until you set it free by acknowledging its validity.

In his book *Nourishing Destiny*, scholar of Classical Chinese Medicine, Lonny Jarrett, illumines the deceptive nature of each organ system when you suppress your emotion:

> ❝ *The (kidney type) tends to be secretive and lie by omission. The (heart type) lies by wearing a false face in the world. The (liver type), in an attempt to always be right, lies by perpetuating the myth that the ends justify the means. The (lung type) lies my misrepresenting the value of things. And the (spleen type) lies by being ingratiating rather than being sincere.* ❞

Here Jarrett eloquently lays out the specific psycho-emotional expression of pathology. He continues with greater specificity:

Possessing the unique ability to find the fatal flaw in everything, [lung] types may come to disdain what is regarded as lowly. Talking down to everyone, they pontificate to the unworthy. What is impure within the self is expressed outwardly as being snide.

[Liver] resentful people act passive aggressively. They avoid direct confrontation and manipulate the world by trapping others into compliance with their plans and decisions.

[As a] reaction to feeling sympathy, [Spleen types] become ingratiating, catering to others' needs endlessly. Excessive sympathy leads to the craving of sympathy for the terrible plight of having to take care of everything and everyone... They communicate disgust by constantly complaining about the neediness of others.

[Kidneys]...secretive people manipulate personal relationships by never quite revealing their intentions. They use their hidden resources in an attempt to overwhelm and intimidate.

[Heart] types may become broken hearted and bitter... [they] are no longer able to trust enough to let another close. Sarcasm and teasing are the resulting forms of communication that may serve to prevent others from becoming too close.

You may see yourself in one or more of these deceptive behaviors, or Jarrett's description may trigger some images of people you know, perhaps those who are passive aggressive or always see the flaws in life.

Deception is how you avoid your emotions. Beneath every behavior is a flood of emotion and a story that justifies the fear of trusting your intuition. When these deceptive behaviors are consistently active, I guarantee that physical signs and symptoms that correlate with a behavior and its organ system are present, *or will soon present themselves.*

MAGNETISM

How you behave is reflected in your body. The lessons you don't complete, you will repeat. Said differently, "What you resist, persists." As long as you suppress your emotions, you will attract situations that help you heal the emotions that you are uncomfortable feeling and expressing. This is the Universe responding to your Heart's true yearning, even if your day-to-day ego self is fuming and grumbling. The people that bother you most are almost certainly expressing the emotions that you suppress. Or they are suppressing the emotions that you express. We're all here to help one another learn.

Basically, the people you don't like are just like you. You loathe what you fear you are, reflected in the people that bother you the most, until you are clear that all you are is Love.

Your heart gravitates towards freedom. Unworthiness hides in the parts of you that have not been freed into Love. The places within you that are devoid of love will attract circumstances in order to help you heal and claim your Divine essence. Physical ailments are the result of you tensing your body against Universal Love. That tension creates physical stagnation and inflammation, which are the breeding grounds for injury and disease.

Resistance is not only the path to spiritual growth; resistance is a natural part of learning anything new. Resistance and unworthiness can transform into places for new love to flow. They are the path to physical vibrancy. Engage with them, rather than avoid them.

Healing is feeling. If you are willing to feel your feelings with the intention to let them move, you will develop the sensitivity to feel how and when you doubt your intuition. As this skill develops, you will be able heal any situation. Unworthiness of Universal Love causes you to doubt your Divine essence. You have been born to heal this. You have the choice in any moment to let go of past pain and allow love to move through your heart. Of all the virtues, forgiveness is the most difficult. We are all capable of forgiveness, and sometimes it requires tremendous grit to let go and trust in Universal Love.

Most people have learned to beat themselves up when they fail. In order to rebel against authority, some people engage in substance abuse as a way to punish themselves and authority (likely their parents). Others self-flagellate with negative self-talk to try to motivate themselves to work harder. Either way, the energy you use to kick yourself when you're down reinforces a deeper sense of feeling not good enough. What if, when you've failed at something, you grant yourself tenderness and compassion or feel gratitude for the chance to practice self-love. To aim tenderness toward your own suffering is a very high level of healing.

❀ THE HEALER WITHIN EXERCISE

Tenderness, Gentleness, Lighthearted, Forgiveness, Compassion, and Gratitude are the shortcuts to Universal Love.

The next time the Universe serves up a lesson and you get worked up:

Pause.

Take a few deep breaths.

Recall one thing you're grateful for.

Feel the warmth in your chest and allow the tenderness of that feeling to sink in deep inside to your spine.

Then, say or think "(Your Name), I love you. You're ok. There's nothing wrong and nothing to fix. I love you. I forgive you. Your Heart is perfect. Rest in the space of your Heart."

You can reinforce this new habit of tenderness and compassion by sending someone in need a blessing by thinking, Love and Blessings to (Friend's Name).

Breathe.

Practice this exercise, so that when the stressful moments come, you are prepared to turn lemons into lemonade. This exercise is how you become your own healer.

The tendency to bury feelings or the belief in the idea that toughness is "locking away your pain and never bringing it up again" can be useful in a survival situation. But you're not running from saber tooth tigers anymore. Grinning and bearing your pain does not help you or others grow. It only keeps you at survival status.

At a certain moment in life, you will be presented with the choice to face your unique life lessons. If you are not in a true survival situation, it will take more courage to face and feel your emotions than to bury them deep inside. To feel your emotions is healthier than to bury them inside. Only you can unearth the unique treasures that allow for the expression of the Universe through you. Though a little uncomfortable, applying these lessons to end the Sequence of Separation, will gain you access to beauty, strength, and free expression. They will begin to arise naturally, and with time, become a constant presence. What was previously uncomfortable can be transformed into peace and centeredness, with practice.

Authentic healing occurs with sustained effort over time. The best example of this is viewed in Nature's growth and decay cycles. Because you are an expression of Nature, her pace is a great marker for growth. The ability to feel through your pain and touch love is a skill that requires practice. You don't have to know exactly where you're headed. Set your intention to align with Universal Love. Do it again and again. Do it when you wake up in the morning and when you go to bed at night. Do it when you are stressed and when you are happy. Make it your habit. With time and willingness to trust the voice of your Heart, confidence emerges and the Universe appears as a constant and loyal companion. I love and support you completely. As I think of your efforts I feel uplifted. Together, united as one family, our hearts stretch to make room for more love.

THE HEART

In Fall of 2005, I led a ten-day retreat on the coastline of Oaxaca, Mexico, that culminated with a sweat lodge ceremony. The ceremony dismantled a core of fear hidden within me. The architects, Gabriel and Maria, had built the bamboo-framed, clay sweat lodge after the rainy season ended in the region, just weeks before the retreat. The lodge was shaped like a clay pizza oven and felt like one as well. Our retreat hosts performed the sweat lodge ceremony in the Zapotec tradition, with prayers to the four directions in the ancient language of the pre-Aztecs. This was my first sweat lodge, and I felt both excited and anxious. We chanted by the fire for hours as the rocks heated in the flames and embers. When the time came to enter the lodge, we crawled naked, belly to the red earth, through the door of the clay oven. The interior was pitch black except for the glowing rocks. No light penetrated into the lodge throughout the ceremony. A musty taste filled my mouth, as air stagnated in the sealed low-ceilinged enclosure. Just as I came from a womb with nothing but my bare body, I returned to the womb of the earth exposed and vulnerable. As I sat upright in the fetal position, a tinge of fear rippled upwards from my belly and caused a choking sensation in my throat.

The door closed and the leader of the ceremony spoke about the sacred ritual. Solemnly he said, "The lodge strips you down to the bare essentials. In the lodge, you see what needs to fall away. If *you are ready, you allow that falling away to happen. If you're not, you leave the lodge for another day. Just as the center of the earth is molten fire, in the lodge we connect with the earth and the red-hot basalt rock that purifies the body, mind, and spirit. To endure the lodge, you must face your darkest fears and pray."*

I held my body tightly in the back of the lodge, which stood no bigger than six feet in diameter and four feet tall. "Pray," I thought, "Yes I know how to pray." The fire tender opened the canvas door and shoveled more fire hot rocks into the pit in the center of the lodge. At first the heat felt comforting. Quickly it became almost unbearable. I began to panic and prepared to leave the ceremony, overcome by fear. I paused and drew in a deep breath ready to announce my decision to leave. With that deep breath I realized I had two possible choices. Leave the lodge, or pray for Grace, and see what happens. I prayed feverishly and recited every Sanskrit prayer and chant I knew for the next hour and a half. The lodge grew hotter and hotter with every dose of re-energized molten rock. The sage and frankincense offered to the coals filled my lungs and tears poured down my cheeks. There was no room in the lodge or even in my lungs for my preferences or opinions. The lodge dismantled my sense of self-limitations. The fire surpassed my tolerance and my vision turned blue. I chanted, sang, and connected with Spirit as I offered the limited pieces of my identity to the fire. I burned physically and spiritually as my faith grew.

Near midnight, after two hours of baking, the clay oven birthed me. Naked, I laid face down, flush to the damp earth somewhere in the humid jungle. My lungs heaved, as I turned to gaze at the sky that appeared so close I could grasp the stars with my fingertips. I rested there for some time, maybe an hour or longer, as my body throbbed. Finally I cooled down, and noticed the crisp, humid jungle air soothe my hot skin. The lodge ceremony taught me that amidst tremendous discomfort, the choice to trust the Universe to support me is always mine. Fire is the great purifier and the element associated with the heart.

THE SUPER RADIANT HEART

The heart allows us to feel a diverse landscape of emotion, but the very highest feeling we can experience is Supreme Love. And this love that is so high, so beyond mental comprehension, is the very source of all life. It is the engine that sustains all facets of life, and transitions us through and beyond death.

Life is for love. Love is the catalyst that brings warmth, heat, and fire to transform life into its highest possible expression. Love added to an impossible dilemma can bear the unexpected, the unimaginable, and the miraculous. Love can take you beyond the limited views of the mind to create something that smashes the heart wide open. Reach beyond what you currently know and let love transform your path with all the wonder, beauty, and mystery that you are.

❀ SUPER RADIANT HEART EXERCISE

- *What is the principal objective of my life?*
- *What is the highest purpose of my life?*
- *Am I willing to have Supreme Love be my constant companion?*
- *Pick an area of my life where I feel stuck or dissatisfied. What is the highest possible feeling that could move me though this current situation?*
- *Will I let it?*

In life there are moments of profound stagnation, sorrow, and aloneness. These moments feel as if they might never end, like there is no possible space beyond their sorrow. And yet love moves life continuously onward.

The heart allows Universal Love to speak through and to you. To experience this inspires trust in the Universe. Universal Love can be known throughout one's life. Your heart is the physical and energetic hub that allows you to know yourself as Divine. One of my favorite mystics, Albert Einstein, extols the wonder of the heart,

> 66 *The most beautiful and most profound emotion we can experience is the sensation of the mystical. It is the sower of all true science. He to whom this emotion is a stranger, who can no longer wonder and stand rapt in awe, is as good as dead. To know that what is impenetrable to us really exists, manifesting itself as the highest wisdom and the most radiant beauty which our dull faculties can comprehend only in their most primitive forms—this knowledge, this feeling is at the center of all true religiousness.* 99

Einstein's words point to a cosmic feeling I call love. Through the human body and mind, you can know, become established in, and be strengthened by love. The heart is the organ and energetic center of the body that discerns messages from the Universe.

Your capacity to hold, refine, and attune to Universal Love propels you along your destiny. Lonny Jarrett, a scholar and healer in the Taoist tradition, says, "The heart aligns us with heaven's will and gives each of us a unique charge to fulfill heaven's purpose." Every human being is born with a purpose. Purpose is the guiding force that acts as a compass for you to effectively fulfill your life lessons. The heart is the beacon that receives and sends Universal signals of healing and love for you and your world.

❁ FLEX MY HEART EXERCISE

- *Am I in touch with my sense of truth when it arises?*

- *Do I suppress my sense of truth around particular people or in particular situations? Who? Where? Why? How does that feel in my body?*

- *Examine my relationship with my parents. On a 1-10, scale how honest can I be with them about anything? (1—completely honest; 10—dishonest, flat-out lying)*

- *Why do I hold back with a particular parent or both?*

- *Write down the story I am telling myself right now in my head about why I can't be totally honest with my parents.*

- *With whom else do I hold back my truth?*

- *On a scale of 1-10, how willing am I to act on what my heart says even if it means creating discomfort for someone else? (1—very willing; 10—absolutely resistant or total rejection of your truth)*

- *How attuned am I to the voice of my heart on a daily basis? Am I confused by this question? Let that be a barometer for how attuned I am.*

Your thoughts, feelings, and actions affect people. Your thoughts, feelings, and actions reflect a field of energy that you emit. People feel your energy and respond to you before you ever open your mouth. The way people show up around you is a response to the energy you vibrate into the ether. The degree of happiness, joy, and satisfaction that you experience is directly related to the degree of attunement to the frequencies, messages, and guidance you receive from the Universe.

The power to be happy and fulfilled rests within you. Your thoughts, feelings, and actions this very moment matter and affect the people in your life. Your ability to amplify Universal Love through your heart is real and is happening, right now.

HEART MEDITATION

Right now, feel your heart, the area in the center of your chest.

Soften your shoulders. Relax your jaw. Breathe gently for a few moments.

Say several times until you feel it in your chest: "The Universe is loving through me." Close your eyes and rest with the feeling for a minute or longer.

Scholar of Classical Chinese Medicine and master clinician, Dr. Jeffrey Yuen says,

66 *The heart burns up the negativity. When there is darkness, you turn on the light. That's why the heart is the fire element. It's all inside of us. It's hard to see that it's all part of the Divine plan. It's hard for some people because they want the world to be only good. The heart means you accept the future. Suffer-*

ing is the result of the conditions we've set for ourselves and others...the human condition...we put conditions on being human. 🙶 🙶

A chief objective of life is to know the deepest realms of Love and share that Supreme Energy with the world. The heart is the cornerstone that links the energy of heaven to the earth. The heart's fire, though at times uncomfortable, allows the forces of Universal Love to purify your limited perceptions and grow the flame of insight and healing.

INTUITION

Intuition is the intelligence of the heart. It is natural and instinctive. Intuition is the ability to respond effectively from the awareness of the heart in any situation. Intuition arises freely when the heart is unencumbered by concerns of the past and future. It is the ability to be present on a subtle level of communication beyond the five senses. Many people dismiss this subtle level of knowledge because it does not rely on logic as its source of knowing. Intuition can be logical, but does not have to be. Intuition uses the direct, knowing experience of the heart. Because intuition is so obvious, your immediate sense of a situation is frequently overlooked by the habit of being logical and reasonable. Everyone is intuitive. It is a matter of pausing to listen and respecting the inner wisdom.

🪷 INTUITION EXERCISE

- *What percentage of the day do I trust my intuition?*
- *What practices and habits help me trust my intuition more?*

- *What practices and habits help me trust my intuition less?*

Western society views the intellectual mind as the supreme tool to grasp knowledge. The pursuit of learning is the necessary function of the thinking mind. But to know something directly requires the attention of the heart, not the intellectual mind. This happens not at the moment of reflection, but in the moment occurring right now. Knowledge known through the heart is superior to intellectual knowledge. Knowledge known to you as dictated by someone else's experience is secondary to knowledge known through your heart.

For example, you may learn of someone's experience of Hawaii and gain an understanding of the islands though a second-hand account. Once you travel there and experience them directly, the words you have heard take on new meaning. You may agree or disagree with what you've heard, but your basis of knowledge will be from your own, direct experience.

Intuition is the process of seeing deeper subtle layers of the truth directly. Your heart knows the truth just as it knows how to feel emotions. Intuition is more subtle; a shift in the texture of energy. You walk into a room and say, "The vibe here is off." That's your intuition. You know the vibe is off because you feel it. You add the explanation with your mind, "Yeah, Denise seemed really angry." The explanation describes the experience, though it is not, and can never be, a substitute for the experience.

Just like any process of education, with intuition at first you'll only see the most noticeable qualities. For example, as with a new piece of classical music, when you listen to it a second time, you'll hear more subtleties of the flute and violin. When you listen a third time you pick up further subtleties of the piano, percussion, and so on. Intuition employs and surpasses the senses of sight, touch, taste, smell, and hearing. As you hear the subtleties in a piece of music, you may feel the emotions of the musicians when they recorded the piece. Other examples are when you notice the delicate features in the flavors of chocolate or in the lips of your partner's kiss. You may even hear people's thoughts and feel people's feelings before they're aware of these feelings themselves.

Clairvoyance is the ability to see the unseen, like a vision of the past or future. Clairaudience is the ability to hear the unheard, like peoples thoughts. Clairsentience is the ability to feel what others feel. As a friend of mine says, "Clair-all-of–it" is the development of the heart's intelligence that stretches beyond the perception of the five senses and into the nonphysical spaces of reality. Just as the majority of the information available on your computer is not visible from the desktop screen, the majority of what you can know is hidden from the perception of the five senses. The exercises and guidance here will teach you how to access concealed knowledge by using your intuition.

The progressive refinement of intuition arises from the practice of listening, seeing, and watching all the ways the Universe speaks to you. The Universe is communicating with you right now. Are you aware of all the ways this is happening? Start to tune in to what messages are coming through. Trusting your relationship with the Universe, empowers the heart's capacity to receive universal guidance. Lonny Jarrett in his opus, *Nourishing Destiny*, elucidates the virtues of the heart, declaring that, "In harmony, the heart allows you to respond freely and spontaneously to each new situation, accepting each new situation as heaven's attempt to cultivate the seed of potential for the further unfolding of the destiny." Think of the wonder, awe, and imagination a child brings to any new activity. This is the spirit needed to open up to your intuition.

My Intuition

When my intuition is really flowing, I get goose bumps. First, I'll feel them along my forearms. Then if the spiritual energy increases, I'll feel a current of energy rush up my spine to the top of my head. The space between my eyes will pulse and sparks of blue light flash as a luminous field of energy undulates around people, plants, trees, and mountains. My visual field becomes crystal clear and I can feel the weight of gravity increase. Every word that comes out of my mouth feels like it carves reality into existence. This experience always shows up when I consciously tune into the energy around my Heart.

Many traditions talk about seeing a mustard-sized, blue light in meditation. After my initial awakening experience in my early teens, I have seen the scintillating effervescent blue pearl spontaneously manifest itself in interactions with friends, patients, and in nature. It appears like a spark of light, randomly within my spatial awareness. For me, seeing the blue pearl confirms a sense of living my purpose, that I am moving in the right direction and aligned with the Universe.

INTUITION EXERCISE PART II

- *When my intuition flows, what do I feel in my body?*

- *What external signs confirm my intuition (e.g., auras, birds, wind, a song on the radio, "coincidences")? These synchronicities are the Universe speaking directly to you.*

Pay attention the next time you feel the Universe move through your body strongly. There is an internal and external sequence to how intuition works through you. The more you notice your intuition, the stronger it will become.

Intuition is linked to the virtue of commitment. Commitment can trigger notions of forever, be it from the "till-death-do-us-part" variety or through feelings of imprisonment. Lonny Jarrett offers a different framework for the frightening word. He writes, "Commitment is the ability to be the one hundred percent present in any given situation." Commitment allows you to be fully invested in the moment regardless of whether you agree, disagree, like, or don't like what's occurring. When you invest your being into the moment, the Universe serves you with the power of its entire resources. That vast ocean of universal intelligence speaks to you through your intuition.

COMMITMENT EXERCISE

- *Can I be committed to the moment exactly as it is right now?*

- *Can I be committed to my partner right now, one hundred percent?*

- *Can I be committed to my job right now, one hundred percent?*

Notice all the ways you hesitate and negotiate to avoid being present in your daily life. Write them down in a journal. One by one, use your intuition to feel out why you avoid being present.

Commitment means you give yourself fully to whatever is in front of you right now. As you surrender to the now, the heart transmits grace to you from the Universe. When you really settle into the moment and stop resisting life as it is, intuition spontaneously comes forward into being. Intuition arises when you accept reality exactly as it is and exactly as it is not.

🪷 INTUITION EXERCISE PART III

- *Am I intuitive?*

- *In which environments and with whom am I most intuitive in my life and why?*

- *In which environments and with whom am I least intuitive in my life and why?*

- *Are the people with whom I experience less intuitive flow like my mom or dad?*

- *When did I stop trusting my intuition? Why?*

- *Am I ready to forgive myself and listen to my heart?*

Intuition is the byproduct of accepting life entirely as it is. Intuition is a gift from the Universe. The Universe honors you when you open to the moment and helps you see what you need to see to make life unfold more beautifully.

Consider that what most bothers you about other people are energies inside of you that you have not fully faced and accepted. The people you most resist reflect aspects of yourself. The resistance is there to help you see where love for yourself can increase.

Closely examine the people and things that bother you the

most. Ask why that is, and then look even closer. Underneath your resistance, you will see the same tendencies that bother you in you. Often, our parents are the first mirrors for this.

As a kid I was scared of Dad's anger. When I learned to express my own anger, I realized that love was underneath it all. Once I fully understood that, I could love myself and my dad and release fear. When anger arises in me or others I have the skill to mix love with it and use the emotion to heal, rather than to diminish. One of my mentors and author of *The Reluctant Healer and Healing*, David Elliott, says, "You are either exactly like the people that bother you or you suppress what they express." When you can own that part of you, accept it and have compassion for yourself, you will heal both yourself and make healing possible for the people around you.

 FEEL INTO IT EXERCISE

(Read through once first; then sit and take a few deep breaths before you begin.)

Pick an issue in your life. Close your eyes and be still. Release the search for answers in your mind. Feel with the center of your chest. Be willing to feel the layers of knowledge with your heart. The experience will not appear like thoughts in your head. It will appear like images that arise from feelings in the center of your chest. Remember that being right has nothing to do with love as love is always right. Trust your Heart.

After a few minutes, write down the exact thoughts, images, and feelings that surfaced without any form of self-censoring. Write down exactly what you may have wanted to suppress, perhaps out of residual fear, shame,

or guilt, as these are the thoughts to go back to and release.
Repeat the exercise to uncover deeper layers of insight.

The Taoist Heart

Ancient Taoists likened the body to that of a kingdom with the heart as the sovereign or emperor. Jarrett quotes the Taoist classic, *The Tao Te Jing*, to illustrate the power of the emperor.

> *With the highest [kind of rulers], those below simply know they exist. With those one step down, they love and praise them. With those one further step down, they fear them. And with those at the bottom, they ridicule and insult them. When trust is insufficient, there will be no trust (in return).*

The text elucidates the power of a righteous emperor, "The best emperor is one whose existence is merely known by the people and whose activities are hidden. The population does not notice the rule directly but observes all is right with the world." In classical Chinese medicine it is traditional that the emperor sits in the north facing the kingdom directly south. The highest level of the rule occurs when the emperor merely assumes position of the throne. The vibrational potency of the emperor, silently and with apparent transparency, emanates order onto the kingdom. On the outside, it appears the emperor simply sits and organizes nothing in particular. Through cultivation and deep trust in the Universe's innate power to create coherency, the emperor's concentrated awareness, stemming from his heart, penetrates into the very core of reality. As such, his presence alone vibrates the smooth flow of reality into being. Though that imagery isn't modern—the concepts hold.

When your heart is aligned with the Universe, reality smoothly flows into existence. To an extent, the degree that the heart is misaligned with universal guidance is equal to the level of control you exert in your life.

Molly Redefined Love

Molly, a patient and a friend, has worked for the last several years expanding her definition of love. She was raised in a family involved in crime and drug trafficking. Molly recounted many stories of drug deals and gun shootings she witnessed as a child. Her mother and father basically ignored her as a child. She never experienced healthy examples of love and affection from her parents either towards one another or towards her. When we first met, Molly had been bedridden from exhaustion for six months. We discussed her upbringing, and she shared her experience of love being synonymous with abuse and neglect. In the past, most of her actions with her own children reflected desperation for love. Molly's four children constantly rejected her attempts for intimacy. She began to see that her expectations for love reflected a deep-seated belief that she was unworthy of love. Molly had trained her children to treat her poorly, just as her parents had treated her. As she realized that her belief around love accentuated and perpetuated the same pattern of neglect and abuse, Molly knew she had to change. She started to love herself independently of her children's lack of affection. She began to see clearly she had the power to love herself and attracted people that willingly and openly shared love and appreciation with her.

Molly's kids still give her a hard time. She has learned to let them have their own experience. Molly knows she can't fix them or help them love themselves, unless they are open to receiving her support. Her kids don't acknowledge her birthday or come over for holidays. As painful as that is for Molly, she trusts that the Universe will allow her to exchange love. She regularly recounts incidents of helping strangers and homeless people, in which she experiences their gratitude for her help. I am inspired and amazed by Molly's efforts to let go of pain from the past and redefine Love in an empowering way for her community and family.

The Universe brings you front and center with your life lessons by design. It's a ride that starts when you are born. You experience achievement and you experience failure. You experience loss. You experience love. No one is exempt from feeling the heart's ecstasy or sorrow. You cannot escape confrontations with life cracking you open. What you do with that opening determines the degree of trust and love that exists between you and Spirit. It also has a lot to do with how much fun or suffering you have in life. Until your last breath, you are in the universal classroom. You are here to learn what love is and what love is not. Then your task is to help others along the way.

Wherever there is stasis or confusion in life, you will find a limited definition of love. Expanding your perspective of love around an issue will make space for healing. It is important to remember that when life becomes challenging, it is never entirely about the people around you. It's always about you. First, fully own your piece. Declare your responsibility to those involved. Then, if others haven't owned their part, let them know what they're responsible for. If you're feeling confused by the above statements, then consider most of the stagnant energy is coming from you. The world that you experience is a projection of what you see as possible and what you see as impossible. If you feel contracted, feel more deeply underneath that feeling and be willing to let it go in exchange for love.

Heart Disease

This section is not about atherosclerosis, high blood pressure, high polyunsaturated fat, high sodium diets, and/or other contributing factors to congestive heart failure, heart attack, or stroke. This section is about the subtle energetic risk factors underpinning disease. Again, illness is a way the Universe gives feedback about your progress with your life lessons. Long before an illness manifests, there are very subtle signs that occur in the body and in the external life to attune you to a disharmony in your body. This is why Chinese medicine and other traditions say: all disease originates from the Heart.

When you refuse to acknowledge the messages that come to you from the Universe through your heart, you begin to sow the seeds of illness. Energetically and physiologically the heart is the center of the spiritual evolution of the soul and the vitality of the physical body. All illness has a life lesson attached to it, which needs to be addressed for the individual soul to grow.

Disease is a way the Universe grabs your attention to help you grow up and open your Heart more. Spirit uses the body as a feedback mechanism to help you evolve. Did I say that already? Let me say it again: *God talks to you through your body. The more you ignore God, the louder, more painful and destructive the lessons can be.*

The 6th century physician of Chinese medicine, Liu Zhou states:

    ❝ *If the spirit is at peace, the Heart is in harmony, the body is whole; if the spirit becomes aggravated, the Heart wavers, and when the Heart wavers the body becomes injured; if one seeks to heal the physical body, one needs to regulate the spirit first.* ❞

The tenets of Classical Chinese medicine view the heart as the very core of the disease process.

The heart-centered view of the origin of illness does not ensure that all illnesses get resolved by learning the lessons accompanied by them. Very often, addressing the issues underneath a physical disharmony improves health. Other times, you may learn the lesson, yet the physical ailment persists or another one arises. Dr. Jeffrey Yuen says, "In spite of heart-to-heart connection (practitioner and patient), the patient tries to change that connection and they lose hope." Dr. Yuen asks the practitioner (in regards to the patient),

> *Will they pull you in the gutter with them? It doesn't matter if someone dies. What matters is how you choose to live. What you bring to death, you bring to life. You can't have the arrogance that you can cheat destiny. You can try to go against it, but you have to learn your lessons. The Classics of Chinese medicine teach us to embrace destiny, including our diseases, or even an early demise.*

The view that all disease originates in the heart is a guiding principle. Sometimes the lesson is to accept the disease, or accept the impermanence of the body.

❧ HEALING PHYSICAL PAIN EXERCISE

- *When I am physically uncomfortable, how willing am I to feel the pain (physical and/or emotional) and learn from it?*

- *Do I numb myself with drugs, alcohol, or sugar to avoid feeling my emotions?*

If your pain is manageable, use your breath to work through the emotional aspect of physical pain. Breathe deeply and feel with your heart. Let go of any fear, loneliness, and beliefs that something is wrong with your body. Your body knows how to heal. Stop perpetuating the belief that it doesn't. Set your body free to do what it knows how to do. Believe in your body.

New formulations of herbal analgesics can be very effective and can even rival the efficacy of pharmaceutical drugs. Not all pain needs to be felt. There is a sensible place for pain relief: to avoid pain altogether is a disservice to your growth and healing. Pain is a message that needs to be heard. Hear the message. Work on the life lesson, and move on. The degree to which you can stay clear and open in the midst of physical discomfort has a lot to do with your physical health, vitality, and long-term happiness.

Consider the role of heart in the context of illness, along with the pertinent and obvious physical presentation of the disease. For example, if the ailment is a bruise or sprain, then by all means treat the sprain physically with an appropriate intervention. And don't stop there—consider the deeper cause of the injury related to the lesson.

✿ HEALING MY BODY EXERCISE

Identify a recent accident or injury, (minor or major). Ask yourself:

- *Where was my attention right before the injury or accident occurred? (If you cannot recall, pay attention to your lack of attentiveness.)*

- *What is the lesson?*

- *Did I learn it fully?*

- *Is there a piece of the lesson that I am avoiding? What is it?*

- *Do I sense the Universe will need to teach me the lesson again?*

Illness is the Universe's way to demand attention. As Lonny Jarrett says, in the language of Classical Chinese medicine, the heart's job is to "discern truth to move you along the course of destiny." To use the example of a sprain or strain, in addition to treatment of the physical symptom, I ask you to look at how present you were when the injury occurred. This is a very simple example of how to take a deeper more heart-centered approach to healing, which, when expanded upon, can be applied to even the most severe disease processes.

All disease originates from the heart. Humans are, at their core, spiritual beings meant to explore life in partnership with Spirit. The body and all its faculties are the vehicle by which you venture into spiritual territory. Furthermore, the heart is the physical and energetic organ through which we may come to know and establish higher states of Love that further a connection both to each other and the Universe.

GRACE

If you have a strong connection with the Divine, you count on Grace showing up in your life, especially when needed the most. Grace is the active spiritual current of the Universe that heals without apparent cause or reason. The spiritual aspect of the Heart acts as a portal for Grace to flow through you. Grace is the catalyst that allows you to face your fears with the intention to experience Love in the world.

When I first practiced facing my fears, which usually involved a confrontation with someone about something I was afraid to say, the resultant anticipation of conflict, anxiety, and lack of sleep was enough to drive me almost mad. Every time I have summoned the courage to have a difficult conversation with the intention for healing, Grace appeared. As my heart opened, the heart of the person I was talking with opened and the conversation lightened and usually ended with gratitude for one another.

The nature of confrontation is often fueled by fear, which causes you to feel cut off from support from the Universe and the earth. Fear causes you to feel uninspired and ungrounded. Then, the mind has a heyday as you project all of your fears and insecurities upon the situation. Your refusal to confront your fears is the source of disease. Within this refusal is an assumption that you are alone and that Grace will not support you. The truth is regardless of your spiritual or religious beliefs; only by facing your fears can you heal them.

Grace always shows up. You can count on Grace to fill in the "*I don't know*s, the *I'm afraid of*s, and *what if*s." Grace will show up and support you when you feel afraid. Grace works a lot better if you acknowledge *it*, and allow *it* to help. You allow Grace to help you by breathing, trusting, and focusing on love. The choice is yours.

Do you think anything good in your life happens without Grace? Grace makes it all happen. Yes, you have to participate. But once you've done your part, get out of the way and make room for Grace.

Every day I work with people who want freedom from pain, anxiety, nervousness, fear, or depression. In severe cases, the body has been worn down physiologically from the efforts to suppress these emotions, in which case pharmaceutical medication may be appropriate, or else some other strong type of intervention. In the instance where medications lose efficacy and there is a call, or repeated calls, for stronger drugs to keep a disease at bay, the patient is showing signs of failing to keep disease in a dormant state. This, in and of itself, signifies a weakened constitutional strength.

For people who are not in severe states of distress, I guide them into allowing themselves to feel anxiety, to feel sadness. "Let it wash through you," I say. Your emotions are not going to kill you. They will cleanse you, if you let them.

Allow your emotions to cleanse you. Feeling your feelings can be very healthy when done in a constructive way that allows Grace to flow through the heart. Author and teacher of Chinese Medicine, Dr. Yvonne Farrell, says: "Though each organ system correlates with a particular emotion, the Heart is the system that feels all of the emotions." As you allow yourself to feel sadness, anger, worry, and fear with the awareness to let them go, you attract Grace, the Divine force that helps heal you.

The Universe does not want you to suffer.

The Universe does not want you to suffer.

The Universe does not want you to suffer.

Suffering is optional. When you stop fighting your feelings, you communicate to Spirit that you are open to Grace. The Heart lets you see and feel the truth. Still, you have the freedom to choose your own path. You can choose to align with the truth in your Heart or choose to go against it and pave a collateral path.

✿ PRAYER FOR GRACE

(Read through once before starting the prayer.)

Feeling grateful for one thing, take a long breath in and a long breath out.

Close your eyes and pray, "Grace, shower your Love

upon me, so that I may serve you in whatever way is most pleasing to you."

(You can say it again two more times silently in your heart.)

Really feel Grace moving through you.

How does that feel? Where do I feel Grace moving in my body?

Build a relationship with Grace, as you would with a lover, best friend, or guardian angel, because, truly speaking, Grace is your Guardian Angel. Right now feel your Guardian Angel nearby. Talk to her and thank her. Receive the love that's waiting for you. Your life is not only for you; it's for those who have yet to experience their connection to the Divine. Your mission, should you choose to accept it, is to be an extraordinary vessel, a thoroughfare for Grace to transmit blessings to those who truly need them.

UNIVERSAL SIGHT

The ancient healers of the East say that your spiritual connection can be viewed in the luster of the eyes. When you look into someone's eyes you can get a sense of their connection to the Universe. You can sense how satisfied they are with life. The eyes tell the story of the past, the orientation of the now, and the view of what's to come. The eyes also speak of what is trapped in the heart, the desires most deeply yearning to be expressed.

The heart is the great facilitator of universal will. Jarrett proclaims, "If an individual has received heaven's mandate but failed to maintain virtue, then heaven, in order to maintain the continuous outworking of its decree, must confer it on someone else." The eyes show the joy of fulfilling heavens purpose and the sorrow of ignoring it. The Universe, whether you're ready or not, will serve up your lessons.

THE NINE HEART PAINS

Classical Chinese medicine teaches there are nine "palaces" that you enter at various stages of life to learn lessons. Each palace helps you make progress within life's curriculum. When you struggle with the lessons in one of the nine palaces, you can develop heart pains that weaken the heart's capacity to interpret guidance from the Universe.

These are the nine palaces from which a heart pain can arise:

1. Health
2. Wealth (or lack thereof)
3. Prosperity (reputation, class, honor, how you are seen)
4. Relationships
5. Children/Creativity
6. Global/World issues (includes travel)
7. Career/Vocation (acquiring knowledge associated with)
8. Wisdom
9. Home/Family

These nine palaces are arenas of life where our lessons appear. Each of us will navigate the nine palaces, and each of us will struggle with a few of them to learn our core life lesson.

When one of these palaces becomes stagnant or depleted, the heart feels pain. The pain serves as feedback to notify that something needs more awareness. To resolve the pain, one must face the issue at hand. These pains will not resolve themselves until you learn the life lesson. If you put off an issue in one of the nine palaces and the issue becomes a heart pain, it can cause significant impairment to health.

Classical Chinese medicine scholar and clinician, Dr. Randine Lewis, cites the classic texts of Chinese medicine and comments on healing the heart pains when she says,

> " *If you don't overcome your heart pains, they will be transferred to your children, unless children are the pain you are faced with. Then it is a heart pain; a palace through which your destiny is urging your spirit to shine through...Long standing heart pains may need assistance through the unconditional love of the Heart and the unconditional acceptance of the Lungs to open and release.* "

Dr. Lewis offers an important warning. You cannot escape your lessons. They will be passed on at the time of conception to your children. Your children will inherit the lessons of your lineage. So, help your kids out and learn your lessons now. Your freedom can affect everyone in a positive way, and the most impacted are those closest to you. I have seen many people discover their connection to Spirit, and the many blessings that flowed to their families as a result. The greatest service you offer for the future of this world is to do your inner emotional and spiritual work. Heal yourself. Heal the world.

❧ HEART PAINS EXERCISE

Recall a current issue.
- *Do I feel any physical sensation?*
- *Does my heart rate or blood pressure rise?*
- *Does my stomach knot up or chest tighten?*
- *Does my throat close up, or do my neck and shoulders*

tighten?

- *Does my heart hurt?*

- *Do I feel sad?*

- *Do I feel the need to become defensive, hide, or put up an emotional wall?*

For now, just allow yourself to feel, and let the pain go. The memory or mental images associated with physical sensations can make emotions more painful. The image of a painful event causes physical tissues to contract, inflame, and secrete stress hormones. Even just remembering the image of an event can trigger pain again and again. When you suppress a painful memory, the emotional pain can become entirely physical. Over time you forget what you were upset about, but the physical remnants of the upset remain as pain. The longer you suppress or ignore your heart, the deeper emotion drives into the body and impairs organ function.

Stefanie's Heart Pain

Stefanie married an older man with an abundance of money and power. She had been suffering from an autoimmune disorder and fibromyalgia for over ten years by the time she first approached me. After a year of marriage, her new husband began to ignore her. He played golf on the weekends and extended many business trips. She confided in me that she was afraid to confront him at the time because she did not want to risk losing her new lavish lifestyle. Stefanie's health began to decline. She experienced more severe muscle pain and fell into a depression. Stefanie had a difficult time expressing her anger. I shared with her that if she did not express her feelings and communicate with her husband, then her feelings would eat her up from the inside.

Stefanie was willing to put up with a lack of intimacy in her relationship in exchange for financial security. She valued financial security and social status over love from her husband, which reflected a lack of love for herself. I taught her breathwork and took her through many healing sessions. She made some progress expressing her feelings, but couldn't really be honest about her emotional needs because of her fear of losing her luxurious lifestyle. She had been dirt poor growing up and abhorred the idea of ever living in poverty again.

Stefanie's husband eventually divorced her because she seemed so unhappy and he didn't want to deal with it. She lost her lifestyle, but is now more open to valuing herself and her ability to exchange love with others. Releasing the illusion that security and money will fulfill you is a difficult arena to heal. The bottom line is, love is the only currency that will truly fill you up, and the Universe will do whatever it takes to teach you that.

Here is a case in which the individual refused to face the truth and manifested the very fear she was trying to avoid. Suppression became a normal and automatic part of her life, yet deep down she knew she was hiding something.

Suppression discredits your intuition. At the heart level, this form of self deception shows up as a flat out lie. You lie because you value what your ego wants over what your heart wants. You refuse to abide by your heart's desire and cling to anything to distance yourself from your inner voice of truth. When you do this, your message to the Universe is, "I don't want what you want me to want." You are granted the free will to make your own choices.

Although, when you go against the flow of the Universe, you do so without *its* support. Going against the will of the Universe burdens the soul. One experiences a partial death that manifests in diminished physical vitality.

When the fear of facing the truth builds overtime, a person will lose the capacity to hold disease at bay because she has spent all her resources suppressing her inner guidance. When the body can no longer contain an illness, disease moves aggressively into a defenseless landscape. For many, death is the next step in evolution. Death is birth into a new life, a new set of circumstances to work out the soul's lessons. Those impacted by this level of separation may take their secrets to the grave. In so doing, they sacrifice a precious opportunity to evolve.

The heart discerns truth. Ignored or suppressed truth creates a sense of separation from the Universe and fosters illness in the body. Illness is not bad. This book is not an endorsement for a puritanical or hyper-vigilant approach to wellness; nor is it a condemnation of suppression. All people become sick and face injuries. Success in life is not measured by perfect health. *Success in life is the realization that you are Supremely Beautiful not because of anything you do or say, but simply because you are an expression of the Universe.* As you listen with greater acuity to the voice of Love inside, you will know the above statement to be true.

In general, people choose to avoid pain. Within each palace of the heart is a lesson. Heart pains serve to return you to your life's lesson plan. Pain acts like a global positioning satellite beacon. It realigns your coordinates with the Universe and your place within *it*. To ignore pain gives rise to confusion. Courage is not putting on a façade of strength to conceal the fear of feeling out of control. Courage is stillness that arises from within. The stillness gives you the capacity to listen to the heart of any situation. From listening with your heart, arises purposeful, confident action. Your external appearance is not meaningful if the Light of the heart is weak. Power comes from connection to the heart. To know your heart is to move through the emotions of sadness, anger, worry, and fear and to choose love. The subtle layers of knowledge gained from being centered in your heart require a fine attunement of awareness. The heart is the only way to know the wisdom of the Universe.

UNWORTHY OF UNIVERSAL LOVE

Suppressed intuition feeds unworthiness. When you suppress yourself at the heart level, the feeling that you are unworthy of Universal Love arises. As you suppress yourself through the sequence of organ systems, unworthiness creates a feeling of separation from the Universe. Lonny Jarrett describes the archetypal behaviors that arise in response to unworthiness. In response to a "reaction of past hurt, people keep the heart habitually closed to avoid pain and display behaviors of control, domination and delusion." Such people can appear as "joyless tyrants." In a state of depletion individuals exude "chaotic, apathetic, submissive or dull" behaviors. They cling to whatever "engenders happiness" to the point of exhaustion. The individual separated from his heart clings to "desires of imagined self." Unworthiness of Universal Love causes one to "prolong pleasure and avoid pain," unable to withstand the confrontation with suffering. Jarrett ends by saying, "all illness is a sign of losing touch with one's heart of hearts." If the heart fails to express its purpose, the end result is disease.

You cannot shortcut love. At some point you have to put the time and energy into what you care about. Short-term pleasure always results in exponential payback, like a debt with a bad interest rate.

- *Which of my habits prolong pleasure to avoid pain?*

- *When I prolong pleasure to avoid pain, what is the impact on my health?*

- *Am I clinging to anyone or anything for my happiness?*

- *Why do I continue behaviors that impair my wellbeing and my ability to be loving and receptive to love?*

- *What am I sad about deep down?*

- *Who am I angry with?*

- *What are the thoughts that spin over and over in my head?*

- *What am I afraid of?*

- *What does my intuition say?*

If you raced through this exercise, slow down, and take a few cycles of long breaths in and out. Do this exercise again, and feel these questions with your heart, the area in the center of your chest. The deeper you are willing to go, the greater the opening you will experience. This is the work.

WITHOUT LOVE

Loss is perhaps the most difficult part of life. The death of people you love is inevitable and unavoidable. All beings meet death. One hundred and twenty years from now everyone you love, including you, will die. This begs the question, what remains?

Werner Erhard, the famous transformational innovator said, the loss of love is the greatest loss to a human being. Werner's teachings reveal that the self-created stories people believe to be true constrict the flow of love in all areas of life. Stories of disempowerment impact health, mood, finances, spirituality, and worst of all, intimacy with people we love. Intimacy is a way to talk about the experience of love, connection, and rapport in a relationship.

Just as Werner's revolutionary trainings exploded around the globe into the late eighties, his past knocked at his door, and the impact of negative stories in the media about his family life caused him to make the most difficult choice of his life—to walk away from the transformational movement he birthed and brought to its early stages of maturity—in order to protect his family from the consequences of his past. Fortunately for the planet, the power of his work lives on to this day in its many iterations of transformational education worldwide.

Werner knew that amidst his hard-nosed, in-your-face style, people ultimately want love. Of course money, health, spirituality, etc., are important, yet, without love the richest person in the world is worse off than a beggar. Whether you agree with Werner's work and methods, his technology is rooted into our culture through the language we use. For example the phrase "got it" comes from Werner. Rather than saying I understand you, Werner taught the distinction of "I got it." That is, "I got that what you just said is true for you. I may not understand it, but I got that what you said is how reality is for you." When it came down to love and connection, Werner believed that if he had to be aggressive with someone to have a breakthrough, it was worth it, because a life without love is a life not worth living.

Love is always worth fighting for, is worth being uncomfortable for, and worth speaking up to preserve. Love is the point, purpose, and reason. It's where we start and finish. Along the way there may be bumps, but we should never go to bed mad at the people we love. It makes for a bad night's sleep, which is a guaranteed recipe for a bad day. Love is why you are here.

Withhold Words, Withhold Love

Withholding love can make you sick. Despite the bumps, I received a bounty of lessons about love through my relationship with my father. In the latest evolution of our relationship, I realize the only thing I have left to share with my dad is love. This realization came to me from a silent interaction I had with my dad not too long ago.

I didn't have much to say about business or spirituality—our go-to topics of conversation. I felt love, warmth and gratitude in my heart for my dad, and I was nervous and vulnerable to speak my feelings out load. I withheld my communication about love because I felt vulnerable.

I later shared this realization with my dad saying, "Dad, I love you so much and feel so tender that it's hard for me to tell you how I feel in words."

He said, "Luke, you are doing great in your personal and professional life and have it figured out." And then he observed, "Underneath my admiration and pride for you, I sometimes feel that you don't need me and don't appreciate me as much as you used to."

I realized that my lack of communication of my love and appreciation left my dad unclear at a deeper level if I did love and appreciate him. This was a profound insight for me that if I don't share my positive feelings with people, they are left in the unknown. Even if they know I appreciate them at some other level, they may begin to doubt my love, which creates disease and a sense of separation in our relationship. When we're in our hearts, we are connected. We are healthy. We are one.

 RECIPE FOR CONNECTION AND INTIMACY

Tell the people you love that you love them and appreciate them often. Notice what happens to their hearts. Notice what you feel in your heart when you speak your love.

Every organ system correlates with a particular sensory organ. The sensory organ correlated with the heart is the tongue. The tongue relates to clear communication. When the resources of the body nourish the heart adequately, speech is clear and articulate. You are able to communicate your experience concisely in ways that people understand. Intimacy and connection are ways to talk about love flowing between people. The key to connection is clear communication. Through words, others know who you are and what you stand for in the world. If you don't share your beauty, people will never know how beautiful you are. When you don't communicate, you leave people only able to assess you by their superficial projections of you. You are responsible for how others view you by how you share yourself personally, professionally, spiritually and so on.

Rate myself as communicator 1 -10: 1 being unclear and incoherent, and 10 being extremely clear and easily understood.

- *With whom is my communication clear as a bell and with whom is my communication unclear?*

- *Does clear communication occur more with the person who is more like my mom or dad?*

- *Does unclear communication occur more with the person who is more like my mom or my dad?*

- *What thoughts or feelings go through my mind and body around self-love when my communication is unclear?*

Trace back to the original memory and feeling from which thoughts of self-doubt and insecurity arise and note how it effects communication. Record what you experience.

Communication is linked to listening.

- *Rate yourself as a listener (1-10: 1 being you talk over people; and 10, truly being able to stand in someone else's shoes)*

- *Do I think about what I am going to say while other people are talking, or am I fully present, that is, am I really seeing the world through their eyes?*

If your experience in any arena of your life is less than satisfactory to you, I guarantee you have held back your heartfelt communication about how you can contribute. Take a chance and share your vision with the people in your life. You may be surprised by what comes from it. If you do nothing, that's all you'll end up with.

LOVE, THE UNLIMITED RESOURCE

Love is the greatest resource in the Universe and all people have equal access to it. Equal access means the wealth of love is equally available to all. Some people are more skilled to access Universal Love than others because they have refined their intuition and safeguard it. This is an ongoing practice for them, and can be for you, too.

You are born on earth to learn about love. Your family, friends, partners, co-workers, and colleagues are in your life to help you learn about love in the unique way that you need to learn about it. Your love curriculum is tailor-made for you. Whether you've wished or not wished to have someone else's life is irrelevant. The life you have is perfectly designed for you to evolve. No matter how old you are, or when you first became conscious of the path, right now the heavens celebrate because you are awake, and you listen to the best of your ability to the Universe. Maybe you wished you had different parents, friends, more money, better looks and so on. You're living the right life to teach you what you came here to learn.

Your life lessons may come in many forms, perhaps around money, health, wellness, spirituality, sex, relationships, and so on. However they appear, life moves you towards the emotional and physical spaces inside you where your definition of love is constricted, impoverished, and limited. Love has nothing to do with limitation, rationing, earning, or proving. Love simply is. And there's plenty of it.

Somewhere along the way, you adopted or created a belief about love that was inherently limiting to what you could achieve in a certain arena of your life. Perhaps it was a belief such as: there is not enough love for others or me. Maybe you've inherited beliefs like, love has to be earned or proven, or that love is something our family doesn't talk about. Or: love is pain; love is suffering, coercion, or manipulation. Love is working till you're exhausted. Love has to be taken. Love makes you weak. Love is standing by your loved one through the destruction of addiction. Likely a parent, relative or role model passed along some of these beliefs. You may be thinking, *No! No! No! Love is not like that for me.* Accompanied in places of your life that feel stuck or stagnant is a limiting belief around the power of love.

The life you have is perfectly designed for you to grow. If you want to have breakthroughs not just around love but around everything, then love your life exactly the way it is. Embrace it. Hug it! Kiss it! Love it!

✿ BELIEFS ABOUT LOVE EXERCISE

- *Breathe deeply and read the following words slowly out loud: mom, dad, brother, sister, husband, wife, ex-husband, ex-wife, boyfriend, girlfriend, Republican, Democrat, etc.*

- *If you feel a twinge of contraction, achiness, or tightness in your chest, then you have a limited belief around love that impacts your health. Did you get that?*

- *Take a few longs breaths in and out. Feel below the physical sensation of your body with the intention to let the sensation or memories move.*

- *If you drift off into another thought, bring your*

awareness back to the word that triggers you. Stay
present. Breathe, feel, and notice what happens in
and to your body. Stay with the exploration until your
body and mind have settled.

- *How is my belief about love related to where I feel*
"stuck" in my body?

- *Am I willing to partner with love to create an*
empowering belief about my wellbeing?

Believe in Love

Charles suffered from irritable bowel syndrome on and off most
of his adult life. The first thing he said to me was, "My gut has al-
ways been messed up. I have a super sensitive system." His system
wasn't strong enough to tolerate herbs, so we did five sessions of
acupuncture to tone his digestive organs. Charles began to feel
better, and we got into an issue about a lack of friendships in his
life. He confessed that he had a group of friends that enjoyed his
company, and another group of friends from childhood that he
wished were closer. Charles realized that he had a tendency to
focus on what was missing in his life, rather than the abundance
he already had.

On our sixth session he said, "I think my gut sensitivity is con-
nected to my sensitivity in my relationships." I was happy that
Charles came to this realization. He recognized deep down he be-
lieved that something was wrong with him because of the grow-
ing distance in his relationships with his childhood friends. He
decided that it was ok to let the Universe hold the agenda in those

friendships, and he let them go with love. Charles's gut occasion-
ally flares up. When he feels into the physical pain, he quickly re-
alizes that he is in a needy emotional place around his friendships.
When he lets go of this old pattern, his symptoms lessen and he
feels love for himself and the relationships he has. Charles is a
great example of shifting old beliefs about love into new healthy
ones.

Love, in its own freedom, can take any form it pleases in order to continually express itself. To believe love to be a certain way and only that way—positive or negative—limits the very nature of love. Again, the nature of Universal Love is to creatively express itself out of freedom: The *free* will of love.

Holding love in a positive light is best. Ultimately, to know what love is and what love is not, love must be allowed to grow freely and unbridled. The irony is that no matter how you try to contain it, like a weed that cracks concrete into pieces and reaches for the sun, love will break through limited beliefs to make itself known in your life. The exercises and practices suggested here support you to gain more access to love. Learn to cooperate with love's natural maturation and receive all the blessings, material and non-material, that come from a life infused with an unlimited flow of love.

Life will present you over and over with the most perfectly orchestrated circumstances to put pressure on those places within you where love does not fully flow. This phenomenon occurs as long as you live and breathe. Some people, many people—perhaps—most people, try their entire lives to fight and resist love's natural impulse to expand. You want to become sick and exhausted: fight love. This is a battle that you'll never win. At some point, perhaps due to exhaustion, commonsense, curiosity, and always

Grace, you may find the path of love.

If you're reading this book, you want to make more room for love to flow to you, through you, and to all the people you love. As love makes a more permanent home in your being, there is less room for arrogance, hubris, false humility, low self-esteem, unworthiness, and the like. The high virtues are emboldened through you as love makes a stand for freedom in your being.

To know Supreme Love, look to how you became bound, stuck and confused. The capacity to hear, feel, and live in partnership with the Universe occurs through the heart, with the support of the other major organ systems. In order to preserve the heart's connection to Spirit, the organ systems will sequentially take on the stress of a given event. Each individual is oriented towards illness in a specific pattern of organ disharmony. The system that takes on the initial weight of a stressful event is the lungs. The lungs facilitate the transformation from pre- to post-uterine life via the breath. The Universe communicates with disruptions to the breath when you ignore intuition.

Take a deep breath. Here we go.

肺

THE LUNGS

Hundreds of years ago, Chinese physicians wrote that, at the time of death, the forces of yin and yang separate. Yang ascends towards heaven and yin descends towards the earth. In the spring of 2006, I led a ten-day retreat on the coast of Oaxaca, Mexico. On the morning of day three, the sun surged overhead as we finished a morning Qi gong practice. The salt water felt warm and invigorating. A group of us jumped in the water and swam into the breaking surf. We bobbed up and down in the turquoise waves, and dove deep below the surface to watch the waves curl above us. From out of the deep blue, a wave, six feet tall from trough to crest, crashed on top of me. Used to surfing big waves, I didn't think much of it, until I looked around at my friends and noticed their contorted expressions as they gasped for air. I caught a glance of my friend Diana. She barely held her head above water. I shouted, "You okay?" Choking on the briny water, she exclaimed, "I'm not a great swimmer." I swam quickly towards her. Because she was unable to touch the bottom, I gripped her waist, and pulled her next to me. I kicked an eggbeater stroke I'd learned on the high-school water polo team. I felt confident and strong. Then I looked back out to the ocean. Lines of swell headed our direction. I didn't have time to think. Turning to Diana I calmly stated, "Alright, we're gonna go over this one." "Okay," she muttered, and we kicked over the massive cresting wave. We repeated the same maneuver, and summited the next wave with a fierce kick. Quickly I became fatigued from the weight of Diana's body, especially as she started to thrash in panic. The set of waves didn't let up, and the fourth wave was larger still. I didn't have the strength to kick us over the peak so I yelled, "This one we're going under, hold your breath!" "No," she sputtered meekly. I pulled her under the thick lip of the wave, and kicked through it like a duck dive on a surfboard. Thankfully, we buoyed through the back of the crashing monster. We were exhausted. I began to panic, as there was another set of waves straight ahead. I yelled for help to my buddy. Before he arrived, another wave crashed overhead. I didn't have the strength to perform the necessary maneuver through the wave. Her body now felt like an anchor dragging us down to the reef below. Under water I could feel my lungs heave and my limbs ache as they reached exhaustion. I began to feel the strangest sensation: as if my body was splitting in two. The life force began to tear away from my body. I could feel death near, as my visual field began to flicker into darkness. The wave stripped Diana from my arms as we tumbled like laundry in a washing machine. Everything went dark just before I strained to reach the surface for a breath. Finally, the ocean released me from its grasp and relieved me from suffocation. Miraculously I was still alive. I coughed up seawater, as the darkness flashed into the Technicolor image of a tropical, coconut tree-laden beach. Frantically, I scanned the beach, praying to see Diana pop up. The seconds ticked by, and, nothing. I held my breath and prayed, "Oh, God, please help!"

My spirit lifted as I saw her walking to shore, coughing up salt water with her arm hoisted around my buddy's shoulders. I extended a few more strokes towards the shore until I could stand flat-footed on the ocean floor. I looked back out to sea in a daze. Twenty feet away, another friend struggled to stay above water. Without a thought I stretched a few strokes back to the open ocean and yelled, "Stand up." She extended her legs and felt the support of the earth beneath her. By the time I arrived at shore, the retreat participants *sat together on the wet sand, shaken and stunned. I wrapped my arms around my good buddy and sobbed at how close we had come to death, humbled by the power of the Ocean—grateful to be alive.*

The transition from inhaling amniotic fluid in the mother's womb to breathing air after birth signals the beginning of post-natal life. The delicate alveoli and bronchioles of the lungs make the preciousness of inhalation and exhalation possible. Of the basic life necessities, air is the most essential. Without air, a human being has only minutes to live (or seconds, as I experienced that morning on the beach of Oaxaca). The breath that is life's constant companion adjusts and calibrates to the shifting demands of the moment. Life begins with an inhalation and ends with an exhalation.

In Chinese medicine, the lungs are the most delicate organ. The lungs are composed of a thin layer of tissue with slender bronchioles, which facilitate the interchange of oxygen and carbon dioxide. They are the organ system most exposed to the outside world. With each inhalation, the lungs bring the external world within. Upon exhalation, the lungs release unneeded gases. They also release emotions. Through the breath, the lungs help connect you to the moment. Every breath is a new opportunity to embrace life or reject it, an opportunity to create something fresh or to experience a variation of the past. *Breathe in, breathe out.* The lungs expand and contract, and fulfill their essential role in supporting life.

The lungs have an intimate relationship with the heart. With inhalation, the cardiovascular system draws oxygen into the heart, and circulates it throughout the body. Upon exhalation, carbon dioxide from the venous system of the heart releases via the lungs. This physical exchange perfectly mirrors the energetic exchange of the lungs. As you draw in the present moment with an inhalation, you accept the reality of the present moment into your heart. As you exhale, your lungs release aspects of your experience that no longer serve you. Carbon dioxide is one aspect of exhalation, and the tension that you hold in your body is another. When you restrict your breath, the body tenses up, particularly around the ribs, neck, and shoulders—the areas that help the lungs expand. Most people experience a tight neck and shoulders because they don't breathe deeply. Breathing helps you release emotions. You may inhale with a sense of satisfaction and contentment after a long day's work; just as you might exhale and release stress, or anxiety, from the day.

Inhale —> Accept. Exhale —> Let go.
Repeat...

The breath resets almost seamlessly and the cycle continues. In the space between the inhalation and the exhalation, a moment of stillness arises, revealing an opportunity for a new possibility. When you become aware of this stillness, it expands. Breath is the doorway to expanded awareness. The opportunity to experience a connection with the Universal Heart is found within the intake and outpouring of the breath. The breath connects us to every soul in this world who breathes. With the first breath out of the womb, the lungs empower spirit in human form, and link the physical to the ethereal. The first inhalation marks the thunder and lightning of the corporeal soul experiencing itself as the body for the first time. The chambers of the lungs are like a bellows, swelling and shrinking with each breath. The lungs enable you to know you are here and alive—that you exist.

The spirit of the lungs is related to embodiment. The spiritual concept of the lungs is unique to Chinese Medicine. The lungs provide the corporeal sense that you are in a physical body, and yet, that you are more than a physical body. You are Spirit. You are the Universe experiencing itself in human form. The lungs facilitate the physical experience of the nonphysical you. Through the lungs, you experience the exhilaration, bliss, and deep gratitude of being alive.

🪷 EXPERIENCE THE BREATH

Inhale deeply ... Exhale deeply. Be present to your breath. The breath maintains life. Without breath, you would exist as consciousness—only, without a body. The breath is involuntary, on auto pilot. When you bring conscious attention to the breath, you actively engage your Spirit. You are a co-pilot with Spirit.

- *What am I aware of in my body right now?*

- *What happens when I forget to consciously breathe?*

- *What happens when I remember to consciously breathe again?*

Be present, feel with each breath how life continues to move forward. The virtue of the lungs is gratitude for the delicateness of life. The organ system that is the most delicate is supremely important because it sustains life in the moment.

GRATITUDE

The inhalation and the exhalation of the lungs perfectly capture the balance of grasping and releasing life. The delicate equilibrium of the breath gives rise to gratitude. The heart also empowers the lungs with gratitude, so the two work in synergy to support life.

When the body is out of balance, choosing to be grateful can be a challenge. Love swells when you choose it in the midst of difficulty. Counting your blessings helps your body return to equilibrium. As you cherish the preciousness of the moment, you align with all the blessings in your life. Gratitude is the practice of seeing the glass half full and giving thanks for both the glass and its contents. Even though it may be especially hard when things fall apart, gratitude dissolves any resistance you have to life. It helps you remember you have a glass, and that it can and will be refilled. When life does turn around, and you have no resistance to overcome, the sweetness of enjoying your life is that much better. Gratitude for gratitude fills your cup and overflows it. A friend told me the glass is always full—it's full of water and air. Gratitude is a choice. In any moment you can see the positive or the negative. Your choice has an enormous impact on how much fun you have in life.

Gratitude for My Wife

I am deeply grateful for my relationship with my wife, Emily. Before I met her, I thought I knew the depths of love. I call her Heart Melter because her presence helps me soften my Heart and be more open to love in the moment. The best thing I ever did was propose to her. I never knew that the depth of love we share now was even possible until we met. When we married, I let go of the fear of losing my independence and feeling trapped. In the place of fear, a new world of freedom opened up before me.

I asked her to marry me on the Oregon coast on a sunny day in late October. I was as nervous as I'd ever been. I scanned the beach in search of a spot to propose. When she said yes, I instantly saw a cocoon of white light surround us in the form of a faint silhouette, and the hazy presence of golden-colored angelic beings standing beside us. Emily said she felt a powerful presence of pro-

tection at that moment.

Our marriage ceremony allowed our friends and family to further embrace us with blessings and love. These layers of protection have permitted Emily and me to open our hearts more and more to one another. Our love provides me with immeasurable strength and steadiness. I can see our love grow like an old growth Douglas fir, with a stronger ring of connection for every year that passes.

It frightens and saddens me to think that one day we will part physically from one another. Yet I know on the spiritual plane that Emily and I knew each other before, and that we will find one another again. We share an extraordinary connection and commitment to family, healing, and love. To hold our Love in my heart, and to let it evolve and teach me, is a supreme adventure. Now that we have had our first child, I am even more overcome with emotion. I am in awe of our baby girl. Life continues to amaze me. To allow this current of awe to move through my body and mind without trying to contain or control is a new lesson in letting go. I am changing. It's not always easy and I try to stay conscious during the process by counting my blessings with every breath.

ONE BREATH

The breath is something we all share. Since the beginning of time, all of our ancestors—the great and not-so-great figures of the past—have inhaled and exhaled the same air that you and I breathe right now. They, too, faced challenges and hardships. The first thing affected when life brings us something new, whether good or bad, is the breath. The lungs, the great organ of vulnerability, the most exposed organ to the external world, holds the utterly important role of meeting the moment as it is and as it constantly rearranges itself.

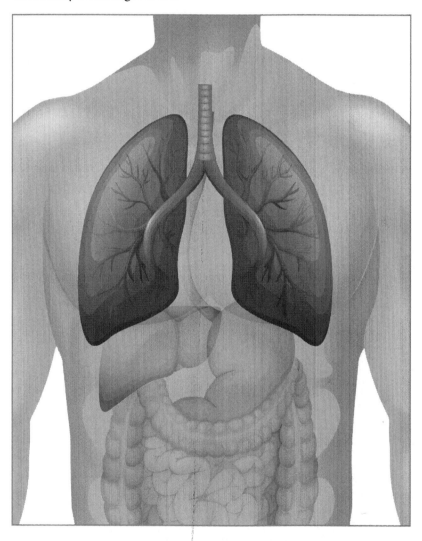

A moment arises in life and causes a catch in the breath. The lungs gasp in the presence of something surprising. Unable to draw reality inside smoothly, the breath constricts, quickens, and becomes short and shallow. The first three ribs barely expand, allowing just enough air to sustain life processes. The deep upper lungs remain deprived of life-sustaining oxygen. The breath turns stale and the body's metabolic output begins to increase, as stress hormones force the heart to pump faster. The diaphragm stiffens firmly beneath the lungs and inhibits receptivity to the present moment. Embodiment is threatened. Something else is filling the lungs. Sadness arises from an unknown source and attempts to find its way to the heart—to be felt and released. If suppressed, the body stores this physiological stress particularly in the tissue around the lungs, the upper ribs, the neck, shoulders and jaw. This tension stagnates blood flow, stresses cellular metabolism, and creates a ripe environment for lung and immune related issues.

Loss is something that happens every day. You underperform on the job and have to come in on Saturday. A patient cancels. The server gets your order wrong. You run out of gas and get stuck in the middle lane during rush hour on the Pacific Coast Highway in five lanes of traffic on the way to an appointment. You have a stain on your shirt after lunch. You rip your favorite pair of jeans when you bend over from recent weight gain. (All and worse have happened to me.) Small losses of dignity: feeling diminished by a comment, gesture, or look occurs almost every day; the smallest things activate an underlying sense of unworthiness.

When not feeling good enough already exists on the inside, and life does something to poke at it, that corrosive, sinking feeling alerts attention that *something is wrong* (and you add to this feeling, these two little words: *with me*). *Something is wrong with me*, you think. The feeling grows inside, and, if left unchecked, eats away at everything good about life. If unworthiness remains over time, physical signs and symptoms arise as an emotion always finds a way to express itself. You can try to keep it away at an arm's length, but unworthiness is still ambiguously there, and may show up as fatigue, congestion, sinusitis, a cold or flu, or asthma. The list goes on. A background feeling of depression, lethargy, and grief colors the lens of life. When you do not honor the intuition of your heart, your feelings of worth associated with being embodied comes into question. You feel displaced from the power, majesty, glory, and unfathomable beauty of your Universal Heart Light.

This book is designed to transform both the sense of unworthiness and the resultant disease processes to which you are made vulnerable. Unworthiness, in essence, is love in a state of confusion. Even if what you're feeling is scary or challenging, push yourself to stay open. You are unwinding precognitive, even past life, beliefs about love. The mere act of reading, breathing, and considering these concepts is, alone, healing. Be open to inhale new "good" into your life, and give thanks for the opportunity.

UNWORTHINESS OF MY BODY

Unworthiness is the seed experience that perpetuates the illusion that you are separate from Universal Love. Feelings of unworthiness, in its various forms, insidiously invite disease in and drive diseases deep into our bodies. We carry feelings of unworthiness into life through birth, and we work to heal ourselves over a lifetime.

Unworthiness around issues of your body is related to the lungs. The lungs bring Spirit into physical form, and are the first system compromised when intuition is suppressed. The lungs take the initial physical brunt of separation from Universal Love. When a given moment is too much to integrate energetically, you stop or slow down your breathing. Your blood pressure increases to pump remaining oxygenated blood through you, which strains your vascular tissue. Over time, the immune system weakens, and symptoms like allergies, asthma, and colds may present.

Physical imbalances in the lungs signify hidden feelings of diminishment. The mind, body, emotions, and spirit are one. Disharmony in any one system will be reflected throughout all systems.

Too often, our heads are filled with negative thoughts about our body. When suppression affects the lungs, you feel separate from your body. You may feel as though your spirit hovers above your body. You may feel stuck in your head, a sensation identified particularly with negative thoughts about your body. These thoughts may be related to self-image or to the occasional strange sensation of being in a body.

Early in life, the first episode of unworthiness is expressed by the feeling: "Something is wrong with me." We then feel self conscious and insecure about our bodies. A sense of being physically insecure in the body can arise. You feel the corporeal spirit detach from the physical as you question your sense of worth. With this initial sense of unworthiness, you may feel that your body is not a safe place for you. Your very groundedness is attacked by doubt, which can become a self-fulfilling downward spiral.

❀ SECURE IN MY BODY EXERCISE

- *Do I feel safe in my body right now? Why or why not?*

- *Have I ever felt unsafe in my body? What part of me responds to a Yes? Does that trigger memories or feelings about specific people, or places, or times in my life?*

- *What does being grounded in my body feel like?*

- *Do I like feeling grounded or do I seek to flee? Why?*

- *What thoughts and feelings arise when I look at my naked body in the mirror?*

- *What is my running commentary about my physical self-image?*

- *Am I mostly positive or negative about how I look and feel in my body?*

- *What is the origin of this view?*

- *How does my critical view of my body affect my relationships?*

- *Say aloud, "I love myself exactly the way I am."*

- *Say aloud, "I love my body. It is a magnificent temple for my beautiful soul."*

- *What subtle sensations and feelings arise in my body around the area of my lungs when I say that?*

- *What agreements did I make with myself about feeling safe or unsafe in my body when I was a young child or even in a previous lifetime?*

Notice even if a question seems strange, just make up an answer or listen to the first thing that pops into your head, no matter how absurd it may seem. See if the response resonates. This exercise may trigger a deep awareness of negative feelings about your body. If so, you can download my Lite Heart Cleanse meditation album for free at lukeadlerhealing.com/products/. Create the intention to heal what came up for you in this exercise. Follow the meditation instructions and do the Lite Heart Cleanse Meditation. If you feel like you need more support, download the full Heart Cleanse album.

THE DECEPTION OF DISEMBODIMENT

Unworthiness of embodiment can cause us to find faults in all things, especially in ourselves. This accelerated judgment and self-judgment is a symptom as well as a catalyst for future suppression. If your sense of self is clouded by unworthiness, you will see it reflected in the unworthiness of everything around you. With this feeling that something is wrong inside, you project the lie that something is wrong with everything. Unable to accept life as it is, instead you may seek to criticize life too harshly. You will begin to see only what is wrong with yourself and others.

When life brings you an event that you cannot embrace, the lungs reject the moment by refusing to inhale fully. Instead, the rib cage tightens, blood pressure and pulse rate increase, and a host of other physical symptoms may appear, such as coughing, wheezing, asthma, and more frequent colds and flus. The more uncomfortable you become, the more critical you are of a world that refuses to cooperate with your preferences.

If left unchecked, unworthiness corrodes self-confidence and trust in Spirit. You will begin to withdraw from life, to reject it. Unworthiness of physical embodiment will slice and dice the world around you as a projection of feeling increasingly unsafe in your body, and more disconnected from the Universe. Like mismatched circuitry, you blast yourself and the world apart with negative judgments when you fight the impulse of the Universe to conduct love through you.

You are here to love. There are times when judgment is appropriate, but you need to discern carefully to know when those instances are. If they come reflexively—from anger, or from feelings that seem based in the unworthiness of yourself or others—they will most likely undercut, rather than facilitate, love. Frivolous and unnecessary judgments cut you off from your divinity and affect your immunity and lung function, among many other negative impacts.

The moment or event that you suppress remains separate from

you—like a call left on hold. The energy used to suppress the past is unavailable for use as tissue repair, new cell growth, elimination, dreaming, and being present to the people you love. When you become aware of how you suppress your truth and let this habit go, you will heal on every aspect your being. When it happens, it will almost feel like magic as your healing accelerates. Your healing will be grounded in your willingness to be present and embrace the moment.

SHAMANIC TRACKING

In the South American tradition of healing, shamans in the Andes perform a ritual called soul retrieval to bring back a piece of an individual's soul trapped in a moment of the past. The Shaman tracks the individual soul through a dream journey ritual, locates the missing piece of the soul, and brings it back to the individual, who may be having a difficult time being present in some aspects of life. Understanding how you suppress your intuition will help you track and reintegrate aspects of yourself like the ritual performed by healers in the Andes.

✿ TRACKING UNWORTHINESS

- *What is my first memory of feeling that "something is wrong with me?"*

- *Was that recollection easy or hard? Did my breathing slow down, quicken, or suddenly stop as this memory surfaced?*

- *Where did my mind go?*

- *What self-criticizing belief did I create after this event?*

- *How do I reinforce that belief on an ongoing basis?*

- *What attempts have I made to change that belief? How have they worked? What supports or derails them?*

See the tools section to learn about breathwork you can do to clear this belief, and the impressions it made on your being. You can rewrite your past and recalibrate your physiology. For now, continue to make inquiries as to where unworthiness has a grip over you in your life.

LAW AND ORDER

The lungs correspond to the element of metal. A "metal constitution" seeks order and justice in the world. Similar to the lungs' equilibrium of gaseous exchange, people with metal constitutions strive to maintain the shifting scales of right and wrong. In a state of disharmony, a sense of justice turns into a sense of self-righteousness. You may be unable to let go of what you deem right and wrong. This often presents physically as constipation because it is difficult to let go.

Deep feelings of diminishment and unworthiness fuel the desire to be right and make others wrong. The desire to carve the world into right and wrong conceals a fear of change. Fear that is pathological leads to desires to control in an attempt to grasp life and keep it from changing. The work to maintain order and organization is constant. Paradoxically, feeling out of control can also show up as an absence of orderliness and general sloppiness. The desires to excessively control your circumstances or apathetically relinquish control are the two polarities of lung pathology. Jeffrey Yuen comments on control with regards to the lungs:

66 *Holding on is why you need to reincarnate. (If you) pass judgment, you put on the weight of holding on to that. The hardest things are to let go of fear and love, the people I love, the fear of losing who I love. The lungs govern Qi. They govern letting go in the form of expiration and exhalation. In a healthy state, the lungs make Qi flow unimpeded. The controlling type cannot forgive or let go. They have to be vigilant and defend something in order for the world to stay in a particular order. They don't just get it done, but get it done right. They are vulnerable and insecure about love.* 99

When self-worth is intact, a deep sense of goodness abides inside and a feeling of natural order pervades the mind and body. You are clear and connected to a deep Intelligence that moves life forward in its highest capacity. You are aware of the forces that seek to diminish and limit life. This clarity of awareness comes through as intuition: clear, bright, and accurate. It is fueled by the lungs' gratitude and acceptance for the preciousness of the moment.

❀ THE KENNY ROGERS EXERCISE

- *Do you know when to hold'em?*

- *Do you know when to fold'em?*

- *Know when to walk away, know when to run?*

- *How good am I at letting good things into my life?*

- *Do I self-sabotage?*

- *Do I let things go because I'm afraid of getting hurt?*

- *Who, or what, do I cling to, in order to make life more bearable?*

- *Where does 'holding on' show up in my body as tension or immune-related symptoms, such as neck, jaw, and shoulder tension, or chronic colds, flus, bronchitis, and asthma, or bowel-related issues?*

- *Where in my life am I good at letting go?*

- *Am I uptight, overly fussy, or even obsessive-compulsive about keeping things in order?*

- *Am I constipated or do I experience loose stools regularly?*

- *How am I with changes in routine, plans, and expectations? Do I have a hard time, or am I easy going?*

- *Do I have trouble forgiving others and letting go of the past?*

- *How often do I get defensive?*

- *How quickly can I let go of an issue when I get triggered: minutes, hours, days, weeks, months, years, decades? Will I take it to the grave?*

- *Am I afraid to take risks? How much do I have to control a situation before I take a risk?*

Jerry and Control

Jerry was in his early sixties when he came to me seeking help with heart issues. He had been taking beta blockers for several years to regulate his heart rate. Jerry had a very strong personality with a desire to connect deeply with people. He was very tuned into how people interacted with him. He had a tendency to project his insecurity upon others and could be set into a rage easily if he felt disrespected. Jerry smoked marijuana almost daily, drank about twelve beers a week, and was addicted to sugar. He wanted me to help him live longer and enjoy the time he had left. He talked to me about the abuse he experienced with his father growing up and more recent tragedies involving his younger brother. He said that growing up, his parents told him he was "a piece of shit" and that he "would never amount to anything." He would often start our sessions by saying, "Luke, your life is so great. You have a beautiful wife and a successful business." He would contrast this by sharing, "I missed out on so much and screwed so many people over." Many times he shared, "I wish I had started the spiritual path younger like you." He often emphasized how little time he had left to make spiritual progress.

I pulled out all the stops for Jerry. I guided him through powerful acupuncture sessions and heart-opening breathwork sessions. I championed and pulled for him to break through his self-deprecation and insecurity. We had confrontations along the way. Once, after not seeing him for several months he exclaimed, "I thought we were friends, why did you not call to check in?"

Jerry desperately wanted to create a way for me to reject him, to reinforce his perception of what he perceived the world had done to him. I was tempted to indulge him because he was so pushy. From the moment he walked into my door and sat in the lobby I could smell his volatility, even from my back office. I knew what Jerry was up to. If I rejected him, he could be right that he was not worth a damn. Instead Jerry taught me something profound. Jerry didn't need mystical acupuncture or deeply mystical shamanic healing. Jerry didn't need supplements or herbs to heal. That's not to say that none of the above benefitted his health. But he needed to be told he was okay to be loved.

In the end, love helped Jerry open up and trust himself. No matter the energetic state he brought with him into the treatment room, I just loved him like a brother. After many ups and downs I actually found him quite endearing. Jerry, like most people, was simply desperate for love. Once I let go of trying to fix him with all of my techniques and just loved him for all his faults and beauty, he started to feel better. I stopped relating to him as though he had a problem and so did he. Now when I see Jerry he is happier whether he is living on fruits and veggies or beer and candy.

THE PHYSICAL IMPACT OF SUPPRESSION

A variety of circumstances may arise that threaten you feeling safe in your body. Separation from your sense of embodiment may occur from an early trauma or abuse, a car accident, the shock of devastating news, or even something minor that, for some reason, is personally significant. The reason something is hard to accept is unique in regards to your particular life lessons

Spirit is a great orchestrator of curriculum. The more you can open, let go, and trust Spirit, the smoother the ride. With every new opportunity to stretch your faith, you become more embodied and grounded into your physical being. Embodiment is not always comfortable and does not always feel good. Challenge is part of evolution. Experience brings confidence that the Universe always supports you. If you're open, life becomes more magical, fun, and full of delight. When you struggle to stay connected to the Universal Heart, the body gives off cues to help you reconnect.

The breath is a barometer for the quality of your presence right now. When the lungs do not draw life in to integrate the moment into the heart, the pulmonary system weakens. Challenging circumstances can trigger shortness of breath, sighing, wheezing, asthma, coughing, and quick, panicky, or heaving breath. When an intense moment arises that you're unable to fully breathe into, your thwarted impression of the moment, stays with you in the form of cellular and energetic tension, which manifests as physical symptoms. These symptoms include stuttering, dry mouth, herpes, rashes, unexplained allergy attacks, frequent colds and flus, increased mucous production, weakened or loss of voice, tightness around the chest, asthma, wheezing, coughing, smoking (to bring warmth into the lungs and heart), loneliness, forgetfulness, obsessive compulsive behaviors, and more.

Every life includes moments that seem too much to accept. The accumulation of physical tension from displaced moments means you are less present to life right now. As this occurs, the health of the lungs and surrounding tissues diminish. Tension builds in the muscle layers of the upper thorax and results in a tightened neck, shoulders, and jaw. Breathing is restricted, which gives rise to the sensation of a belt squeezing around the diaphragm. All the above symptoms are attempts by the Universe to remind you to breathe and to refocus your attention. Generally, the sooner you hear this message from the Universe, the quicker your symptoms will resolve. The more you fight, ignore, and resist the universal message, the more uncomfortable you will become.

Feeling Blue

Suppressed or excess sadness stifles lung function. Sadness is a fundamental emotion from which other emotions originate. The lungs are the storehouse of sadness. When something happens that threatens your feeling of security in your body, sadness is the first response. Anger, worry, fear, and their derivative emotions follow. Many times, lung-related problems have a strong component of suppressed grief associated with them. Sadness is not very cool or masculine. Men (especially in modern cultures) or women raised by masculine-dominant families, tend to push sadness away and either act stoic or skip straight to anger. If you notice a low threshold for anger, remember to stop and ask yourself whether you are responding to what is happening now, or to something old or latent that you have suppressed from the past.

When you allow yourself to touch into sadness and reach through to love, you can heal tremendous amounts of grief. Healing requires the courage to be vulnerable and to let go. That's the only way to make room for love. Do not become lost in your sadness or grief. Sadness can feel abysmal and difficult to free yourself from; acknowledge what you are sad about. You don't always need to dissect what you are sad about or even understand it completely. All you have to do is acknowledge it, and let it go.

Healing flows as Universal Love fills the parts of you that sadness has kept blocked. Love is the goal. Feel your sadness, and remember everything you are grateful for.

The Law of Spiritual ByPass

The law of spiritual bypass states that there is no entry to the next level of growth if you have omitted or failed to complete any previous part of the spiritual path. The law of spiritual bypass means that you cannot skip over vital stages of life learning and expect to grow. Wherever you are is where you need to be to evolve. Sadness is often an emotion people are quick to bypass.

During graduate school, I was so eager to become a great healer. If my friends took a weekend workshop, I asked them to teach me the nuggets of the course. I would then immediately try to apply what they taught me to patients in the clinic at the Chinese medicine school or with my massage clients. The problem was that I didn't understand the guiding principles behind the techniques I learned second-hand from my friends. I had a very superficial understanding, and as a result, the techniques had limited benefits. When I was in high school, I skipped Spanish IV to Advanced Placement Spanish. I was in way over my head. Most of the students were near fluent and I could barely understand a sentence of their quick-paced Spanish. In the past, I had relied heavily on my charisma and enthusiasm to fill in the gaps of my knowledge. When that caught up with me in high school, I learned to hunker down and study the basics.

You gotta crawl before you can walk. The temptation to try to skip ahead in life is a trap. One thing I've learned is to enjoy the ride. All lessons occur on their own time. Nothing that's really worth learning happens without self-effort and grace.

If you are uncomfortable with feeling sad, you will suppress it. Suppressed emotion creates somatization, the transference of emotional tension into physical tension. Tension restricts the flow of life force, blood, lymph, and all other metabolic processes, and creates a ripe internal ecosystem for disease. In order to heal, eventually you need to face your sadness with self-forgiveness and compassion. Compassion for self is sometimes even harder to access and extend than compassion for others. Be easy with yourself if it does not happen easily or quickly. This is tough stuff and worth doing for your complete healing.

Grief Load describes the accumulation of grief from not allowing your self to fully feel and experience sadness. It is the cost for avoiding discomfort in the short-run and carrying it for the long run. It's the accumulated grief and sadness you have tried to avoid, but only through creating the illusion of escaping.

Grief is a heavy physical feeling that weighs on the chest. We feel grief as a response to a sense of unworthiness. You are beautiful, good, and extraordinary. Sadness is the result of failing to stand strong in your worthiness and be in your body right now. Sadness exists as a reminder to honor yourself, as well as to reassert a physical boundary of safety around you and restore the integrity and dignity of your being.

To restore your health and connection to the Universal Heart, you have to clear the Grief Load. For many people, there is a lot of house cleaning to do. The more grief, the weaker the voice of the Universal Heart will be. As a result, you will feel less connected to your purpose and destiny.

❀ TRACKING SADNESS

- *What am I sad about?*

- *Do I hold back feelings of sadness? Why?*

- *How did my mom and dad model feeling sad?*

- *How did my grandparents model feeling sad for my parents?*

- *Feel with your Heart, the current of sadness moving through multiple generations of your family. Where does the sadness stem from?*

- *What is the "story" that keeps sadness stuck in my lineage?*

- *Am I willing to let go of that story?*

Write down what you're sad about. Remember to breathe as you write. Inhale deeply through your nose and then exhale, fully releasing the breath. Keep writing until you begin to repeat yourself. Continue to breathe and read what you've written out loud. Breathe into the emotion. Breathe through the desire to hold your breath. Breathe into the tightening of your rib cage, your neck, your jaw, and your shoulders.

Bring as much awareness to your breath as possible. Re-read your story out loud and consciously breathe through any emotion or tension until you feel relaxed and free from the physical charge.

If the emotion remains intense, you are likely energetically connected to the situation. That suggests there is some co-dependent energy being siphoned back and forth between you and the situation.

- *Am I willing to offer a blessing for healing around this issue?*

- *If you are, then say internally, "I release all energetic connections to (person or situation) and offer blessings for the highest expression of love and healing now.*

Until you disconnect and surround the circumstance with light, you will be entrenched in sadness, which can lead to depression and anxiety. Letting go is not easy. It is essential because it allows you to get out of the way and let the Universe do the healing

Any form of diminishment, whether intentional or due to causes like death, war, atrocity, and tragedy, elicits sadness because all life is sacred. Feeling and expressing emotions like sadness is a natural and healthy part of life. These emotions, which we sometimes think of as downers, are only problematic for the mind and body when suppressed or overly expressed.

As you track the current of sadness through your familial lineage, you will likely find that not much has changed in the patterns of emotional awareness over generations. When I hear people tell me that their physical problem is genetic, I offer another, augmented interpretation: genetics are driven by behavior, and behavior is malleable.

Genetics are the cellular hardwiring of your physiology. When you stretch your awareness to recognize old ways of being, you can update to a new way of being, which changes your genetics and behavior. New gene sequences are known as epigenetics, the ability to change or adapt your genetics to the evolving needs of life. Genetics evolve because you choose to change or life forces you to change.

Nothing is ever just physical. Energy precedes matter. Spirit precedes the physical. You need a soul to have a body. Dealing with an issue entirely on the physical level is more rational and safer than considering how the energetic level impacts the physical, especially if you're unaccustomed to dealing with all of life's emotional and spiritual aspects. Nothing great comes from playing it safe all the time.

To change the past and make a better future, look at the qualities in your parents that especially annoy you. Consider that you're either exactly the same as your folks, or see if you recognize a tendency to suppress that same annoying quality in yourself. A good indicator of progress in changing your makeup is when you can return home for a visit, or an especially focused holiday like Thanksgiving or Christmas/Hanukah/Kwanzaa, and are not annoyed by your parent's comments. The same goes for your reactions to people in your life who remind you of your parents, or those who serve as authority figures in your life. When you see progress in your responses, you will have changed those genetics and begun to address the illnesses associated with them.

If you are asking yourself, *How do I know if I'm worthy of a happy life?* The answer is: you are alive. The fact that you are alive proves you are worthy. To be born is to be worthy of life, even though, paradoxically, your curriculum is centered on freeing the illusion of being unworthy. All life is worthy despite how it may feel at times.

Sadness and Forgiveness

Diana was in her late forties and came to me for help to quit smoking tobacco. She suffered some of the worst cases of child abuse that I have ever encountered. The abuse left its mark on her mind and body. In mid-session, Diana drifted into manic descriptions of the horrible things she experienced, sometimes adding in strange personal connections to famous people that may or may not have been true, but highlighted her trauma. Through years of talk and drug therapy, Diana found a place within herself to get through each day. She recognized that pharmaceutical drugs kept her from fully feeling her emotions, which bothered her, but they also helped regulate manic episodes. We talked about the importance—and process—of quitting tobacco. I shared with Diana that she had a lot of repressed sadness in her lungs and explained why it was hard for her to quit smoking. I said, "The fire and smoke from the tobacco brings warmth to your lungs. Since the lungs surround the heart, the warmth from the smoke also warms the heart. The tobacco herb is also warm in nature, which adds more warmth to the upper chest when smoking it." I continued explaining to Diana that by quitting smoking she would likely begin to feel some of the grief that was being covered up by her smoking habit. Diana completely agreed about the grief she was holding and insisted on quitting. She was highly motivated, so I agreed to help her.

We set weekly goals. She wanted to start cleansing, so I put her on a gradual program to cleanse her blood, liver, lungs, and kidneys. We started slow and increased the intensity of the cleanse weekly. Diana enjoyed acupuncture and wanted to do more work on her own. I took her through the breathing meditation a few times and then she started practicing breathwork on her own daily. Over several months, Diana became more lucid. I was surprised how intuitive and straightforward she became, not afraid to tell me what she wanted or didn't like about the sessions.

I've worked with many people who live with the effects of serious mental and emotional trauma. Diana displayed one of the most severe instances of such trauma I've come across. But she was also highly motivated to heal. Her spirit is strong. When we started treatment she smoked a pack a day. Now she fluctuates between a few puffs of her e-cigarette and four or five cigarettes a day. We're at a place now of beginning to look at forgiveness, so she can move on from the trauma. Diana is willing to go deeper every session. She came to me last week and told me, "I want to become enlightened." I smiled and said, "I'm so glad. I can see the Light growing in you." She seems happier and present to the blessings in her life and less triggered by the past. She is an example that even the most horrible things can be healed with time, trust, and Love.

INJUSTICE AND CONTROL

When you believe the thoughts that say, *I'm worthless* or *I'm not worth it* or *I don't deserve that*, sadness accumulates into grief. For unworthiness to gain a presence inside, you must explicitly agree that you are unworthy. In the quiet space of your heart, you silence the messages of guidance from the Universe. This is an injustice to the soul.

Sadness is the initial physical reminder for you to stand firmly aligned with your intuition. From this injustice, you may seek justice externally in an attempt to control inner feelings of lack of worth. Trying to control the external world is a manifestation of suppressed grief. From here the body becomes weaker. You may feel more bent to reinforce external rules and laws of society and less connected to the Truth of the Universal Heart. In a pathological state, you become the ultimate rule follower or rule enforcer. You need clear rules on the outside, as you are less connected to universal principles of order as dictated by your personal connection to the Universe. Life becomes rigid and unfulfilling.

✿ AUTHORITY EXERCISE

- *Do I have issues with authority?*

- *Do I kowtow to people in positions of authority?*

- *Do I see them as above me?*

- *Do I see myself above other people?*

- *How do I feel at work or in a social situation if I don't know the rules?*

- *How does this manifest in my body? In my behaviors? In my mood?*

In the absence of an authentic connection to Universal Truth, you may cling to societal truth or reject it. The need for rules to feel in control or the need to rebel against rules to feel in control, reflect tension, sadness, and feeling unsafe in your body. To follow the rules, tenets, or philosophy of an external system that organizes religion, spirituality, commerce, or society at large is not a bad thing. Rejecting society is not bad either as long as no one is being harmed. Initially, you learn the rules, and at a certain point you learn why the rules were created. As you become more in touch and in tune with the Universal Heart, you will follow an inner set of principles that often aligns with the rules of a kind and just society. Though if the culture that surrounds you is harsh, you may legitimately rebel against its rules.

The organ system's brilliant design maintains a balanced state that empowers a personal and universal sense of right and wrong. This equilibrium gives rise to skill in action. With time and practice, you may come to improvise and create new rules to evolve your experience. The ability to make a distinction between a deep, inner knowing of Truth and the absence of Truth makes all the difference in your health and how much fun you have.

Po, the Spirit of the Lungs

In Chinese medicine, we say that within each organ resides a spirit or specialized energetic function that relates to an energetic and spiritual sense of being. The lungs house the corporeal soul, called the *Po* (pronounced "Paw"). The Po provides a sense of bodily awareness: a knowing about where your body starts and ends in physical space. Chinese medicine says the Po doesn't take full residence in the body until the age of two. The Po informs you where you are in space right now.

 **PO EXERCISE**

(Read through once first.)

Close your eyes for a moment. Feel your body and what's underneath it with your hands. Notice your body and the sense of being in this space. Observe how, without even looking, you have a sense of what and where things are around you.

Keep your eyes closed and feel the space around you with your hands.

Instinctively, you can sense the location of objects in your environment. That sense is what Chinese Medicine calls the Po.

- *On a scale of one to ten, how aware am I of the space my body occupies right now (1 – being oblivious to my surroundings; and 10 – being completely aware)?*

When shock arises, the Po can literally exit the body. Often in car accidents, people will report painful symptoms of whiplash as long as a week or two after the incident occurred. The Po exits the body during trauma. When it returns, you can feel immense pain that was previously nonexistent. Immediately after a car accident, some people feel high because they are not embodied. Their Po is not anchored in the physical body. Chinese medicine says the Po floats above the body because the Po senses the body is unsafe to occupy. This exiting also occurs with severe emotional trauma. In Chinese medicine, we have specific protocols for this level of shock to the Po that can bring the Po spirit back into the body and accelerate the healing process.

Every time you doubt your intuition, you diminish your connection to the Universe through your body and create less room for spiritual embodiment. To be present, happy, and effective in life, you have to be in your body. Your Grief Load must be addressed.

Being present is not easy all of the time. You can create strength and cultivate the skills to address difficult circumstances as they arise. The key to healing patterns of grief, unworthiness, and self-righteousness are found in the capacity of the lungs. The breath can bring your spirit home to the safety, security, and delight of the physical body.

Sadie, The Glass Half Empty

Sadie was in her early sixties when we first met. She'd had health issues her whole life primarily around issues of digestion and elimination. Sadie was very uncomfortable with her body. She seemed extremely bothered by the smallest of things, like the ridges of her finger-nails. She spoke about her nails with tremendous concern and fear, and often repeated herself about similar physical complaints. Sadie was also a smoker. Many of her physical complaints were affected by her smoking, yet she refused to quit. She held a lot of sadness from past relationships that she was reluctant to confront.

Sadie had seen every type of healer and doctor over the prior four decades. Indeed, she had a habit of going to multiple health-care providers to get multiple explanations for her problems. Sadie seemed always to be looking for what was wrong with her, even as her health improved. Sadie brought her confusion and frustration to her care team. She definitely put me in a fluster our first session.

Sadie's issues were not going to resolve by the right pill, herb, and diet, although they helped. Sadie would find clarity when she herself became clear. After our tenth session, I felt like Sadie needed a major shift in her lifestyle in order to truly make progress with her physical symptoms. I strongly suggested she start a meditation practice. Over the next few sessions I taught her my meditation practice and she attended several of my meditation retreats. After several months of regular meditation, two times a day for twenty minutes, she still had complaints about her health. But beneath her concerns was a sense of peace and steadiness that was definitely absent our first meeting. It became easier for the two of us to find clear direction with her health issues. Amazingly, some of her long-term issues began to shift. As she became steadier with her meditation practice her body began to follow. Sadie is an inspiration to me. She rarely misses a meditation and is going on four years of steady practice. She still can feel frazzled and concerned about her health, though she comes across more content and calm and settled in her body.

SADNESS AND SOCIETY

Society has parameters around feeling and expressing sadness. Society teaches you that you are only allowed to express sadness and grief up to a certain age or under specific circumstances, such as the loss of a loved one, a missed promotion, divorce, or other significant loss. The loss must be deemed significant for others to be okay with you expressing sadness.

The truth is, sadness is a daily occurrence. People feel slighted and diminished all of the time. But unless sadness falls within a generally acceptable scope or reason, many people don't want to hear about it. We live in a culture of suppressed grief, which encourages more suppression. There is a sense in society that *"Your sadness triggers my sadness, and I don't want to feel sad, so 'Buck up, Buttercup.'"*

Sadness must be age appropriate. Emotionally, people develop at different rates. Emotional health is not taught as part of a grade school curriculum. Family and cultural traditions teach emotional propriety. The result of which, in school, is a hodgepodge of cool kids, artistic kids, nerds, intellectuals, and "rejects," where cliques rule and determine the culture of the rest. It's not cool to be sad. It is seen as weak and needy, especially for men. How many middle-school and teenaged kids silently suffer through these years? How many are doped up on pot, antidepressants, or anti-anxiety drugs? For how many youth have pharmaceutical drugs become an acceptable treatment for growing pains?

🪷 CALL THE PO HOME

- *Am I ready to heal?*

- *Am I ready to come home to my body?*

(Read through once first, or have someone read this aloud to you slowly.)

Lying down, close your eyes and feel your body. Using your awareness, sense the air around you. Notice your body and the sensation of being in this space. When sadness arises, the sense of being in your body and the space around you becomes contracted and your Po contracts or leaves. Allow yourself to feel all the past sadness you have buried and give the sadness permission to move.

Remember all the times you checked out, all the instances you left your body because life wasn't safe. All those little moments of feeling diminished by a friend, your mom or dad, your brother or sister; of being picked on, bullied, beat up, teased, mocked, or patronized.

With tender ease invite your Spirit to come home, to come back into the body more fully. Say, "I am ready to heal. I call my Po home. It is safe for you to come home to me now. I love you. I am ready to take care you."

Notice the subtle feeling of energy aligning with your physical body. Breathe in long and deep. Exhale and fully release the breath. Feel with your heart. Say the above and pause for twenty seconds. Feel the subtle movement of energy in your body as the Po returns. Say the statement again, and feel free to add anything that comes to you, and then settle for another twenty seconds as you feel your body recalibrate. Repeat one more time, and any time you do not feel safe in your body, do this exercise.

THE SEVEN PRIMAL URGES

The Po spirit brings with it seven primal urges: fear, anxiety, anger, joy, sorrow, worry, and grief. These emotions are physical sensations that give feedback as to how to interact with the world. They are messengers that bring your attention to whatever needs to be examined. They are designed to be explored, not ignored. If unacknowledged, the urges may turn into physiological imbalances, which further draw attention to a particular life lesson.

The seven primal urges provide you clues to navigate your life lessons. The Universe uses the primal urges to reflect a course change as you navigate through life. The lungs provide your spirit a physical form to engage in relationships with life. Your breath powers your emotions and interactions, and is the bridge to your heart.

As life unfolds, the body, through the seven primal urges, alerts you to something that deserves deeper examination. This occurs in a specific order, moving from one organ system to the next. Each system elicits an emotion to address a particular issue in life. You may fail to fully resolve a life lesson due to a weakness in your constitution, acute fatigue, physiological toxicity, fear of facing the lesson, or a combination of the above.

Physiologically, the fear of facing fear is a process represented by the sympathetic, "fight-or-flight" part of the nervous system, governed by the amygdala–the reptilian, or ancient, part of the brain. The brain is hardwired to support habitual activity. The more you hang out in the fight-or-flight part of your brain, the harder it is to move into a healing restorative state. By intentionally placing your awareness on something relaxing and soothing, you can change this pattern. See the chapter on Neuroplasticity in the Tools section to learn more about using the power of the brain to heal.

CAUGHT IN "FIGHT OR FLIGHT"

I am amazed how many people actually do not know how to rest. I, too, sometimes find myself caught up in activity and have to schedule time to unwind. If my nervous system is wired, sometimes it can take me hours or days to really let go. If you live a go-go-go lifestyle, learning to rest is a necessary virtue. I was impressed when my wife Emily and I interviewed our obstetrician about being present at the birth of our daughter. She said that she makes it to 95% of her births, but if labor begins on her day off, she won't be there. She emphasized that we didn't want a tired doctor at our delivery and we agreed.

🪷 REST EXERCISE

- *Am I addicted to adrenaline?*

- *How much time do I make to rest and rejuvenate my body and spirit? Quantify it in hours.*

- *Am I afraid to rest because I believe if I slow down or stop, I'll never be able to start or get up to speed again?*

- *If I stop to take stock of my life, am I afraid of what I might feel?*

Resting and feeling your emotions is vital to your physical and spiritual health. If you live a go-go life style, try slowing down with some breathwork. (See the Tools section.) Do this every day for one month, and watch your life transform.

LAUGHTER AND A LIGHT HEART

Whatever little or big thing happens in life, if you can't laugh off the sense of loss, or reconcile it in some healthy way, the pain of that moment stays with you until you address it or it addresses you in the form of an assiduous physical symptom. Laughter is a tool the heart provides you with to release the little things that try to displace you from the Light within. Lightheartedness is a skill to artistically and playfully learn from the persistent attempts of the Universe to get your goat. The Universe nudges against the places where you get serious, severe and significant about life. It doesn't do this maliciously. The Universe is always, always, all ways trying to burst forth, to increase its beneficent healing Light through you. It does this to purify everything that blocks the Light from fully expressing itself.

🪷 LIGHTHEARTEDNESS EXERCISE

- *How easy is it for me to be lighthearted, especially when life gets stressful?*

- *What thought keeps me from being lighthearted when I'm stressed and tired?*

- *The ability to laugh it off or laugh at your own seriousness is a high form of forgiveness and compassion.*

David Elliott says,

Sadness is a drop of love away from compassion.

Grief is a drop of love away from forgiveness.

Anger is a drop of love away from passion.

Every aspect of your being conspires for Love. The lungs provide the ability to breathe into life. With a drop of love darkness transforms into Light.

Universal Love will continually try to get your attention. You, of course, have the freedom to ignore Love. A dear friend of mine who does hospice work shared with me that sometimes she sits with people who, even up to the bitter end, still harbor pain, shame, and blame—unable to forgive, let go, or move on. They take their pain to the grave. To those souls, we send love for healing.

To examine what wants to emerge out of the darkness and

be freed into Light takes terrific courage. To merely look, or turn attention toward the unknown, is an act of bravery. I acknowledge your courage for taking up this work, and I am inspired by it. Thank you for affording me the opportunity to share with you in a spirit of healing, lightheartedness, and brother- and sister-hood. My intention in sharing this perspective is that, through understanding the sequence of how disease builds upon itself, there will be less fear and more delight to explore your inner world. To that end, an increased sense of freedom and spaciousness will arise as a steady presence that both serves you and allows you to better serve the world.

肝

The Liver

All life is sacred and worthy of protection. The Pacific Northwest is one of the few regions, which has protected its wild lands despite significant deforestation over the last two centuries. A strong voice for preservation and sustainability is audible from the people who live here. Within a few miles of my house, I can hike to stands of old-growth Douglas fir that are more than five hundred years old. Activists and loggers understand that trees are a renewable resource, and that the ancient forests have a significant historic and timeless value worth safeguarding.

The wood element, represented by the liver, instills life with purpose and growth; it offers a roadmap to achieve one's aspirations. Like the majestic Redwoods in Northern California, the massive Sequoias in King's Canyon National Park, and the sturdy hardwoods of the old-growth Douglas fir in the Pacific Northwest, the liver embodies each individual's hopes and dreams to align with their destiny.

You have a purpose. The liver helps you become aware of that purpose and carry it forward. The liver is the intermediary that conjoins intuition (represented by the heart) with life's curriculum (represented by the kidneys).

The liver is like the peacemaker within the body that keeps opposing personalities in communication. The liver mediates communication between all organ systems, and maintains a smooth flow of the body's metabolic processes. The Light of the heart illumines the hidden life lessons of the kidneys, facilitated by the liver.

Luke Adler

PURPOSE EXERCISE

- *What is my purpose?*

- *What do I live for?*

- *What is unclear about my purpose?*

Create a mission statement for your life. Here's mine:

- *My life mission is to bring love and healing to others through thought, word, and deed, and to help people cultivate a personal relationship to Universal Love that serves to uplift everyone.*

Acupuncturist and author Lonny Jarrett says: The liver holds half of life's plan, while heaven holds the other half. With each moment, heaven releases the insight necessary to illumine your life lessons, which the liver then uses to plan a clear sense of purpose and direction. The liver generates a clear trajectory for your unique life purpose to become reality.

Connection in relationships requires clear communication. The heart is like a tuner that receives insight from the Universe. The liver and heart share information with the kidneys to complete the triad of communication. To reach your goals, it is mandatory to foster communication both within the internal and external ecosystems of life. The liver plays a diplomatic role in translating the unique attributes and impulses of each organ system, ensuring a smooth workflow between all systems. If your liver is balanced everything flows more smoothly. If it is not, it's like a crew of workers building a bridge in five different directions; the results are tenuous, messy, wasteful, and lead to nowhere.

When the liver is balanced, regardless of life circumstances, a sense of "I can handle this" naturally arises. You have an easy-going, calm demeanor throughout the day. The liver's practical nature clearly organizes a strategy and mobilizes action. Difficulty and stress may be present but you remain calm in the middle of the storm. The still point within you remains constant amid a flurry of activity. The balanced state of the liver allows for the smooth flow of reality to unfold. Whether external circumstances are challenging or easeful, your nervous system feels balanced and you possess clarity of mind.

Chinese medicine likes to use the metaphor of bamboo for a healthy liver and wood constitution. Bamboo is very strong, difficult to break, and incredibly flexible. Bamboo is hollow and allows substances to pass through. It grows in dense thickets. In this way, bamboo is stronger together than separated.

A healthy liver reflects a strong disposition. You are able to be responsible and organized and at the same time display the ability to be flexible and change course if needed. The classical text of Chinese medicine, *The Simple Questions*, states, "The liver is the root of stopping extremes."

When fear takes over, you feel cut off from Universal Love, and out of touch with reality. A healthy liver calls you back to the lesson at hand and helps you be practical about how to move forward. The liver stops extreme thoughts and actions, and methodically lays out a way through the chaos. Likened to a general under the direction of a supreme leader, the heart, the liver mobilizes resources to help you address the world. As all organ systems do, the liver's primary role is to serve the heart. The heart's role is to serve the Universe.

A benevolent sense of ambition arises in a healthy wood constitution. You understand that together you are stronger than apart and you value a team approach to problem solving. You're likely to have clear goals, and be able to achieve one and then move on to the next, always in search of something new to accomplish. A master of Taoist healing arts, Jeffrey Yuen cites the classics of Chinese medicine, "The liver is the dawning of the new day." A healthy liver helps clarify new possibilities. It helps you take focused action to achieve greater growth and success.

Healing is Feeling

A friend of mine is a perfect example of the "goal-oriented, better-together" nature of someone with a liver constitution. Zack is a successful businessman in the finance industry. He's always on the lookout for a way to improve and evolve both himself and his company. He routinely seeks advice from other successful people and takes new training seminars to get an edge. In his personal life, he begins one hobby after the next, and thoroughly learns the basics before he starts another venture. Every time he finds something new to explore, he has the same, excited level of enthusiasm and purpose in his expression. Once he understands the fundamentals of a new hobby, the hobby fades into the background, and a new exciting, often better interest arises. Zack has come to see me for healing on and off for many years. He diligently works to become more self-aware and has become increasingly intuitive. His greatest gifts also conceal his blind spots for expansion.

In tune with his body, Zack knows that if a headache comes on, there is something he is unaware of in his life. His goal-oriented nature keeps him busy, and at times blinds him from feeling deeper emotions like sadness, anger, and fear. Zack's liver constitution naturally orients him to do the deeper work, and sometimes, his desire to grow externally keeps him from looking within. Zack came to see me with a sudden onset of sciatica. He showed me where he felt the pain and I smiled at him. He asked me, "Can you fix it?" I laugh and replied, "Not as quickly as you can." He looked at me with a confused expression. "Zack, have you let go of Rhonda yet?" His face flushed red and tears swelled in his eyes. "Is that what this is about" referring to his hip. "I think so," I replied. As he felt the sadness of his recent break up, the pain in his leg became very hot. I put a few acupuncture points in his feet and the pain disappeared instantly. I reminded Zack that he is very intuitive and that if he is experiencing a physical symptom, there is always an underlying emotional and energetic factor that needs to be addressed. Zack understands that in order to heal, he needs to feel. He has a good heart and I enjoy watching him grow.

SEQUENCE OF SEPARATION, THE LUNGS TO THE LIVER

We all have blind spots. Ironically, as people age, the dark spots on their body are called "liver spots." While each spot may not represent a unique event or memory, collectively they demonstrate our ability to push off dealing with certain feelings as we go through life. Recognizing your blind spots takes work. Most of us begin with an initial view that is foggy. That view solidifies with time and attention. When you avoid or resist examining your blind spots, you ignore the Universe.

We address our blind spots differently with each organ. The lungs provide the initial opportunity to process life lessons by fully breathing into them as they arise. Breathing consciously acknowledges the preciousness of life and integrates the moment into the mind and body. Exhale, and you release the feelings and beliefs that no longer serve your wellbeing. When you don't (or seemingly can't) breathe life in, you suppress the functionality of the lung's spiritual and physical systems. You go unconscious into the present moment because you don't feel safe to be present in your physical body. Other organs work harder as a result.

Breathe in long...Exhale long... Say out loud: "I am safe in my body."

The Liver is about expansion. Likened to a tree, the liver grows your deepest dreams and aspirations. When a painful moment from your past gets triggered, and you can't breathe freely in the moment, the burden falls on the liver. The liver is the seat of anger. If you have not cultivated a healthy relationship with anger, the energy of the liver will stagnate. In other words, you will feel stressed. Stress exacerbates all other symptoms exponentially. Stress is inverted anger or anger pointed inwards. For the liver to be healthy, it needs to help you expand. Anger in all its forms is the response to the contraction of your innate desire to expand.

How do I use anger as a tool for expansion and not a tool for contraction?

Anger isn't always "bad." Used skillfully, it provides laser-like focus that can quickly restore order in the midst of confusion. When used improperly, anger can cause massive destruction. Of all the emotions, people have the most difficulty feeling and expressing anger clearly. This is why liver function is often quickly suppressed once the Sequence of Separation is activated.

One can also channel anger to achieve a difficult goal. The Vedic tradition of ancient India declares that anger preserves reality from decay. The Vedas point out that anger used effectively maintains a sense of order and direction in life. Anger is the Heart wanting life to flow smoothly when out of balance.

Anger is a form of creative energy that sets life into motion with purpose. It does not have to be loud. It can be clear, direct, and loving. Anger mixed with love embodies the spark of the creative and reproductive power of the Universe. Physically this manifests in the culmination of lovemaking. Dr. Yvonne Farrell says, the orgasm is an expression of Divine creativity, which is ruled by the liver. The liver provides the explosiveness that allows the sperm to reach the egg and drive the biological and spiritual imperative to impel life onward.

Tough Love

At the end of college, I imagined myself with a clear sense of direction and purpose. After an extremely painful break up with my college sweetheart the last week of my senior year, I felt completely distraught without the faintest idea of what to do next. I fell into a severe depression. Constant mental images of my former girlfriend tortured me day and night. I woke up everyday in despair. I felt incredibly stuck and hopeless. The day the depression lifted came unexpectedly. It had been four months since graduation and I didn't feel any better. One wintery overcast morning at my parent's house, I began to sob into my oatmeal. My mom walked over to comfort me as she had many times before. As she lovingly placed a hand on my shoulder, my dad interjected, "Sandy, don't touch him," he blurted. "What the fuck!" I thought to myself. "I'm fucking dying here, how can you be so callous?" I was stunned. The room seemed to vibrate like the sound of a bullet ricochet, as my mom retracted her soft touch from my shoulder. My mom returned to cook breakfast. Neither my dad nor I said another word.

In a flash, I realized the time of comforting my pain had passed. My visual field seemed to flex like a screen made of plexiglass. I clearly saw that to get out of my pit of despair, I had to lift myself up by my own bootstraps, put one foot in front of the other and start walking. My dad recognized my emotional stasis and realized that I needed some tough love. Later, I learned that my dad had been through a very similar experience around the same age. I suppose he saw himself in my experience and knew what it would take for me to heal. I'm so glad he did. After that incident I consciously stopped replaying images and memories of my former girlfriend in my head and started thinking about my future.

Tough love is an example of using anger skillfully by being clear that you are ultimately committed to love. Being tough with the people you love is one of the most difficult frequencies of love to hold. Most people want love to be sweet and kind all the time. Life gets tough for all of us. I'm so grateful that my father had the courage to be tough with me when I needed it. During my life, he has helped me achieve my heart's desires and overcome a lot of shyness, shame, and unworthiness. A lot of his teachings felt like tough love at the time, but they were the kind of love I needed. I just didn't know it and would not have been wise enough to ask for it.

I've learned to be clear with people I love when I feel like they need a direct reflection to help them move through stuckness. Tough love has been a challenging skill for me to cultivate. I hold space for healing and love to flow for people. If you want healing and love, I can help you. If you don't, there's no point for me to watch you choose to suffer.

Author and healer David Elliott says, "Sometimes you have to be willing to lose someone in order to help them." Being tough with people you love is a very deep and powerful frequency of Love. The liver provides the ability to be strong, even fierce, with people because you care deeply about them. Whenever I use this tool, I remind myself that, *because I love you and see your potential, I lovingly bring this issue to the surface.* Telling people what they don't want to hear with love and compassion is essential to be effective in relationships and helps to truly uplift the planet. The best people in most fields are skillfully honest and clear in addressing sensitive subjects.

Anger is Love

As I shared earlier, most of the personal growth in my twenties, along with some of the most challenging work in my life, was about healing my emotional relationship with my dad. The process sometimes felt grounded in anger instead of love, though with healing and perspective, I see a greater and deeper truth. In my early twenties, I was afraid to confront my dad and to stand up for my vision of my life. When I finally did speak my truth, he began to respect me as a man, and, more importantly, I began to respect myself. When I finally got past feeling picked on by my father, I realized that his persistence to push me to become clear about my direction in life came from his deep love for me, not from anger. When I understood that Dad truly loved me and wasn't trying to shame me, I opened up to his guidance. My life purpose became empowered as I received his love.

Chinese medicine says that the mother's job is to unconditionally love her children to grow the Light of the Heart within, while the father's job is to prepare his children for the challenges of the world. Now that I am a father, I feel more deeply connected to Dad; my appreciation and gratitude for his guidance is immense. I can see now that preparing your children for the world is a monumental task. I'm thankful for the Grace that helped me stop resisting and start listening.

Confronting past pain with the parent with whom you have the most difficult relationship is a key component of spiritual evolution. When I work with people still pissed and hurt from their relationship with their parents, I hold space for them to choose to heal their past and enjoy the time they have left. If you have no idea what I'm getting at, chances are, you have not confronted this area of growth.

Stuck energy in this area of relationships is a lynchpin of suppression, and keeps you attracting partners, bosses and employees that remind you of your folks. This happens so that you can choose to heal. I cannot emphasize enough the importance of healing this relationship. I guarantee the Universe will support you to heal if you are open to moving on. If you are ready to forgive and choose love, your future will be very different.

Any area of life in which you feel diminished, unappreciated, or lack a sense of clear purpose affects your health. To fully communicate with your parents is an act that helps you claim your purpose and direction in life. You take them off the hook for the condition of your circumstances. Said differently, to be fully responsible for your success and failure in life, stop blaming your parents for why you are unhappy. Confronting your parents is not about making them wrong. It's about taking ownership of your life direction. Owning your purpose sets you free from feeling like you have to live up to your parents' expectations or rebel against them. Instead you get to freely choose the course of your life and be fully responsible for that choice.

❀ HEALING MOM AND DAD

- *With which parent do I have the most painful relationship? For that parent:*

- *What am I hurt or still pissed about?*

- *What am I still blaming them for?*

- *What communication have I withheld from my mom or dad? Why? (Notice how your answer to "Why" holds you back in other areas of your life).*

- *Using my intuition, what fear around Mom or Dad is buried underneath my perception of their expectations of me?*

- *Do I bottle up anger, and manifest stomach aches, headaches, breathing issues, or menstrual issues? How does suppressed anger manifest in my body?*

- *Is my anger explosive or implosive?*

- *On a scale of one to ten, how skillfully do I communicate anger? (1–being suppress anger completely or explode in rage; 10–being able to express with love and precise articulation)*

The parent you have the most challenging relationship with may no longer be here. If that's the case, write the parent a letter, and express anything left unsaid. Then burn the letter with the intention to offer your communication to be fully healed and resolved with help from the Universe. Do this as many times as you need to until you feel more whole and complete about the relationship. If your parent is still alive, think deeply about what you have said. When you feel you are ready, send the letter or set up a time to speak to Mom or Dad face to face. If you really want to heal, be prepared to do the work with them. Don't just drop your words on them and run. Seeing a good counselor with your parents can be a safe way to begin to talk about unresolved issues in these relationships. Remember, the goal is to create a space for more love to flow, not less.

BOUNDARIES

The liver in balance provides clear parameters to reach for your dreams, as well as accomplish life's daily goals. Ease with feeling, and expressing anger empowers fulfillment of the deepest desires of your Heart.

Anger is an emotion that accesses discipline. The right amount of discipline enables steady progress in worldly and spiritual life. Suppression can be softened with the willingness of the liver by allowing love to mix with anger. Behind all emotions is the energy of love. You get angry because you care about something. Anger is not about blame. It's a force for love to flow powerfully towards something. Behind your anger is love. Use this powerful emotion to generate love rather than diminish it. It takes skill to set a clear boundary for love to flow. People tend to go one of two ways with boundaries. Either they're rigid, which does not allow love to flow, or they're nonexistent, which leaves you open to being taken advantage of. This has a lot to do with understanding the dynamics of your relationships with others, and of being willing to look at how much you give and how much you take, at where that balance is, and where to draw the line.

A boundary is an effective tool to cultivate love. Skillfully deploying anger allows love to flow in constructive ways to heal the issue at hand. When you're clear about your purpose, you can be clear with a boundary that allows love to flow between you and the person you have the most difficulty with in your life. You can stop disease in its tracks by creating a clear path for love to flow.

Boundaries and Love

Early in my career, whenever a male fifty-five years or older came in the clinic, my blood pressure would rise and I became tense. Anyone who reminded me of my father gave me another opportunity to love the part of myself that was still afraid of Dad.

Gabriel was in his early sixties and wanted to quit smoking. He had a fear of leaving home. Gabriel was a nice man, but beneath his kind demeanor, I could feel a volcano of sadness, rage, and terror waiting to explode. It was a big deal even for him to leave home to come in for treatment. I was very sensitive and gentle with him. We got along great the first few visits. On his fourth session, he criticized me for not spotting a bruise on his left pinky toe. I remember clearly as he exclaimed, "What kind of doctor are you to not notice an obvious injury?" I was a bit taken aback by his quick turn of temperament from kindness to shrillness. At the same time, I wasn't surprised. I knew the monster would come out of hiding at some point.

I've learned many times that as trust grows between my patients and me, sometimes they will test the boundaries of my commitment. Gabriel tested me to see if I would abandon him like others had in the past. I blew off the statement and was more apologetic than I should have been. Four sessions later, he questioned the way I greeted him and said, "Your greeting was inauthentic and not heartfelt." He continued, and commanded, "Greet me again. This time with your heart open." Gabriel didn't like being advised by other people, let alone by someone half his age. He wanted to play a mentor role with me without my permission. This time, he pushed the boundaries of my self-respect. I was clear about looking out for his best interests, and said to Gabriel, "This is not working." He asked for his money back. I refunded the session immediately and we said our goodbyes. I was proud of myself for speaking up.

My early years in practice, the Universe brought me many lessons to further heal my relationship with my father. Many were uncomfortable. The discomfort, however, left me more and more empowered each time I met someone whom I perceived as threat-

ening. Each person that came in who reminded me of my dad helped me become clearer about my purpose to help others heal their pain with masculine energies. This is an arena of healing where I have a lot of confidence holding space for people to love themselves through this kind of pain, shame, and unworthiness.

Pushy people, long to be loved. The skillful healer generates love in such a disarming way that people have no choice but to open up and heal.

A few years later, I got a call from Gabriel. He profusely apologized for his behavior and how our relationship ended. I remember him saying, "Eugene's a small town. It would be nice to run into each other with good feelings in our hearts." I agreed and said, "It was water under the bridge." I wished him love and blessings. We haven't seen each other since.

Boundaries are essential for healing relationships with difficult people. Difficult people are in your life to help you get clear about what love is and what love is not. The people that rub you the wrong way help you see that only you have the power to love yourself.

Boundaries help you become skillful in the midst of the struggle for self-love. A boundary is about you being clear—not with other people but with the Universe—that you love yourself, and that no matter what comes your way, you are not going to compromise that you are a good person deep inside. A boundary is a tool to heal people and places that lack love. When you can offer and receive love to and from the people you have the most difficulty with, you will have made tremendous progress in your relationship with anger and boundaries. The self-love that comes from establishing a clear boundary helps your sense of purpose expand. In my twenties, when I became clear that I loved my spiritual side whether my dad supported my work or not, my love and respect for myself exponentially increased, and my dad respected the strength of my clarity.

The Universe will test your self-love over and over until you are resolute about loving yourself, all of yourself: the insecure, the confident, and the shamed—every last bit of you. A boundary is not something that keeps us apart. A boundary is clarity about how love can bring us together.

❧ BOUNDARIES IN RELATIONSHIPS

- *Do I love myself?*

- *What has been the most painful relationship in my life?*

- *What unfinished business do I have with that person that is reflected in other relationships in my life?*

- *What do I have in common with that person?*

- *How clear am I about my boundaries with difficult people?*

- *How clear am I with other people's boundaries?*

- *Where or with whom do I become shy or invisible?*

- *Do I feel suppressed or underappreciated in any of my relationships?*

- *Am I settling for a version of "love" that is not uplifting? What am I afraid of?*

- *Am I willing to heal?*

Any time you feel either less than or diminished, or inflated and arrogant, you are unclear about your boundaries and self-worth. The polarity of feeling less than or feeling better than others arises as a result of confusion around purpose and self-love. When you suppress anger, the liver has to work harder to move blood through the body. Unresolved painful relationships impact the ease by which the liver can do this. The skill of a clear boundary aids the liver to regulate blood flow and alleviate stress. Life does not have to be hard if you're willing to love yourself. When you are clear about your self worth and feel good deep in your heart, you can communicate your needs to people. That is one way to create a boundary. The liver helps you get clear to align with the oversight of Universal Love.

 HOW TO LOVE MYSELF EXERCISE

Look in the mirror and breathe for a few minutes. Get grounded, and feel your feet on the ground. Say "I love myself," out loud, three times.

Breathe and feel. Then try these phrases:

- *"Hey, you handsome devil." Acknowledge your beautiful body. Breathe through any contrary thoughts or feelings.*

- *"I'm bringin' sexy back." Breathe and feel your sexiness. Let yourself feel good.*

Have fun with these. Notice if you are being too serious, and lighten up.

- *"You are a beautiful soul." See the light shining through your eyes.*

Love is a choice. It's simple. Not always easy, but that's why we're here.

The Myth that Intimacy is Feeling One Another's Pain

In popular culture there is a belief that commiserating with a friend or partner's pain and emotional wounds deepens intimacy. In the treatment room, a patient may become belligerent with me as a way to make me feel and experience their pain. The unconscious idea is "When you feel how bad my pain is, then you'll really know and understand me." This idea actually strengthens and perpetuates seeds of unworthiness that see codependence as a necessary way of relating. If I don't play, I am not perceived as empathetic. If I do, I reinforce a paradigm that needs to heal.

In a balanced state, the liver provides a deep feeling of inner goodness. A healthy emotional expression of the liver reflects through and through without any doubt that you are truly a good person. A resolute sense of feeling good to the core is the clarity required to set a boundary with people who want to inject you with their pain as a form of intimacy. This is where the heroism of healing comes into play. When people close to you or in the periphery of your life insist that you're not good enough, you have a choice to agree with their story as projected onto you or to hold to your awareness of self-love. When you hold self-love constant, you allow people in your life either to choose love or reject it. Just because people in your life don't love themselves doesn't mean you have to be like them. The clearer you are about love, the greater the opportunity for people around you to be clear about love.

A healthy boundary asks people to show up in their Divinity instead of in their pain. Love is not digesting people's pain for them. This is the courageous work of healing. To insist on the purity and power of love is a choice; a choice that will be challenged by the people who are still unclear about where love comes from.

As others seek you out for solace, some may, in their hurt and confusion, want you to feel and be responsible for their pain. They may project their pain onto your sense of self. Notice if you have this tendency in your own life.

The liver gives you the strength to carry your own pain and be clear with others about their responsibility to carry and heal their pain. Taking on the pain of others is a fool's errand. I'm not talking about hearing out a buddy who needs someone to listen to him after a breakup, or when your friend needs to talk about her breast cancer diagnosis. That is beautiful and important work to do. I'm talking about when people want you to be responsible for their insecurity, like my patient Gabriel. Letting yourself be taken advantage of by pushy or needy people does not serve you or them. No matter how uncomfortable it may be, when you set a boundary with people who want you to feel their pain you create a space for love to be cultivated.

Love begins and ends with you. Insist on the goodness of your heart, and others will eventually get the message that you're interested in love, not pain. Enough pain. Enough bombs. Right here, right now, we *must* choose love. Like John Lennon sings, "I may be a dreamer," and I've seen people change.

CLARITY OF PURPOSE

Ultimately, to maintain a clear direction with your purpose, you need to be clear about what energies you want in your life, and what energies you don't. This occurs first on an energetic level and then on a physical one.

When I became a father and endured months of insomnia, I realized that I was done taking on patients who were extremely resistant to healing and unconsciously wanting me to do a lot of the work for them. Being a new dad, I wanted two things: one, to have enough energy at the end of my workday for my family; and two, to have enough energy to enjoy working with people who wanted to improve their lives. As I became crystal clear about these two realizations, the patients that sucked up ninety percent of my energy in a day stopped showing up.

I would be doing a disservice to do your work for you, even if I could. We each have to learn our own lessons or we'll never grow. One of my lessons has been to feel the pain and gain the compassion to let people go through the discomfort of healing. I am clear now that Spirit is doing the work, and it is much easier for me to get out of the way. The only people that I'm willing to take on energetically, albeit to a small extent, live at my house. For my patients, I create a healing space and healing intention for them to show up and choose to do their work, with Spirit and me helping.

Being Uptight and Burnout

Where there is disease, there is unconsciousness. Every day, I work with people to shed light on aspects of the mind-body that seem hidden or concealed from conscious awareness. Seeing and freeing the underlying structures of disease can be difficult when structures of disease are the lenses you look through in search of clarity and direction.

Three years into my practice, I began to experience extreme fatigue, restless sleep, and vision problems. For months I treated myself with herbs and cleanses, and took time off to rest. I felt a little better, but the exhaustion returned quickly if I stayed up too late or had an extra busy day at work. I sought the help of other healers. One of them told me I seemed a bit uptight. He actually told me, "Take the stick out of your ass and let the wild side of your personality come through more." I realized that at work, I was so professional that there was a limited place for my personality, let alone my humanity. Over the next six months, I let my hair down. I told more jokes, laughed a lot, and had more fun at work. Rather than conceal my personal life, I let it all hang out and noticed people felt even more comfortable and safe with me. I had been afraid to be me. I had an image of a very professional young doctor that I thought people expected. Gradually, I realized the goggles that colored my perception had caused my exhaustion. My vision improved, as did my sleep. I'm seeing just as many patients today and having lots of fun.

When the effects of suppression reach the liver, tracking unconsciousness becomes a challenge as the liver falters in its capacity to maintain a smooth flow of blood. As unconsciousness drives itself deeper into the body, a gamut of physical and emotional symptoms arise, such as: anger, irritability, whining, moderate to extreme mood swings, headaches, a tight neck and shoulders, prostate issues, erectile dysfunction, premature or absence of orgasm, gas, belching, acid regurgitation, constipation, diarrhea, small bitty goat stools, breast tenderness, mild to severe menstrual cramps, dizziness, vertigo, obsessive-compulsive behaviors, inability to make decisions, righteous indignation, over-controlling, shouting, sulking, snapping, bitching, and more.

The liver provides the capacity for you to take responsibility for your life. Owning up to your part in the creation of your life circumstances empowers Grace to help you heal. Grace is the guardian of your Divine purpose. Grace protects you from the parts of yourself that try to make you believe that you are not Divine. As long as you breathe, there is an opportunity to let your heart lead the way. The liver has a partnership with Grace that allows you to hand over your individual sense of control, and to experience the relief of accepting just how life is with the Universe as your Copilot.

Symptoms are indicators that you are not attuned to Universal

Love and have been somewhat closed off to receive Grace. This is not to say that when you examine your underlying emotional issues, all physical symptoms instantly resolve. The body will heal faster when you see and own your part in perpetuating your state of health. If the disease process has progressed significantly, long-term work is required to nurse the body back to equilibrium. Again, physical symptoms are often the transference of emotional pain into physical pain, what healers call, somatization.

As you track the disease from the roots to the tendrils to the micro-cellular stirrings of dis-ease, you will find energetic tendencies that are the predictable and patterned ways you interact with life. In your attempts to cope with negative circumstances through the mechanism of suppression, you have become an expert in these patterns. Think about a farmer who tills over the same furrows in his fields year after year. It gets easier each time, and the ruts grow deeper and deeper.

These energetic patterns correlate with your individual propensity for disease. If you're beating yourself up right now, then the liver is definitely having its way with you.

🪷 SOFTEN THE LIVER EXERCISE

Take a deep breath and pause for a few moments.

I am Universal Love. I am open to Grace and receive it fully, as I breathe in and feel God's Love move through my head, mouth, throat, chest, abdomen and pelvis, and into my legs, down to my feet, and deep into the earth.

Read this at least two more times.

RIGIDITY AND TIMIDITY

The liver system can be compared to bamboo, when it becomes compromised by a moment of unconsciousness from the past, two behavioral presentations arise: excess rigidity (wood so hard that it becomes brittle and easy to break) and excess flexibility (or one that is so pliable that it has no strength). These are not the materials with which to build a home or a life. Chinese medicine frequently incorporates bamboo in herbal remedies because it has the ability to transform stagnation and create a smooth energy flow for a healthy body and soul.

In terms of behavior, liver imbalances can show up as belligerence or arrogance and timidity or shyness. Lonny Jarrett says there is great harm in ethos of the arrogant man who believes, "It doesn't matter how I achieve my goal, just as long as I do. Just or unjust, with integrity or not, I will achieve my goal by any means necessary." The opposite is similarly unhelpful. The timid man who rejects his worthiness to achieve goals and pretends that his heart-centered ambitions are less worthy than those of others around him. The timid individual displays no ambition or gives up easily when difficulty arises.

Samantha's Migraines

Samantha suffered from severe migraine headaches that often lasted days, and occasionally, even weeks. Stabbing, knife-like pains behind her eyes were so commonplace, that she adjusted her entire life just to continue her work and social life, even in the midst of tremendous pain. When we first met, I could tell that Samantha was shy. She could be outgoing and funny and had a strong tendency to hold back emotion. I soon realized that she was not aware she withheld emotion. She lived with pain and thought it was normal. Even in the middle of a severe headache, if asked her how she was, she would reply, "I'm fine." When the headaches were less severe, I occasionally noticed a bit of cynicism during conversations. Cynicism is anger with a splash of indifference, and reflects a diminished self-worth. Samantha's severe headaches were a physical manifestation of her suppressed anger that came across as cynicism when her headaches were less severe.

To get at the cause of the headaches, we had to go deeper. I gave her a few acupuncture treatments that provided some relief. After some time working together Samantha shared, "My mom sacrificed her dreams and ambitions for my dad's dreams and she still regrets it to this day." Thirty years later. Samantha recognized this trait in herself, and saw that with boyfriends and friends, she would often go along with their desires, and unconsciously suppress her own. Samantha had developed an unconscious tendency to act in the very ways that her parents' related to each other, while ignoring the voice of her Heart. The result was a very typical liver presentation of migraine headaches.

Samantha now recognizes that if a headache comes on, her heart wants something. She's learned to love herself more through the recognition of this familial tendency. With each new curve ball the Universe throws her, she reasserts and strengthens her capacity to shape a life aligned with Love. To her surprise, when she speaks up and establishes a boundary with people she loves, they don't abandon her. They respect her and appreciate her clear communication. Samantha's story is a great example of the healing power of self-awareness and responsibility.

Luke Adler

UNWORTHY OF PURPOSE

Like sadness, anger is an emotion many feel uncomfortable experiencing, and therefore, are also unskilled at expressing clearly and cleanly. By cleanly, I mean to be able to express anger without diminishing or demeaning others, rather than using anger to help people see your authentic feelings. Anger expressed cleanly is a precise tool to uplift others. Many people have a tendency to express anger either explosively or sideways as cynicism or passive aggression. Other individuals invert anger as shame or project it as blame.

Arrogance and shyness reflect underlying feelings of unworthiness. These behaviors express explosive or passive-aggressive anger as a reflection of a thwarted sense of self. Arrogance and shyness say, "I am greater than you" and "I am less than you," respectively. Both are manifestations of unworthiness misplaced towards the external and internal worlds. The arrogant constantly feel they have to prove their worth to others to make up for an anemic sense of life purpose. The shy feel they have nothing to offer as lack of self-esteem interrupts the livers smooth flow of blood nutrient distribution.

Suppressed anger is corrosive. Anger hides and then explodes. It comes out in little bursts here and there. Part of anger's nature is related to the physical position and structure of the liver.

HIDDEN ANGER

Chinese medicine divides the thorax, or upper trunk of the body, into three sections. Roughly, the upper section includes the heart and lungs and is separated from the middle section by the xiphoid process and the diaphragm. The middle section includes the liver and spleen and ends around the belly button. The lower section of the thorax includes the kidneys and sex organs.

As the suppression progresses, pathogenic factors drive deeper into the body and increasingly diminish intuition. The lungs provide the first opportunity to recalibrate to the intuitive truth of the heart. The lungs can often ward off energetic, emotional, and physical pathogens. When the lungs cannot clear out an energetic or physical pathogen, separation from the heart gains momentum as the breath stagnates and the liver works harder to smoothly move blood. The diaphragm tightens, shortens, and seals sadness in the lungs. The lungs store latent sadness to be released at some future date. This separates and protects any further direct, emotional taxation to heart. Diaphragmatic tension structurally restricts the lungs from fully inflating, which churns sadness into grief if left unresolved.

Old grief is stored in the upper back, near the top, middle corner of the scapula. When the breath stops flowing deeply, you cease feeling intense emotions, and the thinking mind takes control from the intuitive knowing of the heart. In this dynamic, the diaphragm insulates the heart from feeling unwieldy emotions as an instinctive, involuntary act of self-preservation. It is a structural response to an emotional dysfunction.

The flight-or-fight part of the brain is related to diaphragmatic restriction. Asthma, chest oppression, upper and middle back tension, a feeling of something stuck in the throat are some of the symptoms that correlate to diaphragm tension. These are markers of liver taxation, even though they show up in a different sector of your torso.

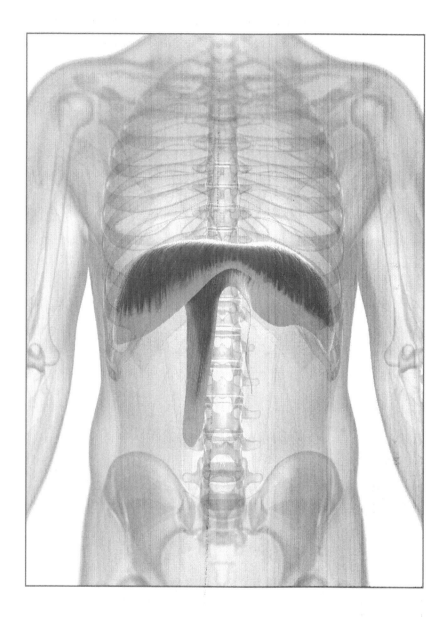

Diaphragmatic tension reflects diminished intuitive knowl-edge of the heart. This progression of the Sequence of Separation is characterized by muffled clarity of communication from the Universal Heart to you. Your connection to direct knowledge is markedly restricted. You may start to reach for philosophy, religion, law, or any external system of rules to guide you, as the voice of Universal Love is more faint. Or your self-deceptive mechanisms may become exaggerated, even to the point of dominating your world. From here the behaviors of arrogance ("I am all knowing") and timidity ("I know nothing") arise, which conceal unworthiness of true purpose, which is illustrated by the statement, "*I don't belong here,*" –as in, I don't belong here in this life.

This deeper feeling of unworthiness of purpose further drives a sense of separation from the Universal Heart. The liver's ability to support a sense of authentic purpose decreases. As feelings arise that support the inner mantra, "I am unworthy of purpose," you may feel forsaken. A feeling that "there is no point to life" shows up. You may think, "What difference can I make, anyway?" or, "My life is thankless drudgery." You await retirement or a quick, painless death. Either way, purpose seems like post-adolescent idealism. You may decide that the real world is full of pain and suffering, and devoid of true joy. Disconnected from Universal Love, unworthiness of purpose robs you of your Divine right to fulfillment in day-to-day work and relationships. At its extreme, there may be suicidal tendencies. But for most people, it becomes harder and harder simply to put one foot in front of the other. Such people present as terminally unhappy, a state that can drive others away, making them feel even more isolated from the love that they need and desire, even if they cannot be in touch with those feelings.

The structure and location of the liver reflects its nature. Tucked under the right lower portion of the rib cage, the liver is concealed and hidden from direct palpation.

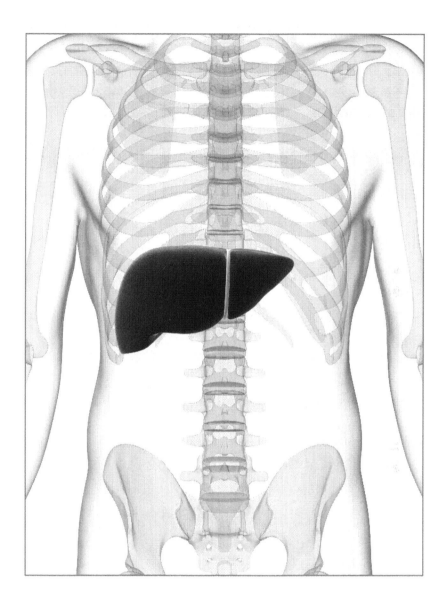

When suppression is active, anger is expressed in a way that directly reflects these deep feelings of diminishment. The sideways or thwarted expressions of anger are completely absent of Love and tenderness. Cynicism, passive aggression, and sarcasm are smoke screens that hide the desperate longing to love and be loved. Like a forest scorched from a wildfire, thwarted anger reflects the burnt and bitter lack of Love and connection felt in the Heart. The concealed location of the liver mirrors the unrealized dreams of the heart. Only by expressing anger with Love do the soul's highest ambitions come true.

❧ SUPPRESSED ANGER EXERCISE

- *Identify places in life where I feel I have-to, should-be, or must-be a certain way.*

- *Where am I shoulding on myself? i.e. "I should be this way. I shouldn't be this way."*

- *What lies beneath these rigid ways of being or believing?*

- *Have I confused humility with timidity by using humbleness as an excuse to not pursue my purpose (for fear of hurting someone's feelings in sharing my achievements and aspirations)?*

- *With whom am I afraid to set a boundary?*

- *Am I arrogant about anything or arrogant around anyone in particular? What insecurity am I hiding?*

- *Am I passive aggressive? With anyone in particular? What am I not speaking up about? Who is really suffering from my withholding of love?*

- *Am I blaming anyone in my life for where I'm at financially, romantically, or spiritually? How do I use blame to cover up not being responsible for my situation?*

- *With whom or with what am I most controlling? What fear am I hiding?*

- *How easy is it for me to choose love when my issues arise and I'm tired, irritable or cranky?*

This is a big list to think about. Go back and do this exercise several times. Watch what happens as you peel away the layers of this onion. If a lot of feelings surface, do one of my breathwork tracks on the Products page of lukeadlerhealing.com. Choice is a powerful concept. Until you uncover all the muck that anger conceals, you have no freedom to choose what you want and be satisfied. You are reacting from past hurt. You only arrive at the ability to freely choose when you've thoroughly examined your fears and insecurities and owned them as part of your experience, if not all of your experience. At the bottom of your insecurities is a desire for love. When you can love all of you, you will gain the freedom to choose what you want and completely love and be satisfied with that choice.

To choose love in the middle of unconscious habitual behaviors is the name of the game. When you can see it, you can free it, make a new choice and generate a new positive pattern. To bring awareness to an unconscious pattern requires self-effort. Meditation, breathwork, and other practices that increase awareness are only useful if you choose to exchange an old, limited pattern for a new, uplifting one. Fortunately, Grace follows closely behind self-effort.

I know plenty of people who perpetually choose a limited way of being, even while being disciplined with life-affirming practices like meditation. To change a pattern requires extra grit in the moment. The task is to reach through a familiar, comfortable choice and select a new (sometimes uncomfortable-to-the-ego) choice aligned with love and freedom. Change also requires that you give yourself Grace. Be generous with yourself, and ease up on self-flagellation. The Universe does not require you to beat yourself up to be worthy of love. Self-flagellation is an old belief that you have to punish yourself to be worthy of love. That belief is nonsense. *Give it up!* Generosity with self is an act of self-love and healing. *Good work! Stay with it!*

THE SPIRIT OF THE LIVER

Chinese medicine attributes a spiritual function to each primary organ. The spirit of the liver is called the *Hun*, translated as the ethereal soul (pronounced "Hon," as in , "*Hey, Hon, I'm home.*"). The ancients say that the Hun stores information about past lives to give you resolution to fulfill your purpose in life. The Hun activates past life information—often during your dreams—to help you navigate your life lessons. The Hun supports your journey to unfold your destiny. The Hun stores memories from your past that are yet unresolved. In order to be fully present and live from your Heart, information stored by the Hun must be processed and resolved as life lessons arise. As Dr. Jeffrey Yuen asserts:

> ❝ *Acceptance of the past, present and future reflects a balanced Hun. The Hun allows intuition, oracles and prophecy. This happens when we are dreaming. It allows us to collect the experience we had today and move them into a depository of memory into the brain. This is important for learning, planning, and maintaining normal flow of Qi. The liver opens us to a level of consciousness before it manifests into the future.* ❞

The Hun is particularly active between the hours of 1am and 3am. The expression "I'll sleep on it," points to a subconscious knowing that during sleep, you'll figure out the answer to your dilemma. The Hun figures out the answers to life's problems, which is why good sleep is imperative to feeling clear and purposeful. People who begin to have sleep issues quickly become agitated and upset with life and their place in it. This aspect of the liver system provides the clarity to be decisive and take action towards destiny. It also demonstrates how liver dysfunction activates even deeper levels of daily dissatisfaction as the sequence of separation progresses.

Dream Journey

Above the quaint towns of Eugene, Oregon, I ran as I usually did along the majestic Ridgeline trail. Lined with gigantic, old-growth Douglas fir, with a ground cover of long-leafed ferns, the ridge-line wraps around the entire southern rim of the Eugene foothills. I was already into my second wind as my lungs heaved smooth, copious breaths of nutrient-rich oxygen from a recent misty rain on the virtual cloud forest. The heavy moisture also meant that the forest trail was a bit muddy. As I rounded a familiar corner, my sneaker plunged into the squishy, ankle-deep mud. The miniature sinkhole suctioned my right shoe and held it hostage as the centripetal motion of my stride moved my body forward. I felt the bare sole of my right foot fall against the damp earth as I turned back towards my shoe. I gasped unable to move or breathe. The sight was somehow utterly familiar and shocking. Next to my shoe stood a huge, brown and black, long-haired wolf. He was beautiful. The wolf looked at me with a stern and peaceful gaze. He appeared rooted deep into the soil by his four, enormous paws. I had never seen a wolf in person. The wolf was as big as a great Dane, and full-bodied like a mastiff.

I stood motionless as my heart pounded and sweat poured over me. I was mesmerized. I took a step towards the stunning creature as if it had something that belonged to me, like my shoe. For a moment

I turned away from the wolf, sensing someone observing the scene. When I looked back to face the wolf, he was gone. I turned the other direction once more. This time, I was viewing the path from about two feet lower to the ground. I looked down at my shoe and instead saw four brown and black paws. I felt warm, powerful and strong. I continued along the trail, no longer jogging, now I was on the hunt or so I thought. I looked up the hillside and saw a massive cedar brown grizzly bear foraging for blackberries. I knew if he caught my scent I was a goner. As I snuck by him some thirty feet below, the gigantic grizzly turned, sighted me and pummeled through the low lying ferns in my direction. I was his potential lunch. Knowing I could not out run him in this terrain, I turned away from the bear and leapt over a forty-foot cliff into the ocean below. I knew I was safe, until I turned to check behind me, and spotted the grizzly hurling himself over the cliff as he flailed towards me. I frantically began to doggy paddle toward the shore. I could hear my predator closing in, just as I began to reach the ocean floor. His claw skimmed the back of my paw as I scurried onto the shore and toward the safety of open beaches.

I awoke the next morning remembering each detail of the dream exactly as I've recounted it. I had earlier that week asked myself if it was time to make my pilgrimage to India. I really wanted to go to India. I felt I would be going only in search of obtaining something, without offering anything in return. As I researched the dream from David Carson's book *Medicine Cards*, I discovered that the wolf is symbolic of family and the wisdom that comes with being a teacher. The grizzly bear is connected with the cave of Lord Brahma of the great Hindu mystical teachings. Although I was hearing the call to make my journey to India, the timing was not right. I needed to bring something to India to offer in exchange for the spiritual guidance I sought. I applied to Chinese medicine school shortly thereafter, and five years later, just days after taking my Chinese medicine board exams, I purchased a plane ticket from Los Angeles to Mumbai, India. Departure date: September 11th, 2007. Return date: unknown. A few friends cautioned me about flying on September 11th. I felt no hesitation. I knew this was the right time to make my pilgrimage.

Dreams discharge karma and guide you on your life path. You work out life lessons in the dream world so you don't have to manifest them in your waking life. Dreams act as a pressure valve to release suppressed fears and worries and help shed light on areas of your life that are unclear. Your dreams reflect areas of your life that lack awareness. Look at your dreams as a way to bring more clarity to areas of your life that seem vague or confused.

❁ DREAMS

- *How often do I remember my dreams?*

- *Do I ever have repetitive dreams?*

- *Have I had any significant dreams that shed insight on my life?*

To help remember your dreams, as soon as you wake up, sit up against the headboard of the bed or wall. Close you eyes and gently focus on your breath.

Rest in this position, and follow your breath. Allow you mind to do whatever it wants. Don't try to control your thoughts. Just allow them to flow. Within the next five minutes, your awareness will sink from waking consciousness into the dream state. You will become aware of your dreams. After a few minutes of being aware of your dreams, take three long deep breaths and gently open your eyes.

Take few minutes to reflect and jot down some notes about your experience.

The Myth that Swallowing Emotion is Strength

Withholding emotion as a form of strength is an outdated virtue that was a bankrupt currency even when it ruled society. Stoicism and bearing through pain is a vintage American value. This mentality may have been appropriate during times of war and famine, but not now, when your basic needs of food, water, and shelter are almost always met. When your fundamental needs are satisfied, you can evolve emotionally. Stuffed emotions are the ingredients of disease. Swallowing emotion does not make you strong. It makes you weak and sick.

If you're in crisis, a war zone, or in the midst of trauma, then putting your emotions on hold is the right call. I had a patient tell me once about a conversation she had with her father before his death. She'd asked him what he thought about his life. His answer: *I've never held a gun. I've always slept in a bed. I've never gone hungry.* He felt his life was a success.

For the blessed individuals who live beyond such challenges, your task is to redefine your relationship to emotion. Fine-tuned anger streamlines the achievement of life goals. Suppressed emotions dull intuitive receptivity. Swallowed emotion is the essential cause of disease. Many people see the ability to compartmentalize emotion as strength, when in fact it is very unhealthy. Healing is feeling. Swallowing is wallowing. Feeling releases trauma. Swallowing stores trauma. To learn more about healthy ways to release suppressed emotion, check out the chapter on Therapeutic Clinical Dialogue in the Tools section.

The ability to understand how emotions move through your body is essential for health and happiness. I want you to know how and where sadness, anger, worry, fear, and anxiety move through your body, and to understand why you store these emotions. As you give yourself space to feel these emotions with the intention to let them move, you will understand how they work in your body and be able to help them along as they arise.

The executive function of the brain allows you to override emotions. Use the capacity of free-thinking consciousness to peer into your emotional life to see more clearly just how and why you suppress anger. Then you can bring more awareness to anger.

An ounce of love added to anger creates passion that can act as an ally to accelerate your dreams rather than an enemy that stifles your purpose. The energy it takes to suppress something makes you sick and disconnected from your purpose. Of all the emotions, anger is the most suppressed and the most volatile.

I always try to be loving and compassionate with people. I use a lot of humor to diffuse volatile emotions. People I work with seem to appreciate a loving approach. When frustration happens, I need time to recharge. I allow people to heal at their own pace. This is a skill that I continually refine. Time is limited for all of us. The liver teaches us that there is a time to grow and a time to decay. Sometimes, I may push someone to break through indifference or inertia. At some point in life you look at yourself in the mirror and ask, *Am I fulfilled?* If the answer is not *Yes*, then you have work to do. The liver provides the gift to achieve your dreams in a way that feels good. Anger can be used to get love and laughter flowing again, as you get clear that love is the ultimate goal and purpose of life.

脾

The Spleen

From the Earth the body arises, and to the earth it returns. The Earth transforms and transmutes all elements to provide the Universe with new materials to evolve creation. The Earth provides the material substance for life. The Earth gives and asks nothing in return, like mother figures who give of themselves to provide children the best chances at life. The earth is the ultimate mother and provider. She gives of her resources without partiality.

In Chinese medicine, the Earth has her own distinction as an element. Earth is the mother of all elements. The Earth contains the other four elements—metal, wood, water and fire—as part of her structure. She is the great container of resources, the one who nourishes all. She takes the shape of all forms, including the human body. The Earth is regenerative. Every cell of your body is completely renewed from the form you were six months ago. Silently, she witnesses every thought, word, and deed of your life. The Earth is the central pillar that is constant amidst activity. She exemplifies Divine order. She is affected by humanity and she affects humanity. The Earth is here, now, listening.

✿ THE EARTH EXERCISE

- *Do I have a relationship with the Earth?*
- *What words would I use to describe it?*

- *How was it when I was a child? How has it changed?*
- *How often do I recycle?*
- *Do I pick up trash on the street?*
- *How aware am I of the resources I consume?*
- *What is my daily carbon footprint? Find out at: http://www.nature.org/greenliving/carboncalculator/*
- *How conscious am I of the Earth's messages?*

One American child consumes fifty times the resources of a Haitian child. At the University of Oregon, I studied globalization as part of my major. The above statistic alludes to one of the most authoritative arguments in the field of globalization known as dependency theory. Dependency theory argues that, to maintain their wealth, developed countries like the United States and European nations are dependent on the poverty of developing nations (also known politically incorrectly as "third world nations"). One example of the dependency of developed nations on developing nations is the outsourcing of cheap labor abroad, which allows the price of finished goods to stay low in the West. The demand for cheap labor drives the suppliers in developing nations to find ways to deliver high quality workmanship at low prices, which keeps the poor in poverty. Many laborers abroad—who work for a few dollars a day—will never have an opportunity to progress financially, because their utility is rooted in the demand for cheap labor. In a global market, as workers become more organized and demand more compensation for their work, a multinational corporation can abandon workers and move on to the next, cheap labor pool. There's always something more cost-effective than the workers they have. So, for example, when workers in China demand more money or improved workplace standards, they're traded in for Bangladeshis, who work cheaper, and are grateful to be out of the fields and into a manufacturing plant.

Another example of dependency theory is when developed countries buy raw materials like metal, oil, and wood from developing countries. The United States, for example, turns raw goods into a cell phone, computer, or car, and sells the finished goods back to the developing nation. This cycle keeps developed nations on top of the economic pyramid and the developing nation at the bottom. It also ensures the continuous consumption of raw goods and finished goods, and depletes the Earth's resources to fulfill ongoing demands for the next, newest, best device. Furthermore, standards to regulate pollution associated with the extraction of raw goods are held to far lower standards in undeveloped countries. The downward spiral of depletion never ends.

Thinking that we are separate from one another with regard to how we care for each other and the planet will be our downfall. Unless and until we, as a species, begin to see the big picture required to sustain life on Earth, and begin to clearly own up to our impact on all living beings and the planet, future generations may have a very different Earth to steward. We cannot stand idly by and worry only about our needs. We must think globally about the needs of others, the Earth, and the impact of our choices. You are not alone. You are an extension of the cosmos and you are made of the Earth.

The Spleen

On a global level, consumption of the Earth's resources mirrors the personal utilization of resources represented by the human body's organ systems. In Chinese medicine, the spleen's role in the internal ecosystem is to process, assimilate, and digest nutrients. The spleen's nutrients come from carbohydrates, fat, and protein. In addition to the digestion of food, the spleen assimilates energetic nutrients from our relationships with others. The spleen gives you the energy to relate with others and is nurtured, or diminished, by how you do so. It provides fuel to physically and mentally digest and contextualize interpersonal exchanges into meaningful relationships.

The spleen helps make sense of life. It is the reason why you do what you do and like what you like. The spleen tells the story of your life. It acts like the mitochondria of a cell—the powerhouse organ system that generates resources to move life forward in the direction you choose. The spleen is the source of postnatal nourishment that fuels the body's daily needs.

One of the most seemingly challenging facets of spleen pathology pertains to self-nourishment. Unlike other arenas of organ pathology, for example the lungs, you can remove an addictive substance like cigarettes and still breathe, whereas if you stop eating, you soon perish. You have to find balance with nutrition to live. Within the spleen system lays a biological imperative to be in relationship with self-nourishment. This is true regardless of whether you want to or not.

The bond to self-nourishment mirrors a certain inescapability to face life lessons until you master them. You can end a dysfunctional relationship or quit smoking to be rid of a challenging situation. And to heal, you must learn the life lesson associated with the relationship or cigarette use. If you don't learn your lessons, and simply remove the external source of irritation, you will magnetize similar circumstances until the lesson is learned. The spleen's perpetual generation of resources fuels your journey to love yourself and evolve.

- *What do I grab out of the fridge when I feel bored, sad, angry, afraid, worried, etc.?*

- *Have I ended a negative relationship, only to find myself in a similar situation later?*

- *How often does this happen? How long has this pattern persisted? Can I recall its origin?*

- *When I eat my next meal ask, "Am I enjoying this meal?"*

- *Am I thinking of my to-do list, or worrying about the past or future while I eat?*

- *Where do I go mentally, when I eat and how does that effect my digestion?*

- *How often do I have gas, bloating, or fatigue after I eat?*

- *How often am I constipated, or experience loose stools?*

Whether you eat organic veggies or pepperoni pizza, your degree of presence while you eat affects how nutrients chemically digest into your body. If you experience any of the symptoms listed in the previous exercise, look at how present you were while eating your last few meals. I guarantee you were thinking or worrying and not present to the smells, flavors, and textures of the food in front of you. Your degree of presence while you eat impacts your ability to digest and assimilate nutrients. Furthermore, the quality of your energy impacts the degree of presence you have in your relationships with others. The degree of presence you have with food and people impacts the vibrancy of your physical health.

Life lessons are repetitive, because human beings are forgetful. We need to be reminded over and over again of who we are and what's important. Also, we need to learn about ourselves in different ways to own and later teach others how to overcome similar roadblocks. Self-nourishment exemplifies the repetitive nature and practice of self-love.

NUTRITION COACHING

How you eat, what you eat, and—to a degree, where you eat—impacts the clarity of your thoughts, intentions and actions. The best food coaching I have heard came from a friend of mine, Mark Dare, who is a nutrition innovator. Marc says, "Chew your juice, drink your food." Chew your food until it becomes liquid and swirl the liquids in your mouth. This releases enzymes from the salivary and parotid glands. "Chew your juice, drink your food" is the most powerful health change you can make to improve your digestion, energy level, and balance your endocrine system.

Organic matters. But, if you eat fast food and take time to fully chew the food until it becomes liquid, you will derive more nutrition than if you eat a raw organic meal that you chew a few times and swallow in small chunks. The majority of the body's digestive power is between your teeth, not the stomach or intestines. Marc further elucidates, "You don't have teeth in your stomach." If you swallow food in chunks, the stomach, spleen, pancreas, liver, and gallbladder have to work extra hard to break it down, which draws blood flow away from other important physiological systems, like the brain. I've passed along this coaching to thousands of people. They are amazed at how such a simple change can remedy or improve some incredibly complex problems.

A powerful way to shift out of any pathological state is to work with nutrition. Food reinforces unconsciousness. Food reinforces consciousness. You won't become enlightened from an organic, paleo or vegan diet, *and* good nutrition will help your awareness stay clear. Your relationship with food supports your journey. The choice to see the glass half full or empty is always yours, regardless of the purity of your diet. See the chapter on cleansing in the Tools section to learn more about this powerful tool.

THE YI, SPIRIT OF THE SPLEEN

Food impacts thought. Thought impacts food. The spleen has an intimate relationship with thought. Chinese medicine says the spleen impacts thought and memory. How you nourish your-self with food is a reflection of how you nourish your mind with thoughts. Food and thought are intertwined. Food is the building block that regenerates physical form. Your thoughts imbue your physical body with energy that can deplete or energize you. How you think is how you eat. How you eat is how you think.

LOVE MY DIGESTION EXERCISE

- *What did I eat for breakfast today?*
- *What did I eat for lunch recently?*
- *What did I eat for dinner recently?*
- *Did I enjoy my most recent meal? Why?*
- *How present was I?*
- *Was I doing other things while eating?*
- *What was I thinking?*
- *Did I chew?*

🪷 BLESS THIS MEAL

Take thirty seconds before you eat to thank the Earth for providing nourishment for your body. Breathe deeply and settle into your Heart. You can say this prayer or speak spontaneously from your Heart.

"Thank you to the people who prepared this sacred food. I offer you blessings and gratitude. Thank you to the plants and animals that offered themselves for my nourishment. May I eat this food in a sacred way that honors my body so that I may be of service to the world."

Pause and rest in your Heart for a few moments

A great health coach I worked with in graduate school taught me the difference between thinking and "thoughting." Thinking is to consciously consider a topic or area of interest. Thoughting is the random, nonsensical, tangential movement from one thought to another without much, if any, awareness. Most people consider thoughting to actually be thinking. When you take a moment to really consider and think about any area of life, you bring the power of the Universe through your awareness to the degree that you've cultivated that power through your Heart. Thinking is a powerful tool for insight. Thoughting is an unconscious recycling of the past that leads to worry and depletion.

The spirit of the spleen is called the *Yi*. It correlates with the intellect, or cognitive thought. The Yi commands active conscious thinking. Thoughting reflects an imbalanced Yi and leads to worry, which depletes the capacity of conscious thought. Chinese medicine says thinking originates in the spleen. The Yi provides the context to make sense of the world, as well as provides a framework to fit within the parameters of society. As Jeffrey Yuen says, the Yi establishes meaning in the world through word and integrates life experiences in a nourishing way.

Meaning requires language. Language is a collection of sounds characterized by symbols that signify an object, subject, or concept. If meaning were stricken from sounds (words), the noises heard would be a fluctuation of tones. Think of hearing someone speaking a language you don't understand or a baby babbling. The Yi assigns and agrees to the meaning of sounds that take the form of a collection of letters called words. When you have a conversation with someone, you're not conscious of the letters that make up the words. As you exchange sounds with one another you mentally see pictures and experience sensations in your body.

Words create hallucinations in your mind. Those images invoke feelings in your body that feel tangible. When you watch a movie you experience a gamut of emotions as you relate to the story from your own life experience. For two hours, you've sat in a chair eyes fixed on a screen. For those brief moments you experience another existence, like stories of people who awaken from very long comas with vivid memories of having lived in another country, and who have full recollection of their families, occupations, and landscape. Who is to say that those feelings you feel watching a movie are less real or significant than events of your daily life? The Yi interprets everything secondarily. You experience life first. Then, in another moment, you give it meaning.

The meaning of a word is only as powerful as you make it. Your agreement with society's definition of words makes words formidable. Your thoughts and words are creative acts that assign meaning to life. Thoughts and words either uplift or diminish both you and the world you construct. The Yi gives you power to create your world by assigning meaning to it. How you see life is how it is. You are responsible for that act of creativity. This creative power is a characteristic of your own Divinity, which is embodied by the Chinese medicine concept of the Yi spirit.

 WORRY EXERCISE

Language is a reflection of thought.

- *Do the words I use uplift me and those around me or do they diminish myself and/or others?*

- *Are my thoughts mostly negative or positive?*

- *Do I connect with others by sharing complaints or wounds from my past?*

- *Do I connect with others by seeing the bright side, the silver lining?*

- *Am I a worrywart?*

- *What's the thing I worry about the most?*

- *What are my worries covering up deep down?*

When the Yi is imbalanced, a tendency to ruminate, or worry, arises. Thought affects biological function, and biological function affects thought. Worry taxes the spleen, which taxes the blood production (a spleen function) and leads to more worry. When your worries are few, blood is abundant, cellular metabolism is balanced, and thought is still and serene like a high mountain lake. When thoughts run wild, confusion engulfs the mind, and energy levels become erratic and polarized.

Constitutionally, I am a spleen type. Most of my pathology is centered on digestion, low energy, and bowel motility. I had a bout of Irritable Bowel Syndrome in high school. My varsity soccer team teased me because I was known to return from a training run with a missing sock (that I'd used in a pinch for toilet paper). It was pretty rough being the butt, pun intended, of jokes. In the middle of a training drill, or occasionally, even a game, I was known to sprint suddenly and without warning across the street to the local YMCA. I'll never forget the tap dance sound of my cleats clanging against the linoleum steps, dirt clods scattering all over the floor, as I dove ass first for the porcelain throne of the beloved Y. To arrive at the toilet was sweet relief as I unloaded (or downloaded) f16 diarrhea, a term coined by my Chinese herbs teacher in graduate school. I never shit my pants in practice, but was a nanosecond close more than once. I was like a CIA agent, but instead of assessing exit routes, I scanned a room or stadium for possible places to take a dump; a toilet, behind a hedge of arbor vitae, trash-cans, a dark corner of an alley, anywhere I could relieve myself in less than five seconds. I became a champion of espionage trying to escape from my own body.

In hindsight, I understand the source. I'd recently moved to Eugene. I was nervous, worried, and really wanted to fit in. My biggest fear the first day of school was walking into the cafeteria, not knowing a soul, and ending up sitting by myself eating my lunch in a corner. Fortunately, that didn't happen. I wasn't fully aware of it at the time, but I felt extremely out of place and afraid of rejection from my peers. The gut instability was a manifestation of my extreme worry to fit in and be accepted. My senior year, all the digestive symptoms vanished. As I became more comfortable

with myself, my bowels completely settled, but my friends contin-
ued to call me nicknames. Old habits die hard.

✿ BM EXERCISE

- *How's my digestion? Any gas, bloating, cramping, fatigue, or acid regurgitation?*

- *How are my bowel movements? Loose, constipated?*

- *What have I been worried about?*

- *When do bowel symptoms show up?*

- *Rate my energy level as of the last 7 days? (1 feeling exhausted; 10 feeling fantastic?*

- *What am I really hungry for in life?*

- *What do I really need in order to be nourished?*

If you're using your digestive energy to assimilate your worries, forget about digesting food. The above symptoms are signs that your digestive organs are weak. Free up your worries, and your digestive symptoms will resolve. Read on to learn how.

Agreement about healthy frequency of bowel movements differs among health care providers. My view of healthy bowel movements is two to four formed bowel movements a day, with the consistency of toothpaste. One bowel movement a day is okay, a sign of some constipation. Less than one is a sign of constipation. More than six bowel movements in a day is a sign of loose stools, and perhaps malabsorption of nutrients. The last section of the large intestine absorbs water from the stool. If the stool hangs out in the descending colon for too long, toxins from the bowel are re-absorbed into the blood stream and refiltered by the liver. Healthy and regular bowel movements are essential to overall health.

GOD OF WORRY

Separation from your intuition at the level of the spleen marks the mounting effects of suppression. Until this juncture, the emotions of sadness and anger present intense visceral messages that signify separation from Universal Love. As the spleen aids to suppress intuition, the field is even easier for the intellect to churn thought into worry. Of all the emotions, worry is the least physically agitating. In general, people are more comfortable feeling worried than feeling sadness, anger, and fear. Worry is a type of excessive thinking or rumination. Excessive thinking is the safest emotion in the wheelhouse of feeling, which is part of why western society bows to rational thought as the supreme source of intelligence. Meanwhile, intuition is considered less valid to espousers of the intellect.

You have the free will to empower whichever sets of thoughts you choose. You can do this regardless of whether Spirit supports your choice or not. You have the power to be your own sovereign god of thought. When you're suppressed, more often you try to think your way out of an issue rather than trust your intuition. You assign meaning to a circumstance that is not empowered by your intuition. You may even have to work very hard to do so, or if your self-deception is already strong, you can rely on old stories to comfort and mislead yourself. You go against the will of your Heart and pave a collateral road that diverts your destiny away from its optimal course. Thought without love is mental masturbation. It lacks power.

The power to assign meaning to life is only useful if it unites you with others. If the meaning you create in life isolates you or pushes people away, it's time to open your heart and get on with healing those relationships, which starts with healing the wounded energy in you. Change your thoughts. Change your words. Create a life you love.

The Sequence of Separation when it lands in the spleen is a further departure from the insight of the heart. As emotion becomes more subdued and takes the form of excessive worry, a tightened diaphragmatic tendon and shallow breathing mark the sense of separation from the heart. This creates a physical sensation that can be summarized emotionally by the statement, "I am on my own." Society's worship of thought as the highest form of intelligence is born at this level of separation. Excessive worry is the absence of faith that the Universe is the ultimate and only provider of resources. Rumination creates a false sense of responsibility for life. When this occurs, the spleen begins to operate much more autonomously from Spirit.

When repetitive thoughts abound, they may take on the appearance of care and wisdom. This is part of your attempt to feel safe "on your own." In actuality, repetitive thoughts signify that you are cut off from divine knowledge. Instead of access to All, you only have access to the knowledge from your own, limited, experience of the past. Worry is a projection of the past onto the future or obsessing on regrets. Worry is the interminable replay of should-have, would-have, thinking of past regret that is better left where it belongs, in the past.

WORRY EXERCISE

- *Do I rely more on my head or heart to make choices? Why?*

- *"It happened before, so it may happen again." Have I had this worry before?*

- *How much energy do past fears and traumas influence me when an opportunity arises to be open and trusting?*

I'm not saying all worry is bad. A degree of concern is healthy. But when worry makes you physically or mentally sick, it has gone too far. You can find a million reasons to justify any choice in life. Ultimately, your heart knows the right path, and trumps all other forms of thinking. Very intelligent people often have a hard time trusting their hearts. Their minds are so clever. They try to think their way through life. At some point, all of us, even the most genius among us, must approach and receive the Universe with our heart and allow the intellect to simply be in awe. When you do, you will gain clarity and a sense of fulfillment that only comes from the heart.

Co-Dependency

Progression to the spleen is arguably the most significant step in the Sequence of Separation. It happens not just when you have internalized your own emotions too often, but when you begin to feel responsible for the emotions of others, or think they should heal your wounds. Being overly responsible for the pain of others or needing others to be overly responsible for your pain turns the switch of autoimmunity on, where the body sees itself as the pathogen. This exemplifies the spleen out of balance.

If—as a healer, friend or partner—I carry your pain, I keep you from learning how to care for yourself. I rob you of the lessons you need to learn to evolve as a soul. I offer you a disservice. If you carry my pain, you keep me from learning how to care for myself. You rob me of the lessons I need to learn to evolve as a soul. You offer me a disservice. If we carry each other's pain, neither of us learns our life lessons. We remain co-dependent for meager crumbs of love embedded in one another's pain that only further stagnates our growth.

For the person with the imbalanced spleen, the disease of co-dependency is the hardest lesson to learn. Your task is to redefine love in order to be able to witness a loved one struggle (and that loved one could be you) with compassion, respect, and dignity. Encouragement, empowerment, and prayer go a long way when it comes to moving through life challenges. We must never underestimate the mysterious and total power of Grace to support the expansion of Universal Love.

What may appear as a curse is often a prayer away from a blessing. Time, deep intention, and showing up for healing are required to transform this cycle.

HYPOCHONDRIA

Excessive worry thrives on the two-way street of neediness. The person who worries needs something to worry about to feel needed. Sometimes patients present with an illness, and I wonder if they really want to heal because they have an obsession with everything that is "wrong" with their body. They seem committed to "figuring it out." And they sometimes miss the seemingly obvious point that the illness is asking to be ended, not transmuted into another illness. Like a dog chasing its own tail, such patients expend a lot of energy without making a lot of progress.

Dire forms of need can morph into hypochondria, the addiction to worry. These patients move from one complaint to the next in search of some fatal flaw. I am weary of this level of pathology, because if you look hard enough for anything, you'll find it—or worse, create it. This progression is a mark of concern that even further separation from the intuition of the heart will occur if suppression is left unchecked.

 NEEDINESS AND HYPOCHONDRIA EXERCISE

- *Am I good at carrying other people's pain?*
- *Am I good at getting people to carry my pain?*
- *What do I get out of it? What or who would I be without it?*
- *Am I a hypochondriac?*
- *Where does that current of energy come from in my lineage?*
- *Am I willing to heal it?*
- *Where does neediness show up in my life?*
- *What void am I trying to fill?*
- *Am I addicted to the thrill of worry?*

Neediness is a place to focus self-love again and again.

THE ART OF REST AND EXCESSIVE REST SYNDROME

Most people in the West, especially in the United States, do not know how or when to rest. Anytime I'm online or listen to the radio, there is an advertisement for a new energy supplement or weight-loss protocol. If you treat your body like a credit card, when it comes time to pay the piper, you may not have money in the bank to heal yourself.

Spending all your energy today and planning to heal tomorrow is a bad strategy for longevity and enjoying the moment. The only way to recoup energy is to learn the art of rest. Professor of Chinese Medicine Giovanni Maciocia says, "The spleen rules the muscles of the four limbs." When you are tired and barely able to lift your arms over head and/or dragging your heals on the floor, the spleen is not able to maintain blood production to keep you going. The body begins to prolapse, which shows up as mouth sores, hemorrhoids, excessive uterine bleeding, sagging skin, erectile dysfunction, and more. You can take the longevity cocktail of supplements:

- Vitamin C,
- Vitamin D3,
- The entire complex of B vitamins,
- Omega 3 oils,
- Adrenal Support—desiccated bovine adrenal or herbal ashwaganda, rhodiola, licorice root, and others,
- Curcumin,
- Chlorella and Spirulina,
- Chinese herbal tonics.

But the only real way to deeply restore your wellbeing is rest. You can take the right supplements, eat the right diet, but nothing can substitute rest. They say that after having kids, sleep is the new sex, and they're right. Good sleep is the cornerstone of health. The body does most of its cellular repair at night. If you're not getting sound sleep, the entire health equation goes out the door. Good sleep is essential.

Rest Time

If you're tired, close your eyes and rest. A short catnap in the afternoon will give your adrenals time to reboot. The life force energy of the body flows through the entire meridian system in twenty minute intervals. Set a timer. Lie down and close your eyes for twenty minutes at lunch, and you'll save your glandular system from depletion. If you lay down for longer than twenty minutes your sleep cycle will reset, and you may have trouble falling asleep at night. Twenty minutes will leave you refreshed and ready for the evening.

Learn to rest rather than push. Western medicine may be able to keep you alive longer, but what will be the quality of your life if you're taking ten or more pharmaceutical drugs to stay alive? Imagine living a long vital life with very few or no Western medications. It starts now with rest. Begin to see the long view of your life and take care of you, now.

Resting helps you assimilate and digest new life experiences. Your capacity to ingest and assimilate life is determined by the strength of your physical and energetic digestion, which is, again, ruled by the spleen. The right amount and quality of rest is the most essential nutrient for thorough enjoyment of life.

Too much rest is not a good thing either. Among people suffering with chronic diseases like cancer, many patients suffer from Excessive Rest Syndrome, whereby too much rest makes the body stiff, weak, and achy. The remedy is movement. Gradual movement over time can bring back mobility and strength. One imbalance characterized by the spleen is inertia. When the go-go-go energy runs out, laziness, inertia, and lethargy can show up as a mechanism for the body to enforce rest.

The balance here is to strive not to rest too much, but just enough. Once inertia has a hold of you, it can be difficult to shake.

Luke Adler

Looking at the balance in your activity-rest cycle is a great way to measure your healing progress. Watch how you feel when you wake in the morning. Are you eager to rise, or do you cling to your pillow? When you go to sleep, do you look forward to rest or just collapse? Both ends of the paradigm can become symptomatic if you see them too often.

For years, I have struggled to get out of bed in the morning. I've learned that if I get out of bed and go for a short run, my body wakes up. Some cold air in my lungs takes the edge of sleep off me and I feel alert for the rest of the day. Fatigue due to deficiency resolves with sufficient rest. Fatigue caused by stagnation improves with movement. If you don't know where you're at, go for a brisk walk for twenty to thirty minutes. If you feel energized, it is because you were a bit stagnant. If you feel tired, you need to rest and ease up on activity.

The most difficult part of healing for most people is to ease up on activity, especially when you start feeling better. To temper and preserve the hunger for life requires some restraint. Healing from an injury, physical or psycho-emotional, is most often compromised by secondary injuries. You start to feel good about that shoulder sprain, and decide to play a game of tennis. You take a big swing to win the game and end up with a tendon tear worse than the original injury. An emotional example is ending a relationship and quickly getting into a new one, only to repeat the same patterns. Be thorough, patient, and listen to your body and to your heart during active healing to avoid the need to relearn the life lesson you hoped to be done with. You can hit your head against the wall all day long repeating the same broken patterns. Tune in to what the Universe is teaching you. Then get ready for the next lesson.

Fatigue, lethargy, and inertia are symptoms of aversion to the present moment. You can find a lot of agreement in the world that validates fatigue as a response to hard work. People who work hard often use fatigue as a way to avoid listening to their bodies and hence to Spirit. Just because you work hard and have responsibilities doesn't exempt you from being responsible for your wellbeing. You cannot abdicate that responsibility, either actively or passively. Your body is your perpetual witness.

At spleen-level Separation, people are caught in the cycle of hard work, and at some point think, *"Who is going to save me, help me, or appreciate me?"* The answer sometimes is *"No one,"* and other times, *"Yes, people will step up to help."* Be careful of the need to prove to yourself that, *"No one loves me,"* or try to guilt people into loving you. Whether people do or do not show you love, self-pity inhibits both the receptivity to, and perception of, love. You might not notice love even if it's staring you in the face or kicking you in the butt.

In order for love to move through your heart, it must begin with you, cycle to Spirit, and flow back to you. It is only then that you can offer love to the world around you. When you begin to see yourself the way that Spirit sees you, the way you exchange time, attention, money and love becomes imbued with tremendous value. The responsibility for your wellbeing and experience of Universal Love starts and ends with you.

🪷 FATIGUE EXERCISE

- *How do I use fatigue to avoid being present and/or responsible to the needs of my loved ones and myself?*

- *Am I lethargic? Is it hard for me to get my energy moving throughout the day?*

- *Do I get enough rest?*

- *What does rest look like for me?*

- *When is the last time I had a deep restorative sleep?*

- *Why do I push myself so hard?*

- *What unconscious fear do I cover up with my busy schedule?*

Ingratiation

Ingratiation is a form of deception that arises at the level of the spleen in the Sequence of Separation. Ingratiation means pleasing others at your own expense and/or acting against the will of your deepest needs and desires.

I view ingratiation as being overly kind and or generous with attention, time, and resources, which includes gifting money to avoid triggering feelings of diminishment, disappointment, and abandonment in one's self and others. This deception conceals a deep truth of the heart; for example, ignoring the desire to say *No* to a request and instead saying *Yes*, just because you are afraid to hurt someone's feelings. The inauthenticity of being agreeable when you disagree (or vice versa) leaves people with an unclear understanding of where you really stand. Ingratiation conceals a sense of unworthiness of love in relationships. Lack of self-love is translated into the need to please others to fulfill the vacancy of love inside. Love between people only flourishes if everyone has a personal source of love from which they exchange.

Ingratiation can appear as being very sympathetic. Over time it can turn into extreme neediness, summarized by the statement, "I give so much to everyone else, what about me?" With an inauthentic representation of your own needs, the world around you is left to think, "You can handle it all." When and if you articulate your need for support, which is a rare instance, people are often surprised by the dire nature of your need, as no previous actions demonstrated your resources running low.

In Chinese medicine the spleen makes the lion's share of blood for the body. Excessive giving or ingratiation depletes the resource of blood. As blood contains emotion, depletion of blood destabilizes emotion, which results in excessive worry and rumination. When the Sequence of Separation reaches the spleen, it draws on the resource of blood to "finance" ingratiation.

Ingratiation covers up a deeper truth of the heart that you sacrifice to preserve being liked or remain in someone's favor for a hidden (from yourself) reason that always comes down to a lack of self-love and a lack of trust in your intuition. When you allow intuition to take the lead and the intellect to follow, it sometimes creates discomfort for yourself and others. Intuition fueled by Universal Love is not interested in you always being liked. It's interested in your healing. Sometimes healing requires the capacity to withstand not being liked. Getting comfortable with the notion that *sometimes not being liked* is absolutely necessary to expand the influence of Universal Love through you and to the world. If you tend towards ingratiation, not being liked can feel like emotional torture. The fear of disappointing others causes you to put your needs second even to your detriment.

Ingratiation is tricky. It appears to be a kind, generous, and loving quality. Bottom line, ingratiation is a form of inauthenticity. By not being forthright about an issue, no matter how big or small, you withhold the truth. Spirit places truth into your heart to help you and others grow. Ingratiation withholds and delays life lessons from you and others. The longer you withhold truth, the more doubt you cast on intuition. To finance the energy required to deny your truth, you may ingest substances like french fries, sugar, alcohol, dairy, or marijuana to dampen down your intuition. These foods create phlegm, which dulls your intellect and ability to see life clearly. The truth then begins to seem mentally unclear. With ingratiation, you trick yourself into believing that your intuition is not the truth. Withholding the truth from yourself and others comes at a physical cost. Ingratiation stresses the spleen's capacity to produce blood, which inhibits the efficacy and function of all other metabolic processes. Essentially you have less energy to enjoy life, because you're spending that energy ingratiating. When you withhold truth, you withhold Universal Love. The most important ingredient to make life flourish is love.

As my primary element is the earth, ingratiation is my blind spot and indicator when I am out of balance. This quality is deceptive, in that I am generous, loving, and kind, and I truly care about people. I always have people's best interest at heart. I'm not consciously interested in being liked or loved, though in the past the need to be liked drove many of my close relationships. Now that I am more self-aware, I'm consciously more interested in you loving yourself. In the past, I found myself ingratiating others, because I was afraid of people feeling rejected or hurt if I spoke my truth. I see ingratiation as an indicator where Spirit wants to work through me to increase Universal Love. As a loving person by nature, enabling others by not sharing information that they need to hear in order to grow is a delicate balance that weighs discrimination, kindness and courage.

The question *Can I comfort you in your hour of need and remind you of your highest capacity for Love?* neutralizes the desire to ingratiate and allows me to love you, but also allows you to hold yourself accountable to your divine potential. Asking people to be responsible for their blind spots does not have to be done harshly. I remember feeling shy and embarrassed as a kid. I remember not feeling good enough and looking at my body thinking, *I'm ugly and awkward.* Unconsciously, at times I became afraid to trigger feelings of diminishment in others, because I did not want them to feel the same. So I held back truth. I can see a lot of improvement in my honesty with people. I can be kind and humorous when I point out someone's blind spot if I choose to see ending ingratiation as an opportunity for Universal Love to expand.

In the past, I've felt frustrated when I gave lifestyle tools and coaching, and people continued to choose harmful behaviors and then complained about their health and personal life. Everyone has to make the choice to change their free will. I am clear that allowing people to use my energy as a pick-me-up to continue the same limited patterns shows a lack of faith in the Universe. If I sense people want to pull energy from me to finance their stagnation, I might pull my energy back and give less. If people don't want to participate to the degree that I am willing to give, I will titrate my energy to their level of exchange. There is nothing more exhausting than to give without the blessing of the Universe flowing through the exchange.

Money and Ingratiation

My clinic is run on half-hour appointments. Occasionally, I go over the allotted time because someone really needs more attention, and I'm fine with that. I used to have a few people who pushed the boundary of their appointment time, and tried to squeeze any extra drop of my energy they could muster. As I've become clear about the value of my energy, my schedule runs smoothly. The people who are the most volatile, needy, and emotionally shut down will have issues with money. They're the first ones to give my office manager a hard time about the cost of a treatment, workshop, or retreat. If you have issues around not feeling appreciated or valued, and ultimately appreciating and valuing yourself, then you will likely have issues around money.

Money is a tangible representation of energy that many people have contradictory intentions around. Money is an outward expression of self-worth and a good barometer of where your sense of worth is contorted and inconsistent. At this point in my life, I know the value of what I do. As I write this, I can hear the Universe telling me, *What you do is worth more than you think.* I know that Universal Love is doing a lot of the work. I am confident that Universal Love finances my business and encourages me to expand. Part of being a good facilitator of Love is allowing your self to trust that flow and to flow with it.

🪷 MONEY EXERCISE

- *How does money come to me? (i.e., through work, inheritance, investments, gifts, theft...)*

- *Are money and love intertwined in my beliefs?*

- *How much does fear rule my choices around earning and spending money?*

- *Have I ever felt manipulated over money?*

- *Where do I feel that in my body?*

- *What does that bring up for me?*

- *Do my beliefs about money come from my mother or father?*

- *What do my relationships between money and food, money and love, and money and sex have in common? Write about each one and compare.*

- *Do I believe the Universe will support me financially if I do my part?*

Write down the amount of money you have plus or minus debt as close to the actual number as possible.

Now look at the number? (pause 20 seconds)

- *What am I making that number mean about how I handle money? Now write down what's in your head without censoring:*

- *Do I put money in tip jars? How much do I tip at a restaurant? How does that feel?*

- *Do I give money to homeless people on the corner? How does that feel?*

- *Do I donate to any causes or charities? How does that feel?*

- *Do I buy lottery tickets? How does that feel? What message does that convey to the Universe about how money flows to me?*

- *Is it prestigious to have no debt?*

- *Compared to how much money I earn, do I give abundantly or just a little?*

- *Do I ever give up something that I want in order to give to someone in need?*

- *Have I paused to see what came up for me regarding the above yes or no questions, or did I gloss over my responses?*

Dig deep into these questions and you will see a plethora of unconscious energy around money and self love.

I acknowledge that I do not always see the big picture and that the Universe has a better idea of where people are headed than I do. I honor people's pace on the path and let Spirit hold the agenda.

I remember harassing myself for more than a decade to be more disciplined and dedicated to the spiritual path. I have compassion for people's struggle to overcome limited habits. When my life became conscious of service to others, I stopped worrying about myself and paid attention to the voice in my heart. As I trust deeper into Universal nudges around my worth when it comes to money, abundance continues to flow to me. I don't follow a formula to be receptive to the Universe. Being in a relationship with Universal Love is not about having the right attitude or eating the right diet, although both may help. To listen and trust requires taking some risk around being honest with your desire to grow. Life will bring you opportunities to trust the Universe more. Money and finances can be a big area for trust to grow.

Bonus question: When faced with a choice/opportunity to expand or contract around Universal Love, do I recognize it, and what do I choose?

To recognize that you are responsible to care for your Divine nature is a significant marker of maturity in life. To be responsible for your success and failure in every area of life is a high level of evolution. Because many people really haven't experienced their own Divinity consistently, they lack the trust and faith that Spirit will support them. This is especially true around finances. Trust in your humanity and your Divinity magnetizes Grace. Trust allows the Universe to flow energy through your body in an uplifting way. I strongly encourage a consistent spiritual practice for many reasons. One of the most important is to grow trust that the Universe is, has, and always will support you. Spiritual practices, like daily meditation, help you recognize how the Universe helps you grow so you can forgo frivolous efforts of resistance that leave you exhausted, confused, and stagnant. To learn meditation with me, come to a Roaring Silence of the Heart retreat or Healer Studies course, or go to my website and download the latest guided breathwork album.

Suppressing My Truth

Remember the story of my depression after the break-up with my girlfriend in college? The "rough" break-up was in large part my responsibility. She wanted us to move to San Diego after graduation. I really loved her and wanted to move in together, but a persistent voice inside said, "She's not the one." I was devastated by the voice and tried to negotiate with the Universe. I said, "God, please change my heart, change my destiny, I want to be with this woman." It was a gloomy day in June as I kneeled on the damp sidewalk outside my campus apartment. I clearly heard the answer to my plea from the Universe, No! like a clap of thunder. My heart wrenched as if clenched in a vice. If I moved in with her I had to consciously go against my destiny.

I had a beer with her the next day, got a bit tipsy, and told her I would move in with her. Half of me felt great, while my heart sank in despair. My head screamed "Shit, I can't move to San Diego with her. We just aren't meant to be. I really messed up." I knew I couldn't go through with it. I tried to get behind the move to San Diego, without the blessings of my heart. A week later I told her my Truth. She ended the relationship later that afternoon and started dating one of my buddies a few days later. Yeah, karma is a bitch. I had it coming. So I've learned to listen well and do what I am told as soon as possible when God has something to say. Delay only makes the payback worse.

Ingratiation is a misallocation of your energy that shows a lack of trust in the Universe as the true provider of resources. By not valuing your sense of truth, you're supporting the notion of giving physical, emotional, and spiritual energy from a perspective of being less than Spirit. The exchange is contorted and devalued by ingratiation. Ingratiation makes a case that you are not worthy of experiencing Universal Love in relationships. The result of this argument is the creation of intellectual, logical, or illogical stories that justify why you have to ingratiate, and why you can't listen to your heart. The voice of your heart will sober you. The truth will become more accessible. Furthermore, when you really acknowledge that the guidance you seek is within and already known to your soul, you will also become aware of the instances when you've ignored this inner wisdom, and the impact that they've had on your life and the lives of others. You will see more clearly why you ignored your heart, and become skillful at truly listening to yourself.

Truth not only sets you free, truth sets the world free.

As I said in my opening paragraphs of *Born to Heal*, disease is born when you ignore the voice of your heart. The weight of the world is not yours to carry. Tell the truth about anything and everything in your life and it will set you free. Always lead with love when you speak your truth. It helps the medicine go down, especially if that medicine is bitter or hard to hear. Ninety-nine percent of the time, truth is straightforward and seemingly so simple that you may dismiss it, because it doesn't seem complex or sophisticated enough. The Universe is always right, and sees the big picture. *Trust it.*

 **SPEAK MY TRUTH**

To re-establish sovereignty as a spiritual being in a

physical body, take some deep breaths and speak your truth to yourself or to someone else. There is nothing wrong with standing up for you. Remember that when you need to speak your truth to someone, you're choosing to do so when s/he is going through unique challenges as well, despite how it may seem. Best to start any challenging conversation with compassion and respect. It helps open the heart and the ears to allow Spirit to flow through everyone.

When having a potentially emotionally charged conversation ask, "Am I more committed to love and healing or being personally right about my position?"

You rarely get to be right and have love and love what we're born to nurture.

Ask: Is my truth better delivered in a letter than face to face?

Taking the time to formulate your truth and giving someone time to respond allows space for the intense emotions to burn off and really hear what each other is saying. Feel love inside and speak from your heart.

The world becomes very small if you feel obligated to be the provider, fixer, and rescuer. Ingratiation is akin to martyrdom. When you put yourself last on the priority list, you are of no use to others. It may seem like there is a fine line between self-care and care for others. Actually, when you deeply love and value yourself, you not only exemplify self-love for others, you radiate the potency of Universal Love, and people are uplifted in your presence without you exerting much effort.

David Elliott talks about healing as learning to take on your own pain and teaching others to do the same. If I take on your pain, you never get the opportunity to become strong. If I shelter you from the harshness of the world, you'll be afraid to leave home. True compassion and respect allow the people you love to struggle and grapple with life. You give them the opportunity to develop resilience and strength in the process. You also give yourself the space to release control and trust the Universe with other people's healing. This is a high level of healing and Love, worthy of effort and further study.

Gu Syndrome

Gu Syndrome is a pathological presentation that results from the accumulation of poor nutrition, suppressed emotions, and physical stagnation over time. It is a recipe for serious disease progression if left unchecked. The spleen transforms and transports nutrients throughout the body. The spleen loathes phlegm. Gu is the inertia of metabolic life caused from lack of movement through the gastrointestinal tract. The result is the individual feels stuck at every level of their being. A marker of Gu syndrome occurs when an individual becomes accustomed to that sensation of stuckness.

Gu stems from avoiding your fears. Rather than addressing the life lesson at hand, you choose to ignore it, stuff it, and insulate yourself from it with any barrier possible, almost always through food. The fear of confrontation eats away at your self-worth, and you may fall into a space of self-deprecation, self-loathing, and/or seek out others to fulfill your inner void. The accumulation of Gu leaves a "*guey*" or slimy energetic residue that people who are sensitive can feel from you. As a result people may not want to be around your sticky energy field, because they feel "Gu-ed" by you.

Gu exemplifies the spleen out of balance and reflects a high degree of devaluing Universal Love's imperative to express through you. Gu syndrome communicates to the Universe that you are terrified to trust your heart and you would like to take a break from your life lessons.

🪷 GU EXERCISE

- *Do I ever feel Gu-ed after an interaction with someone? (tired, yucky, sticky, depleted, blurry vision, headache).*

- *Do I ever Gu people? Do I unconsciously verbally or energetically vomit on people?*

- *Is there a confrontation in my life that I am avoiding?*

- *What negative habits have I taken up to support the energy required to not confront this issue?*

- *Am I willing to trust the Universe?*

Everyone is afraid to confront something or someone throughout life. The Universe needs your voice, arms, legs, and heart to move people into alignment with their destinies. You are a vessel for the Divine to express love. You get Gu-ed when you step out of the presence of your heart and become critical of the limitations of others and yourself.

Negative judgment creates a separation between you and me, between you and the Divine, and leaves you vulnerable to Gu-ey energy. Gu is fueled by the sense of unworthiness we generate when we are out of spiritual alignment. You magnetize the negative and positive judgments you make. I'm not saying to avoid judging others if they're really out of line. There certainly is a time to point out when people are not being responsible for their Divinity. But be clear whether you are speaking with the intention to generate love or diminish it. Hold the space of love. Speak from your heart. Be honest. Be clear and kind, and the Gu will not stick. It will be transmuted into Light.

EXCHANGE

As you value your relationship with the Universe, and increasingly trust that the Universe is your provider, the flow of exchange arises. When you hold the value of your connection to the Universe constant, you illumine the world in the Light of your worthiness. I love David Elliott's definition of exchange. He says,

> *Exchange is giving and receiving with people, plants, animals, the ocean, mountains, and the Universe in a way that feels whole and balanced. It is a feeling of respect and reverence really flowing inside you and your relationships in a way that feels good. Exchange can refer to goods, services, and money, but really is all about the flow of conscious energy, respect, value, appreciation, and love.*

Exchange is clarity about your worth as a facilitator of Universal Love. Your worthiness is reflected in the unique way you exchange love with the world. Your role in society has zero impact on your ability to be clear about your worth. You do not have to hold a high position in society to be worthy of love. Your worth is not relative to what you do or who you are in the world. Your worth comes from your connection to the Divine. How you exchange your energy in every arena of life is a reflection of the depth of your relationship with the Universe.

- *With whom do I ingratiate the most in my life?*

- *What are my complaints about this relationship?*

- *What happens to my relationship with food, drugs, or alcohol when I ingratiate with this person?*

- *What do they mirror for me?*

- *What is the definition of love in that relationship?*

- *Where does that definition come from? (Lineage often passes down antiquated definitions of love; like taking on people's pain in exchange for love, or "love is suffering" and "being burdened.")*

- *How does the exchange feel "off" in that relationship?*

- *Am I living their version of exchange in my life or mine?*

- *Am I imposing my definition of exchange on the relationship?*

- *Am I giving more than I'm receiving?*

- *Am I receiving more than I'm giving?*

- *Does one of us have an expectation that the other is unaware of?*

- *Am I aware of how the unspoken expectation is affecting the other person?*

- *Who is a support person in my life? Someone who listens, consoles me; someone I go to for advice, someone I respect. Are they ingratiating me? Am I taking more than I'm giving? Would they tell me if I was?*

- *What kind of people do I surround myself with? What do they mirror for me about the energy I attract?*

- *Do I have any relationships where I take more than I give? How does this undermine the relationship?*

- *What is the effect of that on the relationship and the feeling of respect that flows between us?*

- *Am I aware of how that dynamic affects the other person?*

A healthy expression of exchange is knowing that the Universe deeply loves and cares for you and needs you in a unique way to fulfill *Its* mission, which is to evolve all beings on this planet. When you meet God's Love for you with your own love for you, the integrity of exchange naturally manifests as an expression of this balance.

The Universe is going to support you, and yes, you have to participate for the exchange to work. You have to show the Universe what you want, what you stand for. Life lessons are inescapable. If you refuse to choose or resist what's being asked (for example, in a career or relationship) then the Universe will choose for you. For instance, I've worked with many people who stay in relationships that are unfulfilling, who feel afraid to move on. A few individuals that hang onto the stagnant relationships have manifested pregnancies while using birth control. It is amazing to see how bringing new life into the world gets your shit together. Couples either work it out and stay together or separate. I don't believe there is a right or wrong way to bring a child into the world, and I'm not judging this particular scenario as good or bad. But there are a lot of difficult feelings that have to be worked through, and in this example, a child's life can be greatly impacted.

If you do not listen to the voice of the Universe in your heart, the Universe will find a way to get your attention. Pregnancy is only one way I've witnessed. Others include everything from bankruptcy to a car crash. If you aren't clear with the Universe about your preferences, you usually get a mish-mash of things, half of which you don't want, and some of which will require you to very quickly get your act together. The best things to desire in life are those that bring the Highest good in any given situation regardless of how much they benefit you exclusively.

❀ EXCHANGE PRAYER

Dear Spirit, whatever you want for my life is what I want. The only thing I want is to serve You more skillfully and with greater delight. May I serve You with devotion, one pointedness, and honor my human needs as a spiritual warrior in the world.

Exchange: The value of Universal Love expressed through you to the world and back to you in a self-generative cycle of well being.

THE KIDNEYS

A sapphire jewel, Crater Lake sits nestled atop Mount Mazama's dormant caldera. From the Crater's pristine source, the emerald headwaters of the Rogue River begin their steep course through basalt canyons, before surging onto Gold Beach to finally unite with the mighty Pacific Ocean. A section of the Rogue River— from Galice to Fosters Bar—is protected under the National Wild and Scenic Rivers Act. This section of the Rogue is one of the most beautiful places on the planet. It is rich with lore and history of skirmishes between settlers and Native Americans, gold miners, and perilous white water adventurers. Nature abounds with bald eagles, osprey, turkey vultures, blue herons, salmon, green sturgeon, trout, river otters, beavers, deer, and black bears. Riddled with class III, IV, and V white waters, the wild and scenic Rogue is a thrill seekers' paradise.

The green water of the Rogue is a place of great rejuvenation, celebration, and a test of will, skill, and courage. The river can also be a place of great sorrow and loss. The final class IV rapid on the Rogue is named Blossom Bar. Blossom is infamous for its "picket fence," where large cylindrical boulders are set like fence post across the width of the river. Even the most skilled guides have pinned or sunk their rafts on the picket. The lucky ones climb to a boulder and wait for help, if water levels allow; if not, they are swept through the narrow chutes, and swim to a rescue boat or the shoreline. *The unlucky make Blossom their final resting place. My best friend's dad, an accomplished river guide, once pinned his steel McKenzie River drift boat on the picket fence. He had to be helicoptered out of the canyon with his wife and daughter. Later he hired a wedge to pull out his old boat from below the rapid. The hydraulics of Blossom Bar requires the utmost focus and respect. A few weeks prior to my own trip down the Rogue, three people died at Blossom Bar. God rest their souls. On a 2011 summer Rogue adventure, some of my buddies and I led five inexperienced rafters down the river, which culminated in dramatic fashion at Blossom Bar.*

Normally when I go on adventures, it is with people who have a lot of outdoor experience. After two huge class III rapids within the first half-mile, my friends and I quickly realized we were in a serious situation serving as guides for the less experienced rafters moving down this powerful river. We were on high alert, constantly making sure everyone was safe, with life jackets snug, and rafts properly inflated. During the first day several people flipped their kayaks over in small standing waves; they easily climbed aboard and paddled on with smiles from ear to ear.

Day two of the trip we began our descent to Blossom Bar. The river carved through the tumultuous Coffee Pot rapid of Mule Creek Canyon. We floated through the canyon cautiously, as the river narrowed from one hundred feet across to a mere twelve feet. As the river walls confined, the water quickly deepened from a few feet to over one hundred feet. This quick drop in depth creates massive turbulence that can pull boats and people underwater for long periods of time. We wanted to avoid a loss of thrust in the canyon, which would allow the hydraulics of the rapids to suck boats below the surface of the river. A few kayakers flipped over on a standing wave at the threshold. My friend and I pulled the flailing kayakers from the sucking whirlpools. This slowed our river caravan to a halt, and caused our crafts to smash into each other in the narrow basalt canyon. The party leader and I were extremely frustrated and stressed at our debacle as we began to approach the high intensity run of the Blossom Bar rapid. Fiercely we organized the rafters and pulled the oars aggressively to create some momentum through the heavy downward current. Our entire party made it through the tight canyon a little shaken up, but relatively unscathed. The terminus of Mule Creek's still waters open to the magnificent expanse of Blossom Bar.

Back at the Bureau of Land Management ranger station in Galice, I had asked ranger Todd about the recent deaths at the famed rapid, he said that one of the boats from the deceased remained wedged up on the boulders of the picket fence. Sure enough, as we rounded the corner to Blossom, we saw a huge antique wooden drift boat lying mounted on the three boulders of picket fence. It looked like a jewel compressed perfectly in the boulder's shoulder. The river level had subsided since the incident weeks before, which now elevated the beautiful drift boat out of the water several feet. It was an ominous sight. With the water level so low, navigating the picket fence had to be very exact. We scouted the rapid for some time, and watched three guide boats and a kayaker flawlessly eddy out into the channel just right of picket fence. They glided their boats smoothly into the slender opening just right of the picket fence onto the main flow of the river below. After several minutes of planning and instruction from our party leader, it was our turn.

My co-leader led the maneuver through Blossom with two people in the front of his kataraft, followed by another friend, while two other kayakers and I picked up the rear. My friend Josh, the most experienced of us, drew a perfect line, avoided the picket fence and glided into the six-foot waterfall and onto the river's main flow. My other friend, along with his crew, set off to cross the main channel to enter Blossom Bar on the left. My sister, as wild and free as she is, followed the lead kayaker, but was unable to cross the swift current pushing into the red wall on the left side of the river. Instinctively and wisely she turned toward me on the river's right-hand shore. I climbed over a cliff and down to her. We hiked, kayak in tow, up and down the basalt canyon, back to my kataraft. I tried hard to keep my cool. I was a bit shaken up by the last minute change of plan, and additional weight to my raft.

Moments away from running a very technical Blossom Bar with two people I love dearly, my heart pounded visibly through the life jacket. I was filled with a mix of emotion, exhilaration, terror, love, joy, anger, and grief. I'd been in dangerous situations before while surfing, but none where I had so much time to think. The summer heat beat down on my shoulders while I strapped my sister's raft to the back of my boat, and unpacked and repacked the dry bags and trash. With so much adrenaline surging through my system, I could not cool off. I submerged myself completely into the cool river. Then I did some fire breathing, inhaling and exhaling sharply through my nose. Just as we were about to push off, on a rock below picket fence I heard my friend Andrew yell "Bear, Bear!" With the words of my friend, I felt Nature's blessing surround us.

I pushed off the rocky shore with my sister and dear friend Juliette on the front of the kataraft and eased across the channel bearing river left. We ferried into the mouth of Blossom Bar. The starboard side of the raft loomed closer to the teeth of the picket fence and the remains of the antique drift boat. I pulled hard on the fiberglass oars to make the eddy just above of the picket fence. The kataraft heaved towards the rushing waters. Still in the cur-

rent, I pitched the oars once more, giving them my full strength and then heard a frightening noise that rang through the canyon and cracked like a gunshot. My right oar snapped in two, like a broken wing. "Shit!!" I screamed. My raft spun 180 degrees now heading straight at the last post of the picket fence. The right oar attached by only a few fiberglass threads provided just enough resistance to lick the water, and float the kataraft near the chute away from picket fence before breaking off completely. Everything happened so fast. I gazed down at the kayak paddle strapped to the dry box just below eye level. I remember thinking that maybe I could unstrap the paddle and use it for my right oar. I didn't have time. Somehow with the positioning of the raft amid the weave of hydraulics, I didn't need the oar anyway. The left oar clawed at the rivers flow and nudged us against the last post of the picket fence. We did not pin against the fence. The kataraft kissed the flat granite boulder as if in jest, and we slid into a slender chute and onto the river's main flow. We made it through the legendary rapid. With one oar, we pinged our way through the boulder field below before beaching the kataraft on an outcropping of small boulders. Our friends cheered, waiting with a spare oar and the biggest smiles I'd ever seen. I was amazed, relieved, and grateful to be alive.

My friend was able to catch the whole thing on video. You can't see it from the angle of the camera, but right below my buddy was the tattered antique drift boat. After my oar cracks in half, my friend drops the camera and yells an expletive. So you actually don't get to see the most dramatic part, but check it out here:

http://www.youtube.com/watch?v=vzX8U7e6nP8.

Thirty minutes later, a huge mama bear eating salmon twenty feet away from the river smiled at us, as a warm breeze swept over our party. A little later, Andrew found himself just twelve feet away from a cub with his mom in tow. Five bears in three hours. Words cannot capture the beauty of the river. To live with the river is to know it. To all of you seeking adventure and communion with nature, greet the black bear with an open heart, laugh as much as you can, and watch over each other with gratitude in your heart.

My love of water likely reaches back to my Mom swimming beyond the breakers of Santa Monica beach with me in utero. Water has taught me to respect it many times. Until that late afternoon on the waters of the Rogue River, I never knew how much and how deeply I could respect the power of water.

All life comes from water. Life begins within the aqueous fluids of the womb. Like the earth, the human body consists primarily of water. Our intra and extracellular fluids transport nutrients to and from the myriad cells of the body. Water is the medium that carries the entire range of metabolic processes for all living beings. Even our blood consists primarily of water. The greatest resource on the planet is water. Protecting the availability, accessibility, and purity of water is the greatest concern of this generation and for many to come. Water nourishes life. Contamination of water threatens life. Most water in our nation's most populous state, California, has water piped in from Colorado.

Why does the state with the largest population have such tenuous access to life's most essential resource? People are attracted to the state's coastline, mountains, and beauty. Its fertile farmland grows a huge percent of the country's crops. Southern California's mediterranean climate is one of five on the planet, which heightens the demand for fun in the sun. I remember it seldom rained growing up in the suburbs of Los Angeles. I didn't understand as a child the contradiction of warm, pleasant weather co-existing with an abundance of water. As an adolescent, I thought I could have it all.

Today, food, water, fuel, clothing, and more are delivered from distant lands to supplement local shortfalls. When we are out of touch with the source of the resources we use and the energy required to deliver them locally, we perpetuate the illusion that the extra-long shower, the high powered toilet flush, leaving the hose on by accident, or dumping toxins into the rivers and oceans, does not make that much of a negative impact on life. If the majority of people are unaware of their relationship with water, then the quality of life diminishes exponentially for all people.

Water represents the unknown. Even in clear water, there are deadly microorganisms and toxic heavy metals that are not visible to the naked eye. Invisible from the turbulent surface of the ocean, is a vast world teaming with life. Water conceals, nourishes and sustains life. Water is powerful and demands respect. Water is the keeper of fear. Occasionally, water checks to make sure you know who is in charge.

Water sustains life. It is the basis for physical health and absolutely essential for evolution as a soul. In the same way that the air you inhale has been breathed by life forms since the beginning of time, the water that contains the resources of your body has similarly circulated through the blood vessels of your ancestors. We are connected through water. In an elemental sense, there is nothing new under the sun. Yet your Heart is ever new, fresh, and vitally necessary to bring forth more love and connection on the planet. Water holds the mystery of life. Within the mystery, is the fear of facing the unknown lessons of your life. In the physical body, water is ruled and represented by the kidneys. The kidneys, water, and fear are the means that contain the life lessons that must be explored for the soul to evolve.

- *What is the most frightening event I've experienced?*

- *Did I remain present during the event or leave my body? (If you don't know what that means, then you left your body.)*

- *Am I still impacted by that event?*

- *Where does the impact of that event live in my body?*

- *What energies trigger the physical sensation of that event in my body? (i.e., manipulative, domineering, controlling, or startling behavior).*

- *How do I work consciously or unconsciously with that energy in my body?*

- *How does that energy make me go unconscious at times?*

- *Where and/or with whom do I feel in danger in my life? Why?*

- *How can I feel safe?*

- *How do I practice being present in the middle of a dangerous feeling in my body as it's occurring?*

Tip: remember to breathe, keep your eyes open and move your awareness to your heart.

The more consciousness you bring to this area of your body with the intention to let go and forgive yourself or another, the less triggered you will feel around this memory. The breath is a powerful tool to become present to a moment from the past that you've suppressed. Breathe.

Post Traumatic Stress Syndrome (PTSD) is the result of a very powerful stressful imprint on the mind and body that limits your ability to be fully present and enjoy the moment. PTSD is a Western diagnosis for the impact left on the mind and body when something traumatic happens to you. Whether you are aware of it or not, whether you can see, feel, or touch it or not, such impacts linger. They may be whispers or they may be shouts. But as long as you are still reacting to them, you have not yet healed.

The authentic desire to move past the trauma is crucial to healing. The work to heal deep impressions of fear requires the willingness to stand face-to-face with the fear in your body, to stay present, and to find a healthy way to relate to that energy.

Snake Spirit Medicine

Most of my life I've had an intense fear around snakes. Growing up in the San Jacinto Mountains, I had numerous encounters with coiled rattlesnakes as a child. I remember coming home from school as Mom stood on the porch, rifle in hand, pointed at a six-foot rattler. "Get back," she yelled. Then, pow! She blew the snake's head off. I learned that you had one chance to kill a snake with a headshot or else it could strike you if you only landed a body shot. As a child, I had nightmares with snakes slithering everywhere I turned, until they wrapped themselves around me. I lay cowering in terror. For a long time, I tried to avoid any environment that might have snakes, but I love the outdoors, so occasionally I run into one. Then it finally dawned on me that snakes are one of my animal spirit guides. As I befriended them, I started to feel their energy as a powerful ally in the spiritual and physical worlds. Whenever I feel a tinge of fear, I call upon my snake friends. When I do, they help me feel grounded and rooted into the earth. Snakes are powerful medicine to face fear, and I'm glad I've found a way to work with them in my life.

ANIMAL SPIRIT GUIDE EXERCISE

- *Who are my animal spirit guides?*
- *Have I identified them yet?*
- *What do they look like?*
- *How can they help me do my work in the spiritual and physical worlds?*
- *What are their messages for me?*

Your animal spirit guide may be any animal in your personal landscape. It could be your pet, or an animal that's always frightened you, or one that appears over and over in your path, or in imagery when you are thinking about deep matters. Start to interact with these powerful spirits. Talk to them with an open heart and your intuition will light up with messages and guidance from them. Animal spirit guides are powerful allies to support your journey. They are messengers who bring you gifts. Notice when they show up in your head, eyes, and heart. Listen for their voices.

THE KIDNEYS AND THE HEART

The kidneys are the foundation of life. They rule growth, reproduction, and development of the body. The kidneys represent the shadow self, from which all of life's lessons await manifestation. Life lessons can be likened to genetic information stored in your DNA, which Chinese medicine places in the category of the kidneys.

The kidneys and heart have an intimate relationship. The connection between the heart and the kidneys represents the relationship between your ability to see (or intuit, as influenced by the heart) your life lessons (kidneys) clearly. The insight of the heart has the power to shift your predispositions of disease towards new patterns of wellness.

Your kidneys are located behind the hollows in the small of your back. Ball up your hands into fists and place them there. Then breathe, and feel until you can sense them pulsing with life force.

For the heart and kidneys to maintain a connection, one must acknowledge and make peace with one's fears. Courage, or any other quality of the heart, allows you to face your fears and discover what lies beneath them. Like a body of water, much is hidden below. Until you befriend your fears, their powers to transform are not available to you.

When the heart and kidneys fail to communicate, or miscommunicate, your ability to move through your life lessons stagnates.

You've inherited the lessons of your ancestors. The lessons live within you. They will not go away. You were born to heal the behaviors, points of view, and habits that feel restrictive and non-inclusive. You were born to break free, break through, and break down the limitations of the past and birth new ideas that bring people together to heal.

Suppression at the stage of the kidneys gives rise to the feeling of being unworthy of your sacred lineage. This form of unworthiness is a result of resisting the lessons that your ancestors passed on to you. This aversion leads to feelings of apathy and dispiritedness. These feelings are relentless, and can turn into dread, depression, anxiety, and isolation.

The relationship between the heart and the kidneys plays out in the aspects of your life where you feel the most resistance. Resistance is a place that your heart wants to illumine, and that your fears want to conceal. Your heart will give you the qualities you need to move towards the resistance (courage, gentleness, kindness, strength). Your job is to trust your heart, which is akin to trusting the Universe. Start to see fear as an opportunity for you to expand. Instead of shrinking from it, move towards it. Greet it. It may feel hard to welcome and embrace. Resistance will only deepen the difficulty of resolving the lessons, whereas bringing it into the light makes it possible to grow and transform.

THE CREATIVE POWER OF FEAR

The kidneys are the seat of fear. As the kidneys correlate with the water element, fear is the ice that fuses emotions together. Fear makes you see life as an unsafe and dangerous place. Located in the lower back, the kidneys are the furthest major organ system from the heart. When we are afraid, we hold fear tightly in the muscles of the lower back. This is part of the reason why lower back pain is the number one chief complaint in America. The kidneys hold the regret of life lessons not faced. Ultimately, the kidneys store the depression of dreams unfulfilled. Suppressed fear congeals your life force, which silently turns into volatility, waiting to either implode or explode.

The divine impulse to create is innate to all life. Fear is a raw state of creative energy that is frozen and stuck. Suppressed fear feeds depression and anxiety. It is summarized by the statement, "I would rather be stuck than confront the fear I feel in my body." This level of suppression is characterized by feelings of entrapment. Fear propagates the illusion that you are not responsible for how you respond to your circumstances. Fear magnetizes the archetype of the terrorized victim unwilling to be self-empowered, and instead, seeks to make others accountable for their victimized plight. Not only are you stuck and afraid, but you are also resentful at everything external onto which you project blame for your situation. The absence of personal responsibility reinforces the fear, and the cycle deepens and progresses. You can drift into a downward spiral almost without noticing, because you are so disconnected from your body, your soul, and your heart.

When you feel unworthy of your divine lineage, a deep feeling of pointlessness about life can arise. It can progress until you hit rock bottom: a sense of separation from the Universe. To heal, you eventually realize an ultimate truth: *You have no control of your circumstances, and you are responsible for how you respond to them.* As you begin to trust Spirit, Grace shows you that you are not alone.

Fear and the Tyrant

Many hundreds of years ago, an infamous Mongol leader invaded China. News of this ruthless warlord quickly traveled to the high monasteries of western China, with stories of massacres and the destruction of temples and other holy sites. A very wise monk heard the warlord was within hours of attacking his monastery. The warlord arrived, seized the wise teacher's crimson robes in his fists and pinned his body against the cold, grey stone monastery wall. With sword at the monk's throat, the warlord roared, "Do you know that with one flick of my wrist, I can sever your head from your body and end you life?" Calmly, with utter repose, the monk replied, "Do you know with one flick of your wrist, I can allow you to sever my head from my body and end my life?" The warlord was stunned. The monk's koan penetrated deeply past the rage of the warlord into his heart. Completely defeated, he lowered his sword, left the temple, and returned to his homeland. The warlord derived power from instilling fear into the heart of those he terrorized. When the monk replied, "I can allow you to sever my head," the warlord realized that even with all the power of his mighty army he could not make this humble monk fear him.

 CONFRONTATION EXERCISE

- *How do I handle confrontation? Write down the first five words this question evokes.*

- *Am I afraid of confronting fear? Why?*

- *Do I muster courage in the face of fear? How?*

- *Do I have the courage to confront the person that is most volatile in my life?*

- *Do I believe Grace will show up to support me to confront this person with love and skillfulness?*

- *Do I know how to use fear as a catalyst to generate love?*

Hint: believe in yourself, love yourself, and then feel your fears as you breathe and trust love to show you the way.

How you choose to work with fear is directly related to how creative you are. You remain stuck in fear, because you are unwilling to be one hundred percent responsible for your life, and more specifically, responsible for your insecurities. Sometimes people ask me, "How can I be responsible for things outside of my control?"

It starts with being aware and admitting that you are afraid, sad, and angry. The fear to embark on a new path; the fear to write a story, paint a picture, have a child, leave (or begin) a relationship, return to school, or pursue a new career, all require some risk. Fear lets you know how important something is to you and what you're willing to risk for it.

Emotion is a response to what you feel in your heart before you have a chance to consciously think. Beneath your feelings is the doorway to your intuition. Feel your feelings and then notice where you are not taking responsibility in your communication with others. You have communication problems and breakdowns with others because you don't trust what the Universe is telling you. When you are not honest with yourself about how you feel, you will not communicate authentically with others. This can take many forms. But when you wonder why things aren't working, look at yourself first, before you proclaim, "It's all her fault!"

Be a responsible adult about conflict. Own your stuff. Only then can you make requests of others to show up as responsible adults.

Facing the truth and the fear of change is a paradox. People usually know what does not work in their lives and will readily admit that it affects their health. Yet, the familiarity of dysfunction can be more comfortable than the *perception* of discomfort to face the truth. Fear is the gateway to expansion, even if it's scary! So many athletes I know would rather run a marathon, triathlon, or compete in a strong man competition than confront their mother, father, or boss about their feelings.

Nature ensures that all beings will face their fears one way or another. Confrontation with physical and emotional fear is built into the structure of life throughout the entire cycle of birth, life, and death. The difference between fear that propagates disease and fear that generates creativity is a matter of practicing the act (or art) of facing your fears and learning to partner with Grace in the moment. To channel the energy of fear and to allow it to transform into creativity is an intense process that calls you to withstand the alchemy of Love and fear.

May you face your greatest fear with lionhearted courage and compassion in your heart!

This is the ultimate call of life. If you have not yet faced tremendous difficulty in your life, you will. I charge you to emotionally and spiritually practice facing your fears, so when big life events come, you are ready and able to hold a presence of love.

Corazón's Birth

The best day of my life occurred the 5th of May, 2014, at 8:02 a.m. On Cinco de Mayo, my stunning wife Emily, birthed our daughter Corazón Grace Adler. "The best day of my life" comment is such a cliché. If you've experienced the birth of your child or a child close to you, you know with utter certainty the cliché is true. I've experienced many transcendental spiritual expansions that blasted my heart and mind open beyond my capacity to imagine. Never have I experienced such outrageous Love, healing, transformative Grace, and power on the physical and spiritual planes as I did on the fateful day that Corazón journeyed beyond the womb and into Emily's and my loving arms.

On May 4th at 3:30 p.m., I spiked a fever twelve hours into Emily's labor. Fortunately, our doula had just arrived, so I was able to get a few hours of rest as Emily continued to labor. In bed, my body began to ache as my stomach churned. The diarrhea was brutal, and my vision blurred and swirled like a bad trip. I hadn't been this sick since I had salmonella poisoning as an exchange student on the coast of Ecuador. I felt just as sick as I did then, where I ended up in a dilapidated hospital with an I.V. duct taped

to my arm while local farm animals jumped through the emer-
gency room window (no, I was not hallucinating!). I wondered
why I manifested such a horrid illness on the day of my daughter's
birth. At 6:05 p.m., my wife cried out from downstairs, "I need
you!" I pleaded with Spirit, "Either give me the strength to support my wife and put this sickness into latency for another day
or help me heal quickly." No matter what, I was committed to
being there for my family. I came downstairs to my wife crying in
pain. I comforted her as best I could with strong waves of nausea
and fatigue circulating through my body. I was in disbelief at my
state during the time of my wife's dire need for support. We both
needed help. We decided to transfer to the hospital. Slowly and
carefully, we departed home for the last time as a family of two,
excited to return as a family of three.

As we approached the on-ramp, I began to cry uncontrollably
like a baby. We merged onto Interstate 5. The crying turned into
shrieking and I remembered myself wailing like this as an infant
in the back seat of my parent's Volvo station wagon. Emily yelled,
"Pull over, you're going to throw up." I swerved onto the shoulder of
the highway and wildly flung open the car door. Diesel trucks ca-
reened alongside me as a gentle rain poured overhead. Projectile
vomit erupted all over my grey sweats and neon green Nike's, an
outfit I had chosen months earlier to wear for my daughter's birth.
Another diesel truck blasted by, and sent gallons of water that
crashed over me as I vomited again. Snot and mucous frothed
out of my nose and mouth. I looked up at the overpass, as rain fell
onto the Interstate in the twilight. I took a deep cleansing breath.
"Damn, I feel great," I shouted into the traffic. I blew my nose into
my sweatshirt. My fever seemed to vanish along with the body
aches. "Let's go have a baby," I declared triumphantly.

My own birth had been traumatic, as my Mother and I nearly

died. Though I processed my birth trauma many times before, I projected my birth experience as a fear of Emily and our baby's deaths in childbirth. This fear lived intensely inside me in a dormant state that became activated the closer time came to Corazón's birth. I'd always wanted the fear to be purged from by body. The day of my daughter's birth was the right time. My wife put labor on pause to support me. After vomiting on the Interstate, the ghost of my birth was gone. I was ready to support my family. I felt relieved and confident afterwards that my wife and daughter would be fine.

At 7:55 a.m., Doreen, our labor and delivery nurse, lovingly offered to Emily in her South African accent, "You can reach down and touch your baby's head." I watched my wife touch Sona's (baby's nickname) thick head of black hair for the first time. A wave of relief washed over Emily and vanquished a sliver of her exhaustion. Emily and I knew in that moment that she would give birth to our daughter.

Sona's head crowned at 8:01 a.m., and Emily asked if she could switch birthing positions. Dr. Martha and I looked at each other and agreed with a nod. "One more big push," Martha responded sweetly and calmly. Emily was certain she would tear in two, though she had enormous faith in Martha's guidance. With Goddess might, force and determination, after twenty-nine hours of painful yet, strangely graceful, labor, my wife pushed our little girl into existence. The back of Sona's head burst forth like a desert flower blooming with the first dawn's ray, as her sturdy shoulders quickly twisted ninety degrees into my hands. The most beautiful cry erupted from Sona's lips as Martha, Doreen, and I lifted Corazón onto Emily's chest. My wife and I, wide eyed, mouths agape in sheer bliss and celebration, exclaimed, "We did it!" On the 5th of May at 8:02 a.m., I was born as a father. Emily was born as a mother. Corazón was born as our daughter. And the three of us were born as a family.

The mystery of life and death is loaded with fear. How you choose to work with fear determines the quality of your life and how much you'll enjoy it. Fear and love alchemize into creativity. Fear alone creates numbness and terror. The choice is yours to make.

❀ BIRTH EXERCISE

- *What are you making with the cards life deals you?*

- *Can you describe your birth experience?*

If you have no way to learn about your birth, sit quietly for a few minutes and ask yourself, "How was my birth experience? What happened?" Let yourself feel the answers with your heart.

How you enter this world impacts how you live your life. As you place awareness on this primordial event you can unlock energy that has imprinted on your early life. Birth is your first major life impression. Take some time to review this experience. If you don't know much about your birth, ask someone who does. If you've given birth to a child or had a miscarriage, review these experiences to heal any tendrils of trauma and fear that live within your system. Take this examination into a breath session with the intention to heal the cellular memory.

On the other side of fear is love. Sometimes the only way to reach love is through the gatekeeper of fear. If you're crystal clear that you're committed to connection, unity, and love, then you stand a good chance to move through your fears with a lot of ease. If you're looking to fulfill your ego, then fear can make your journey miserable.

Wager fear for love. Love is what you want. And in order to get it, you have to be willing to face your fears. The beauty of this bet is that love wins ninety-eight percent of the time. The other two percent of the time, you may have to wait a bit longer for love to prevail. It's a matter of faith and trust in the Universe. Love always makes its presence known at the right time. Often, you can't see what the Universe sees for your life and have to take the lesson at hand with a willing and open heart. Over time, faith increases your trust in the Universe. Fear can be an ally that grows love rather than an enemy that incarcerates you from love.

Facing Fear

Margaret had been working for the local university for over twenty years, when the job of her dreams came open in her department. The university never made the job posting public and hired someone less qualified than her. Margaret was angry and distraught. The dilemma fed right into her story of never being good enough, which manifested in her chronic poor digestion. I encouraged her to fight the decision and plead her case. She was terrified of the idea. "What if they reject me," she said. "They already have," I replied. "What have you got to lose? This is your life Margaret. You don't have what you want because you don't ask for it." Margaret brought the issue to the Dean. They reviewed the hiring process and deemed it unfair. Margaret got an interview and eventually landed the job. She faced her fear and trusted her heart. Since this instance, I've seen Margaret face fear after fear, and with each instance grow stronger and more confident in her heart's ability to guide her.

Dr. Jeffrey Yuen says,

66 *The fear of change makes you more rebellious.*
The fear of being wrong makes you more right.
The fear of being hurt makes you more angry.
The fear of disappointing makes you worry. 99

Dr. Yuen points to a fascinating energetic anatomical distinction that illumines why it is unhealthy and impossible to release fear by containing it in the body. He makes it clear that we cannot heal by hoping fear will just evaporate and magically go away. Dr. Yuen points out the pathological structure of suppression and why the kidneys are the lynchpin of disease.

He continues:

66 *We can say fear is the motivation force behind all things. Ultimately we face the fear of death. There is no recourse through fear. Fear is not something you can let go of through the diaphragm because the diaphragm anchors things back to the kidneys. The diaphragm longs to let go. The kidneys can't release fear by itself—even though [they have a] pathway to the lungs that ultimately goes to the heart—The heart gives us the language to dialogue with our fears, elevating us to the light. We let go of fear through our words. Releasing the diaphragm will not release fear.* 99

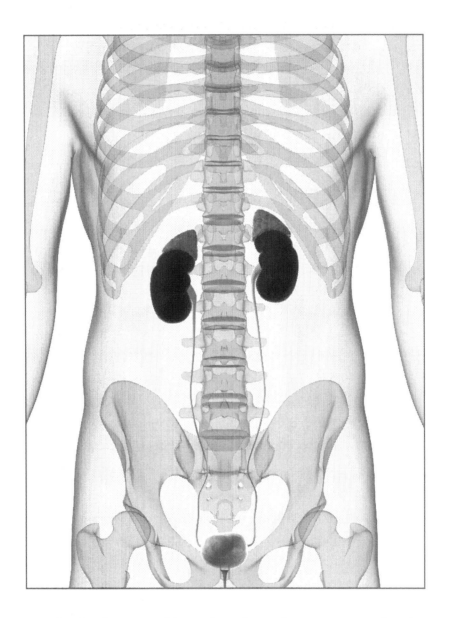

The diaphragm is like a dam that releases emotion for the heart to feel. The channels that govern fear have only an indirect pathway to the heart. The heart is the system that distinguishes all emotions. The heart is associated with the tongue, which is responsible for speech and articulation. It is only through the articulation of your fears, aided by movement of the tongue, that you can let go of fear. Dr. Yuen adds, "You only let go of fear by acknowledging it. No clinician can make you let go of fear. You have to work it out yourself." See the chapter on Therapeutic Clinical Dialogue in the Tools section to learn more about releasing stagnant emotions.

Releasing Fear

Marissa, a mother of three, has struggled with alcohol for twenty years. She recently started attending Alcoholics Anonymous. She said, "I love going to meetings. For so long, I avoided going to AA because I had so many stereotypes about it that just weren't true. It's so freeing to openly talk about my shame and fear with a group of people having the same experience. Talking about these deep emotions in a group quickly allowed me to let go of them and I'm feeling so much better." Marissa has been sober now for nearly six months and feels confident she can keep it up with the support of her meetings.

The power to heal is a choice that requires courage and faith. There is no short-cut or back door. Your body is ingeniously designed to heal, thrive, and be vital throughout life. With every new fear, the choice to address it and release it is yours.

ARMAGEDDON EXERCISE

- *In the midst of a difficult situation, how do I respond?*
- *What happens when the fastballs of life come, and when something horrible appears even more horrible?*

Do I align with love and blessings or do I align with fear and despair?

- *Where am I still comfortable, bored, and complacent in my life?*

- *What am I afraid to risk?*

- *Do I procrastinate anywhere in life? What am I afraid of achieving?*

- *Where am I resigned or apathetic? What hurt am I afraid of releasing?*

- *Am I willing to face the turmoil within myself?*

- *Have I cultivated the strength to face my demons?*

We all face incredibly difficult circumstances in our lives. Every moment prior to a terrifying moment is preparation for this confrontation. Whenever there is a down economy, there is a rise in zombie apocalypse and vampire films. I remember these topics trending during the recession of the late eighties and the more recent economic slump. In fact, I know people who are preparing for Armageddon.

We don't have to destroy the world to test our courage and see what we're capable of. Learn to meditate with me at one of my Roaring Silence of the Heart retreats and you will face your self in a safe environment. You will be strengthened and transformed in a wonderful way by the profound journey within.

Love and Depression

Depressive energy seeks to keep the individual soul stagnant. Whenever I come across depression, the degree of its strength is reflected in how much resistance it puts up to remain stuck. Usually, the degree of resistance manifests as noncompliance with any or all suggestions that would shift a patient's state of mind. The commitment to being stuck often accompanies depression. The fear of repeating past trauma causes the individual to doubt herself to the degree that she would rather stay in limbo, even though it's miserable, than move forward and risk the potential repetition of pain from the past.

Miranda and Denise presented with remarkably similar forms of depression. I tell the story of both of them together in this case study because the energy of depression they displayed was nearly identical, which illustrates the pervasive characteristics of depression.

Miranda and Denise's stories were eerily and sadly similar. Both had been through abusive romantic relationships and came from abusive families. I took them through many sessions of acupuncture and breathwork, as well as seated meditation, which I had taught them. Whenever I suggested an herb, cleanse, or meditation practice, I heard an excuse about lack of money, time, or simply a lack of interest. Anything that I knew would change their state was met with resistance. The deep sadness and depression had an incredible grip on Miranda and Denise. On multiple occasions they said to me separately "I have the worst life of anyone alive." They both had good jobs, plenty of food, water, shelter, and extra money to take vacations. I was tempted to show them pictures of starving children in Africa.

Their depression was parasitic. Miranda and Denise didn't want to get better. They wanted to have someone witness their misery and feel sorry for them. At a certain point during one of my own exhaustive attempts to find ways to support them, I realized there was nothing I could do except be a steady presence of love and support in their lives.

A funny thing happened, within weeks of this clear realization. I gave up trying to fix them and rather than come into the treatment room sulking in despair as they had so many times before, they showed up with smiles. When I asked, "How's life?" they said, "Not bad, I had a better week." "What the heck!" I thought. Here I was kicking myself to give my best care and releasing my desire to help them made the difference. It made so much sense and, at the same time, none at all.

Miranda and Denise were good at pushing people away. They built fortified walls to insulate themselves from intimacy. They didn't need to be fixed. They needed to experience a steady presence of love that wouldn't abandon them, and that had no agenda attached to it. When I understood that my agenda to "help" gave them something to resist, I let it go and let love flow. Almost instantly, their depression began to lift and they became open to my guidance. Now when we see each other, we tell some jokes, and laugh about the latest life issue. Miranda now helps others through depression, and Denise has made amends with her family and has made new friends.

One of the toughest tasks for humans is to watch others choose to suffer when you know there is a way to freedom. The second hardest task is to get out of the way and let God do the work. Sometimes my grounded nature causes me to miss the obvious. It took some exhaustion, but I finally got the message from the Universe: love is the medicine.

JING

There is a saying in Chinese medicine "A chronic disease will inevitably reach the kidneys." The energy required to suppress your inner truth will eventually consume resources from the lungs, liver, spleen, and ultimately reach the level of the kidneys, your constitutional reserves. The kidneys are the last resort before the heart becomes vulnerable. They are the body's last-ditch effort to reconcile pathology driven to the deepest depths of physiology. Fear is the engine that allows pathology to eat away at the vital substances of the body such as blood, extracellular fluid, glandular fluids, skin, and so on. At the level of the kidneys, the most refined vital substance is called *Jing*, which Chinese medicine considers one of the three treasures of the body. The other two are qi and blood.

Some ancient texts say that Jing is a limited resource. Like a candle, once burned down, it is very difficult if not impossible to regenerate. According to Lonny Jarrett, Jing is your genetic endowment, the constitutional strength inherited from each of your parents. You're born with a specific amount of Jing. When that is depleted, it's very difficult to replenish. Only with time, the right nutrition, and healthy gentle living can the Jing be restored. In males, sperm is considered pure Jing. For women, gestation and giving birth consume tremendous stores of Jing. Western medicine acknowledges that it is unhealthy for women to conceive within a year of giving birth. Many classical texts say that excess ejaculation for men can severely weaken the body and manifests as blurry vision, burning dry eyes, feeling of hollowness in the head, irritation from loud noises, lower back pain, knee pain, and more.

Everyone inherits a certain amount of Jing. Some people have such hardy constitutions they can eat poorly, maintain lascivious lifestyles, and still have long lives with relatively few health concerns. Still others with weak constitutions can barely derail from a healthy routine without impairment to energy levels, gastro-intestinal function, and mental and emotional clarity. For the sensitive type, deviation from a healthy regime often requires weeks of healthy living to correct. Most people do not have the hardy, work-all-day-party-all-night constitution. For most people, a good indicator of how much you can indulge in sense pleasures is the length of time to recover from indulging in them. To operate at higher levels of awareness, conservation of Jing is essential. The Universe conducts Grace through the refined vital substance of Jing to strengthen the nervous system and enable higher frequencies of love to flow through the body.

KIDNEY ZHI

The spirit associated with the kidneys is called the *Zhi* (pronounced Zhir, like *sure* with a z). Zhi is willpower, the motive force prior to action. The Zhi calls upon willpower to complete tasks when life does not flow smoothly. When you're almost done with a huge paper, a thesis, or a marathon, and you want to throw in the towel, the Zhi of the kidneys provide the will to complete your goal. There is often a sense of digging deep within your self to face fears or complete monumental tasks. The space you access to achieve something great is your Zhi, your willpower. As the kidneys govern the energy of fear, they also provide the will to face fear. Just as Jing is a limited resource, so too is Zhi. Some people are born with more Zhi than others. In order to conserve the Zhi you have, be aware of how you use your willpower, and take time to replenish your stores of Zhi regularly. For example, in the scheme of things, it's just a college paper. Life is going to present you with far more important challenges.

ADRENAL FATIGUE

Adrenal fatigue is an epidemic that plagues a majority of people in the United States. Americans are exhausted due to long hours at work, irregular exercise, mediocre or poor diet, and lousy sleep. Over time this lifestyle creates profound fatigue that gives rise to: autoimmune issues, gut inflammation, nutrient malabsorption dangerous to heart function, weight gain over the abdomen, and depression. Deficiency of adrenal hormones leads to hormone deficiency in the sex, thyroid, thymus, and hypothalamus glands. The endocrine system is a complex neurochemical network that supports organ function. When the endocrine system goes awry, secretion of the wrong hormone at the wrong time of day leads to exhaustion in the morning and alertness at night or a variation of the two throughout the day. It's a recipe for hard times.

America's addiction to caffeine, sugar, and alcohol is a symptom of this deep fatigue. Caffeine draws on cortisol, the long-acting adrenal hormone that makes you feel awake. Caffeine depletes your natural stores of cortisol and pulls on ancillary sex hormones like DHEA, testosterone, estrogen, progesterone, and pregnenalone, which can impair sex drive and create more fatigue in the long run. Sugar and alcohol are sedatives that calm the central nervous system and temporarily relieve anxiety caused by hyper cortisol production. One downside of regular sugar and alcohol consumption is an excessive draw on insulin production, the hormone that stabilizes blood sugar. For some, this aspect of blood-sugar destabilization can lead to adult-onset diabetes. Excess sugar, alcohol, and high cortisol levels cause storage of belly weight that is particularly hard to lose and which compromises cardiovascular function. Sugar and alcohol are also inflammatory, which impairs immune function and gives rise to excess mucous production, the beginning of an autoimmune response. The stimulant-sedative cycle of caffeine and sugar is a downward spiral of depletion.

The above describes the biological picture of the high-paced, high-stressed, American lifestyle. Your Jing—your constitutional strength—determines how long you can maintain an unhealthy lifestyle. But whatever your level of health, it is all relative to self-care and time. When the kidney system loses its stores of vitality, the doorway to serious, aggressive illness and disease is near.

Most people know that with the addition of regular exercise, the consumption of vegetables and vitamins, and the avoidance of stimulants and sedatives promote a healthy lifestyle. Knowing this, why do you and/or people you know continue to choose unhealthy lifestyle habits? Something deeper anchors unhealthy habits in place.

Uproot disease at the source and you will find a remedy.

Supplements, diet, and exercise are important. I use them all in my practice. But ultimately, to create lasting change in health, you must examine the underlying patterns of disease, which almost always boils down to some form of fear. When fear is chronically suppressed, there is nothing you can do enough of to maintain a vibrant system. If you are afraid to face fear, it will inevitably get the best of you.

Fear yearns to be transformed by the warm light of the heart. The more it is kept in the dark, the more disharmony it generates. Until fear and love are alchemized, disease builds momentum.

❧ EXHAUSTION FROM FEAR EXERCISE

- *Is my lifestyle exhausting me?*

- *What fear am I covering up with the exhaustion?*

- *Am I ready to feel and bring love to fear so it can heal?*

Not all fears need to be faced. The fears that we are meant to move towards persist. The Universe brings them to our attention in a way that says, "You need to face this issue in order to grow." We may try to dismiss these feelings, but like a weed, they reappear until we learn to use them as allies. These fears are related to our life lessons. Fear is like birth: it wakes you up to a part of yourself you didn't know was there. If you have a lot of fear inside you, then you work hard to keep it suppressed. You may be very disciplined or out of control in your life as a response to fear. To move skillfully through fear, the best thing you can do is learn to meditate and do breathwork. These two practices will help you release the fear in your body, as well as, help you address fear when it arises in your life. See the Tools section to learn more about them. Besides the practices, understanding these five principles is essential to forming a healthy relationship with fear.

1. The Universe loves you and wants you to succeed.
2. Despite what your mind says, deep down your core nature is good.
3. You were born to heal anything that limits your sense of goodness. The core intention of the Universe is to help you with this.
4. You are more courageous than you think.
5. It's okay to be awkward when facing your fears. It's not meant to be comfortable. Do it anyway.

Fear has a way of eating you up from the inside. I can't think of a more uncomfortable experience than being afraid to face something. My school of thought when it comes to facing fear is to just do it. Summon the courage and have the difficult conversation, quit the job, take the job, leave the relationship, stay in the relationship, and trust the Universe to fill in the gaps. At some point you'll be forced to face your fears. You might as well open up a little and try to cooperate with the Universe. You will find it's not as scary as you thought; you're stronger than you imagined, and people are generally much more generous than you believed. And…I love you. I've got your back. Go for it!

WITHHOLDING

People do not like to admit they are afraid. Fear is not an attractive emotion. It does not inspire strength. Suppression at the level of the kidneys appears as withholding, surmised by the idea, "Rather than admit what I'm afraid of, I'll pretend it is not real by saying nothing." You know the *mysterious type* that people find attractive. "He's so mysterious," you hear people say. Yeah, the mysterious dude that you find attractive is at least as scared as you are, but he has learned to dissemble and hide the fear in bravado, style, glibness, or some other distracting behavior.

Withholding information, feelings, and love is a form of suppression that separates the heart from empowering Universal Love throughout all dimensions of your self. It is a marker for expansion. The thing you are afraid to admit will set you free.

People don't need to know all of your thoughts. Discernment is needed. Will your thoughts and feelings uplift the situation and set people free even if they create discomfort? If yes, then sharing your truth would be a good thing. If your fear diminishes what's possible, feeds insecurity, or demeans people's inherent goodness, it's probably better for you to ask someone neutral to help you process or spend some time alone in nature. Complete transparency is not always appropriate. We don't want our fears to feed fear. We want to mix love with it and use fear's powerful energy to create more love. You don't need to share things that insult people's Divine essence. Never tell your partner "Those pants make your butt look big." Or that he is fat. If you need a rule of thumb, don't be a jerk. Think before you speak, and when you do say something, be kind, friendly, and loving with your words, even when you need to tell someone a hard truth.

Fear is a way the Universe gets your attention that something needs to change. It's a two-way process, because it helps you and others. Spirit needs you to help others grow. Fear has a lot of affinity for Grace. When you find yourself trying to bury fear or feeling ashamed of feeling fear, offer yourself Grace and invite the Universe to shower you with Grace. Say, "I invoke Grace upon this situation. Thank you Universe, God, Love, and [your favorite name for the Divine]."

In the West, most people were taught since childhood to suppress every emotion except happiness, and even then, to express happiness only to a degree. You don't want to annoy people by being too happy, right? You don't want them feeling badly if they are less happy than you. And you fear that if you subject your happiness to their scrutiny, they may burst your bubble. So we sometimes suppress exactly the happiness that would make the whole world better. Only when we are falling in love and cannot contain the glow, does our supreme happiness shine through.

Suppressed emotions undermine wellness. Every time you are kind with yourself and allow your feelings to flow, you change the culture of emotion in society. When you choose to love yourself, you grant Grace to your being and lift up the world. You break the imprisonment of negative self-talk. The highest form of gratitude is absorption in self-love. What you omit, will not quit. The things you hide from others, you also hide from yourself. Over time the energy required to conceal truth will exhaust you and suck up your creativity.

- *To whom or to what do I give my energy? (i.e., work, friends, family, drugs, sex)*

- *What am I afraid of in that arena of life?*

- *How does that fear show up in every area of my life?*

- *If my first response is, "I'm not afraid," look closer. The nature of fear is to try to remain hidden.*

- *If I'm feeling tired or wired: What fear am I covering up with my busy schedule?*

Suppression that reaches the kidneys activates a polarity of archetypes: the rebel and the conservative. It's primal. Fear makes you fight or flee to protect yourself from potential threats. The rebel devalues fear through lofty fantasies not rooted in reality. The rebel seeks out danger and taunts fear at every turn in response to feeling out of control. The conservative person constructs life to prevent anything or anyone from coming too close without strict rules. Fear restrains the conservative person who sees life as dangerous and chaotic.

🪷 THE REBEL AND CONSERVATIVE EXERCISE

- *What is my life theme around fear? Some familiar scripts: I'm afraid of nothing. I'm afraid of surprises. I always have to watch my back. When will the other shoe drop? I don't need you. Leave me alone. I have to be perfect. I have to be the best. I have to be unique. I have to be better than anyone expects me to be.*

- *Do I embrace fear or hide from it?*

- *Do I relate to being a rebel in any way? How is being a rebel tied to a deeper fear around giving and receiving love?*

- *Am I rigid and strict with myself? Do I impose nearly impossible standards on myself and others?*

- *How have I constructed my life to avoid feeling fear? How does this impact the relationships I choose, the places I go, the food I eat, the risks I take?*

Both rebels and conservatives suppress fear. Fear cannot be overcome by rebelling against it. You cannot protect yourself from fear by building a castle of conservatism to insulate you from your fears. Fear is within you. In fear, you'll find strength, but you have to be willing to feel through it and choose love on the other side.

The key is this: fear will not kill you. Feel it. Breathe into it from your kidneys (down in your hips) and pull it up to your Heart. Feel your creative power pulsing from below your belly up to the center of your chest. Fear is power that can be used to fuel your dreams. Feel it moving through your heart.

The kidneys provide the opportunity for mastery. Joseph Campbell's writing about the Hero's Journey captures this. Luke Skywalker faces Darth Vader, only to realize that his greatest nemesis is his own Father. Essentially the darkness that the Jedi tradition charges Skywalker to defeat is within himself. Luke realizes his job is not to kill his father and banish the darkness; his job is to skillfully face the darkness within, and restore the balance of Light and Dark in the Universe. He emerges from the journey illumined as a Jedi master, capable to face the darkness with skill and Grace.

Dark Night of the Soul

All beings are on a path of healing. For most of us, there is a period when one feels completely isolated and separated from the Divine. The seeker feels as if God does not exist. St. Francis of Assisi is a shining example of an exalted being who radiated Divine Love. His teachings talk about this time in a seeker's life when one experiences the "dark night of the soul." This is a very healthy and necessary journey. During the dark night of the soul, faith is tested. Can you endure the void, the sense of nothingness? The dark night is an adjustment to the dark form of Light. Yes, darkness, too, is a form of Light. Just like entering a dark room, at first you cannot see, and you may feel disoriented. Then, after some time, you begin to see amid the darkness.

The capacity to work with darkness can only occur if you have experienced it firsthand. At various junctures, Spirit demolishes your limited views and beliefs about life and ignites a burning desire within for freedom. This is the dark night set in motion.

Can you find faith when you feel nothing? This is a skill to cultivate that enables the spiritual warrior to emerge.

The dark night of the soul is a normal and important impasse on the spiritual path, one that signifies that it is time to face your life's deepest lessons. There is no quick fix to make it go away. You simply have to endure. More importantly, you want to learn from it and ultimately allow it to strengthen the tides of compassion within yourself for your own suffering and the suffering of others. The dark night allows you to hold increased light for the planet. And there are ways to abate the intensity of its magnetism.

DARK NIGHT OF THE SOUL EXERCISE

- *Have I experienced the dark night of the soul?*
- *What helped me through it?*
- *Am I experiencing the dark night now?*
- *What seems to help move it along?*
- *What seems to hamper it?*

If you've never experienced the dark night of the soul, it doesn't mean you will. Not everyone does. You do not need to wish it upon yourself to advance on the path. Sometimes people abandon healthy life practices when life gets hard. This is a mistake. The practices that strengthen you in your evolution strengthen you even more when you are in the midst of challenges. The darkness is a catalyst for freedom, and can be especially empowering when you choose uplifting practices during hard times.

NEFARIOUS ENERGIES AND ADDICTION

The kidney system is the body's last ditch effort to reconcile health within the Sequence of Separation. When pathology reaches the constitutional depths of the kidney system, preservation of physiological strength is essential for healing. In other words, to fend off a pathogen or heal from an advanced disease, you need to have some vital reserves. No reserve, no resolve.

Submission to negative lifestyle habits leads to weakened physiology and lends the body to possession by nefarious energies. I'm not trying to frighten you or be too dramatic with a line like, "possession by nefarious energies." This is not a joke or an attempt to indulge a fetish for the paranormal. These energies manifest as thoughts and habits that seek to destroy life. In the same way that humans gather to celebrate Light and Love, there are places where people gather to exalt hate and cruelty. Look at any group of people who hate other people for the color of their skin, sexual orientation, culture, or religion.

Known as the "King of Medicine," physician Sun Simiao of the seventh century Tang dynasty wrote extensively on treating dark energies that possess an individual with his famous protocol called the Thirteen Ghost Points. Today we consider this protocol an approach to treating mental illness, which is another way to talk about possession. One of Sun Simiao's contributions to healing is his pristine commitment to seeing the best in people. He said,

> 66 *I will be devoted to the task of saving the sacred spark of life in every creature that still carries it. I will strive to maintain a clear mind and be willing to hold myself to the highest standards.* 99

Sun Simiao words speak clearly about how to relate to all people, even those who are entrenched in dark thoughts and feelings.

You likely know someone who has gone down a dark road in life and has been consumed by that darkness to the extent that his or her previous positive qualities have been eclipsed by negative ones. Maybe that person is you. To watch someone's inner Light become dim is one of life's greatest tragedies. It can trigger feelings of helplessness, as well as sadness. Ask the Universe for Grace and compassion. No one is alone, no matter how it may seem or feel in a dark moment. Though we make this journey as individuals, we do it together.

Possession and Andre

Andre came to see me after a major healing crisis spurred on by the night that he tried to destroy his life. Andre, a 48-year old CEO of a multimillion-dollar company, had worked eighty hours a week for two consecutive years and had taken terrible care of himself in the process. Brief weekend blowouts in Las Vegas were his only repose from the extreme stress of his life. Andre shared, that when he arrived in Vegas and descended down the airport escalator, he faced a picture of the Welcome to Las Vegas sign. Every time he saw that familiar sign, a wave of peace washed over him and all his stress disappeared. Vegas was Andre's Holy Land.

The night Andre tried to destroy his life was like any other night in Vegas, except the momentum of the years of stress overpowered his will. After another eighty-hour work week, Andre hit his favorite club on the strip. The drinks started flowing along with the cocaine. Andre recounts that, "At a certain point into the evening, I was high on coke, drinking, and felt the heaviness of all my stress and responsibilities weigh down on me. I said, 'Fuck it!' and in that moment, the force of feeling trapped by responsibilities and my desire to be free from them imploded. I couldn't stop the energy inside me that wanted to destroy my life. I knew the destructive energy had to run its course and there was nothing I could do to stop it. I did more cocaine, cheated on my wife, got arrested, and thrown in jail."

Andre's ability to contain and process the stress of his life completely collapsed, and the force behind his unhealthy lifestyle tried to kill him.

Later he shared, "I was ready to die that night." A destructive force possessed him. His poor self-care had weakened his resilience to such a dire extent that he could not stop the destructive force within *him. Andre had created a pattern of destruction in his life that he could not control. Fortunately for Andre, he found help, forgiveness, and Grace. He realized that his wife and child were more important than money and power. The Universe gave him a second chance with his wife, his business, and his health. Andre is now learning balance and is grateful to have so many blessings around him. He attributes our sessions with helping him find new healthy ways to deal with his stress and is now looking to retire and enjoy his family. But Andre admits that while he does miss the high of Vegas, he is going to seek healthier ways to allow himself to enjoy some of life's edges.*

The more you choose to align with the frequency of Universal Love, the more you redirect power from sources of diminishment towards sources of Light. In the same way that you can create habits of destruction in your life, you can create habits that uplift and heal. The highest form of service to humanity is immersion in the Light, which is why I believe in life-affirming practices like meditation that enhance your ability to hold and radiate Universal Love.

Everyone is born with an innate hunger for freedom. The hunger for freedom and for love cannot be stopped or impeded.

The part of you that feels insecure, self-conscious, and doubts your self-worth limits the expansiveness of your Divinity. Some traditions call this the ego, as if everything ego-related possesses a bad connotation. I see the ego as a necessary aspect of self. In part, the ego allows you to function in the world and uphold your responsibilities. Behind all of the ego's fleeting desires is the singular and elemental desire for Universal Love. That desire is what heals.

Possession by destructive energies marks the full impact of suppression. If left unchecked, the ego magnetizes the limited and unconscious aspects of itself. Sadness, anger, rage, doubt, worry, and fear magnetize similar energies. When the body is extremely weakened, the kidneys and the heart do not communicate, and one's dreams are left unfulfilled. This is where magnetizing tragedy arises.

If you hate life and yourself, suicidal thoughts may emerge. The energy of suicide is complex. Says David Elliott, "Adults find more complex ways to commit suicide than young people." For example: alcoholism, drug addiction, or car accidents that were not accidental. In these instances, one begins to give power to an inner voice of destruction. Kidney-level separation is most common among adults, though it can appear at younger ages. If drugs are involved, either illegal or prescribed, the prognosis is grim, unless there is a comprehensive, integrated healing team involved, along with a desire from the individual to heal.

Mary Overcoming Darkness

Mary came to me with an addiction to white foods. Her diet consisted of white bread, pasta, ice cream, candy, and the occasional hit of marijuana. With a history of alcoholism, and a self-proclaimed "addictive personality," sugar had taken the place of alcohol, but was keeping her in a suppressed state. Her energy was low (two on a scale of ten), and sleep was nonexistent without sedation from a pint of Ben and Jerry's and several hits from a vaporizer. She had chronic pain along her cervical spine and took a cocktail of drugs for anxiety, restless leg syndrome, pain, high cholesterol, and allergies. Her demeanor appeared dull and lifeless, almost zombie like. Her tongue presented with a thick turbid white coat and her pulse was weak, thin, slippery, and empty in the kidney position.

I'll never forget how, after five minutes into the intake, Mary announced, "I think I'm pretty healthy." I was amazed to hear her blatantly declare something her body so blatantly contradicted! I didn't know if there was much hope, because of the depth of her addictive tendencies and her nearly comatose demeanor. I sensed a deep grief and sorrow in Mary that seemed to possess her. Her high sugary diet that had replaced her alcoholism had encapsulated all her emotional pain and kept it from surfacing. She was in a vicious, self-reinforced, and, ultimately, self-defeating cycle.

I had treated patients with a history of addiction before with some success, but they tended to require a lot of my time and energy. When I met Mary, I had come to a place in my healing practice where I was valuing myself more and sensitive to the exchange of energy. I was clear that I would give only if she was willing to do the work. We started with an Aggressive Energy acupuncture treatment developed by Lonny Jarrett. The purpose of the treatment is to clear extraneous stagnation from the entire system. The next treatment Mary seemed slightly more lucid. I told her if she really wanted to get better she needed to reduce her sugar intake. Surprisingly she said, "I'll do whatever it takes." I had heard patients say this before without conviction and I wasn't sure that Mary had the strength to carry out her declaration. Sensitive to her state, I suggested she take a supplement called Vitamineral Green to help stabilize her blood sugar while also cleansing her blood and detoxing her liver.

On her third visit, I was amazed. Mary sat in the treatment room happy with a spark in her eyes. She said she hadn't had ice cream since her last visit, her pain level was down from 7 to 3 out of 10, and the restless legs had stopped completely. The Vitamineral Green was working. There was an increased level of vibrancy to her being. We continued with acupuncture and herbal therapy for several more weeks. About two months into treatment, Mary opened up about a history of verbal and physical abuse as a child.

Luke Adler

She was ready to do some deeper healing. I was hesitant to introduce seated meditation and breathwork, because her physical system was still fragile. She expressed an eagerness to heal that was truly heart felt. She came to one of my healing events. In the middle of the breath meditation she burst into tears and wailed uncontrollably for several minutes. The next day she called the office with so much gratitude in her voice. She didn't think she would ever feel happiness again. She said the breathwork opened her Heart and she remembered that she really is a good person.

For the next six months, she had her ups and downs. Mary became stronger physically and emotionally, and is now developing new relationships. As a talented musician, she began composing prolific works that were filled with joy, nostalgia, and hope. After a year of working together, she is completely unrecognizable from the person who walked into the clinic a year before.

In extreme cases, an individual possessed by darkness can appear zombie-like, and resemble a living human only in form, not in being or vitality. Mary displayed some of these attributes. Hair falling out, pain throughout the body (particularly in the knees and low back), loose teeth, hollow appearance in the eyes, her body a mere shell of what it was; a perfect opportunity for a foreign entity to inhabit. By foreign entity, I mean a parasitic toxic energy that seeks to feed off a human being's life force.

To arrive at this point of separation from your heart, you have to doubt the Light of the Heart enough times to cause a split from Universal source. The Universe respects your freewill. Should you choose to ignore Spirit's input, eventually Spirit honors your choice, which leaves the body vacant for other energies. Other illnesses may ensue. These include autoimmune disorders, like complex regional pain syndrome, fibromyalgia, Epstein-Barr virus, and cancer in its various forms related to specific tissues and organs.

I'm not saying all chronic disease is a form of possession, though there may very well be, or there may be some component of possession or parasitic energy that accompanies a chronic disease. Spiritual death can be followed by physical death as parasitic energies consume vital reserves. The Buddhist tradition calls these dark forces Rakshasic energies. These energies appeal to your insecurities and diminish the capacity for the Light in your Heart to increase.

The Universe never abandons you. Should you turn towards Grace, even at your lowest ebb, the Universe will support you.

DARK ENERGY EXERCISE

- *What habits, relationships, or addictions make me vulnerable to dark energies?*

- *Do I have people in my life that trigger or stimulate dark energies in me?*

- *The desire to seek affection, praise, admiration, and appreciation from external sources can cause one to do things that are misaligned with the Heart. Am I vulnerable in this way?*

- *When I feel negativity, do I tend to reach for something uplifting, like meditation, an inspiring book, a glass of water, or a healthy snack; or do I reach for something that feeds the negativity, like sugar, alcohol, violent or negative music or television?*

- *What energies do I allow to vibrate in my mind, body, and spirit, and why?*

Possessive energies seek to destroy your body, mind, and spirit. These energies are negative and may disguise themselves as positive. Ultimately, you are responsible for what you allow to vibrate in your mind. The people with whom you choose to spend your time and energy can uplift or diminish. Diminished patterns of being and addictions are rooted in negative thoughts. Negative thoughts are virulent diseases that seek to replicate themselves. Think of them as energy-sucking vampires, black-holes for your vitality and joy.

I sometimes work with people who are addicted to their emotions. They gravitate towards situations that allow and encourage them to feel sadness and anger. They feel unworthy and seek experiences to validate their unworthiness. They amplify and recycle past hurts to fulfill this pernicious belief. I remember being this way at various points in my life. Playing the victim is a seductive role, partly because there's a rush of endorphins associated with sadness, anger, and fear. Society esteems the victim archetype, especially in the legal system, so this is a reliable way to get the attention that such people crave to support their emotional habit.

❀ NEGATIVITY EXERCISE

- *What are the most predominant negative thoughts that circulate through my mind?*

- *How much (in terms of percentages) do I believe in these negative thoughts in a given day? (How frequently do such thoughts occupy my mind?)*

- *How well am I at allowing negative thoughts to float by?*

- *Which thoughts trigger me the most?*

- *What makes me buy into a negative thought pattern?*

- *Does this happen more when someone agrees with my negative thought or disagrees and challenges it?*

- *Do I play the victim role anywhere in my life?*

- *What am I not being responsible for? Who am I blaming for my circumstances?*

Pay attention to where negative thoughts resonate in your body. The thoughts that trigger you the most point to where disease lives in your body. Notice the sensations, changes in your breath, and what memories arise. Be willing to use your imagination to sense what past lives are connected to these sensations. Record your experience and then take it deeper with more inquiry and breathwork.

Even darkness is a form of Light. The purpose of spiritual practices like meditation and breathwork is to build strength to face the darkest of the dark energies and free them into the Light. After some strengthening of the energetic body from meditation, it will be more difficult for nefarious energies to stick to you. Your being will become so suffused with Light that negativity has nowhere to attach.

Spiritual practices are not an escape from the stresses of life. They fuel and fortify Universal Love and keep the mind and body laser sharp. They transform life's lessons into healing frequencies. Meditation fosters freedom and leaves you at peace wherever you go. Regular meditation transforms you into a person who radiates Love, goodwill, and healing.

SEX

In Chinese Medicine, the kidney system includes the sex organs, marrow, and the brain. Sex is utterly natural and obviously essential to the continuation of life. Why is it, then, that sex is so suppressed within our culture? Why is pornography one of the most common search terms on the Internet? I remember feeling embarrassed about sexual attraction as a teenager and remained awkward about sex in my early twenties. High school sex education scared me stupid about contracting a sexually transmitted disease. I learned to communicate with women about safe sex and was extra sensitive to their comfort level regarding how quickly we moved forward in a sexual relationship. I have incredible respect for women around the exchange of sexual energy.

Sex is amazing. The pleasure and energetic connection between partners can reach transcendental levels of energy exchange and soul communication. The pure essence of sexual energy is the desire and provides the fuel to merge with the Divine. Sex, when approached from this perspective becomes a spiritual experience and can become a spiritual practice that heals all aspects of one's being.

My first time was with someone I loved. I'm not sure why, maybe all the years of meditation did it, my vision transformed completely into white light, and blue light poured out of her eyes into my heart. Explosions of white light arced, refracted, and expanded out of the center of our solar plexuses. Tears poured like a torrent of rain from my eyes. The whole scene blasted into sonic explosions of white light with streams of blue auras outlining our bodies. For days afterward, I could feel a strong pulse of energy emanate three feet from the center of my chest around my heart chakra. I was intoxicated by the experience and in love with my beloved partner. She made me feel so safe to express and enjoy myself as a sexual being. Through our connection, I learned to view sex as an expression of love at the level of the soul. Later, if that level of trust and openness was not there with a partner, I moved on.

Sex is not the most important thing in a relationship for me. I enjoy it, no doubt. The deep Heart connection with my wife is ultimately why we're together. Making love with Hearts connected is utterly powerful and strengthens the connection to one another and to the Universe. The relationship I now have with sex and my sexuality feels very comfortable and free. I am a one-woman man, and honor the many variations of sexual connection. I respect other people's sexual choices, as long as there is nothing harmful taking place for either partner.

No matter who you love, the most important thing before, during, and after sex, is that Love and respect flow first to self and then to your partner. If you are looking for someone to fill you up spiritually through sex, then sex is just another addiction, such that the more you use it, the less it gives you.

Shame, embarrassment, and awkwardness around sex is completely natural, given society's portrayal of sex as both something pure to be saved for marriage and as something dirty. These sexual polarities reflect the two extreme behaviors of the kidneys out of balance: conservatism and rebellion. Because sex is something society suppresses, sex expresses itself within the two polarities of the kidney system: as the puritanical virgin who regards sex as the most holy symbol of spiritual worth, or the prostitute, whom society rejects as an outlier, even an untouchable.

❦ SEX EXERCISE

Where do I fall on the spectrum of sexual expression?
1   2   3   4   5   6   7   8   9   10

Addicted to Sex, Perverse, Comfortable, Free, "Sex feels Healthy," Conservative, Rigid

- *What am I afraid of with regards to sex?*

- *What fear around sex do I suppress?*

- *Does that fear originate from Mom or Dad?*

- *Where does the fear live in my body?*

- *What's my earliest memory of feeling that fear?*

- *Feeling into my lineage and using my imagination, how far back does that fear go, and how did it arise?*

- *Stretching my intuition, what was my relationship to this type of fear in previous lives?*

My Sexual Healing

I began to notice a shift in my experience of sex a few years into my healing practice. After sex, I would feel tired and irritable, with dry eyes and a hollow feeling in my head. I would need a few days to recover my energy before I felt balanced again. The worst was if I had sex on an evening before work. I felt like I had a decreased capacity to run energy through my body, like I was frying my circuitry. I became possessive of my sexual energy and only wanted to have sex on a Friday, so I had time to recover before work on Monday. My sex life became tied to my work life. I went to see a naturopath, checked my testosterone and adrenal levels, which were slightly low for my age, and began taking DHEA, fish oils, and B vitamins, among other supplements. This helped a bit, but when I tapered off, all the symptoms returned. I struggled with this issue for another five years, and I began to lose faith in my body. Sex became a love-hate relationship and through it all, my wife was very supportive and patient with my process. At times, she couldn't understand why I was rigid about sex, but held the space for me to explore why I felt so drained by it.

An opportunity came up to see my chief mentor of Chinese Medicine, Jeffrey Yuen. The only catch was I had to present my case to fifty of my peers and have Jeffrey diagnose me. I flew to San Francisco and told my story as I choked down tears of shame and embarrassment. After questions from Jeffrey and my colleagues, my mentor announced to the class, "Luke is working too hard." Fuck! The sinking feeling in my gut was immediate. My wife could tell me this a hundred times, but coming from Jeffrey, the words sank in deep. The phrase was simple and I knew it had a deeper meaning.

Then, I worked with a healer in Eugene on the issue. She asked me about masturbation, sexual shame, essentially how I felt about sex. I thought "I've masturbated maybe five times in the last five years. That was something I did as a teen and young adult. Married men don't masturbate." Wow! I realized that I had a lot of suppression around my sexuality. As I looked deeper, I saw I had a list of rules that I followed. My sexual energy was tied to a fear of failure. I feared that if I didn't use that energy for healing, my patients would leave me, and I'd end up on the street, or worse, have to ask my parents for help, another layer of fear. I had tremendous shame around masturbation. I saw it as dirty and ugly. I began to see that some part of me resented that I had to deal with sex at all. As I unpacked all of this deep suppression, I realized the symptoms I was having were not because I was exhausted from working too hard. The symptoms were coming from stagnation of sexual energy, that when expressed, was like an unwieldy dam breaking open that I then quickly rebuilt again. In a sense,

I had become extremely conservative with my sexual energy. I began to actively heal this energy by embracing it, breathing into it, and having more sex. In the beginning it was very emotionally painful, because I allowed myself to feel all the feelings I had suppressed; feelings of shame, embarrassment, rigidity, and fear. As I breathed into these feelings and mixed them with self-love, I began to find balance with my sexual energy.

In the midst of this breakthrough, my dear friend, Dr. Juliette Mulgrew, taught me that in Ayurvedic medicine, the three pillars of health are nutrition, sleep, and sex. Holy Shit! No wonder I'm so messed up. I was taking sexual advice from one of my spiritual teachers who is essentially a monk. He doesn't have sex. His teaching is to have sex once a month to maintain equilibrium on the spiritual path. When I finally began to listen to my body as a teacher, it taught me that his advice was wrong for me. I learned that for me, healthy sex isn't about always having an orgasm. It's about circulating the energy, feeling it in my heart, and feeling good about it. I'm still working on balancing my sexual energy. It is the most powerful energy in the body and essential for health and vitality. Healthy sexual expression is an essential aspect of progressing spiritually. They are not two, distinct parts of life. They are interdependent. My next book will go more in depth on this subject. I felt it was prudent (pun intended) to be upfront about this level of my healing, because it is current; it represents the deepest part of how suppression can affect someone, and is one of the most important aspects of one's mental, physical, and emotional health to address and heal.

Sexual energy is powerful. To work with it consciously requires a lot of awareness. Sexual energy is the fundamental energy that creates life, sustains life, and exits the body to permit death. An expanded level of awareness helps discern the nature of sexual energy when it is active. I'm very aware of sexual energy within myself especially when I'm working with people. I'm very careful not to allow this energy to move through me toward a patient in a sexual way. I always bring the creative energy of my sexual organs up to my heart by breathing and focusing the energy on the center of my chest. The sexual energy of the kidneys (the water element) alchemizes with the fire element of the heart. The metaphorical steam that's created through the union of fire and water is very healing to both practitioner and patient.

Creative people are often vulnerable to addiction. This happens because the creative energy stemming from their sexuality stagnates. Rather than ascending sexual energy to the heart to be expressed, they spend it recklessly with drugs, alcohol, sugar, excessive sex, or something else that diminishes their constitutional strength.

Everyone is creative. The Taoist value of longevity comes into play here. Work consciously with creativity to preserve your congenital resources. Allow Universal insight to flow through your heart. You have God given talents. Use them to channel your love, and the Universe will guide you.

When sexual energy is suppressed, it operates independently from the wisdom of the heart. David Elliott talks about sexual predator energy, as a force that seeks to gain power over or from others by manipulating people with sexual energy. If your sexual energy is not connected to your heart, you may be vulnerable to sexual predator manipulation, or you may use sexual energy manipulatively to get what you want.

❀ SEXUAL PREDATOR EXERCISE

- *Am I aware of sexual predator energy in me?*
- *Am I aware of sexual predator energy from others*

towards me?

- *What unresolved wound attracts sexual predator energy towards me?*

- *What unresolved wound activates sexual predator energy in me?*

In high school I was known as a flirt. Not understanding the power of my sexual energy, I remember looking at women in a particular way that expressed an interest in sex. I didn't really know what I was doing with my sexual energy other than letting a woman know I was attracted to her. Later, I realized I was playing the I-want-you-to-like-me game of cat and mouse. I wanted to be liked, because I was insecure. As my self-love grew and I understood how I used sexual energy to fill a wound inside, I stopped sending this energy towards women, and chose consciously when I would open these energy centers.

SEX AND CREATIVITY

- *In what ways am I sexual? Is it for pleasure only?*

- *Am I trying to run away from or towards something to avoid being in my heart?*

- *How am I creative?*

- *Where is my creativity blocked?*

- *How do I act when it is? How do I get my creativity to flow? How is this working for me?*

- *What are/were my parent's views of sex? How have they influenced me?*

- *Where in my body do I carry pain, shame, or guilt from past sexual experience?*

- *Using my intuition, from what generation does shame or guilt originate?*

- *Do I feel comfortable expressing my sexuality?*

If you don't know the answers to some of the above questions, feel into them with your intuition. If you're noticing or sensing strange currents of energy, breathe and work into them with your awareness. Write down what you see and feel in your body. Be as specific as you can. Work to separate the different currents of energy. Feel into what era of your life they come from.

The more you know how sexual energy moves through you, and how you suppress it, the better you'll be able to access your creativity and help others do the same. Sexual trauma, toxic sexual shame, and unhealthy sexual practices usually arise from some sort of abuse as a child or a latent impression of abuse from a past life. Often people are shut down sexually and may be numb physically, and/or hyperactive sexually in response to this pattern from a young age.

 CLEARING SEXUAL CONNECTIONS

It is essential to clear sexual connections from the past that are still active in your subtle system in order to be present in a healthy sexual way with your partner.

- *How do I know if I am still connected to past partners?*

If the mention or thought of a past partner's name triggers a contracting or diminishing sensation in your body then there is some unfinished karma to address.

Listen to my Lite Heart Cleanse track, which you can download at http://www.cdbaby.com/cd/lukeadler

After the Lite Heart Cleanse is over, mentally trace back to your most recent sexual partner. If you feel a physical charge in your body when you recall their presence, either think or say aloud, "I'm sorry if I hurt you or caused you any pain. I offer you Light and healing and I release you with Love."

If you were hurt in the relationship, say "I forgive you and release you with love and blessings." Inhale long through your nose and exhale long through your mouth. Breathe until you feel the sensations clear from your body. If the sensation gets stronger, return to the three-part breathing until the energy has cleared.

It is essential to declare to the Universe that you release this partner. Energetic cords connected to past relationships drain one's life force energy and siphon energy from our vital reserves. Be clear with the above declarations to reclaim your life-force energy. With this meditation, you communicate to Spirit that you are ready to be in partnership with the Universe to create in an uplifting and wholesome way. When you've tracked through all your partners that you were still connected to sexually, and you feel complete say, "I open to Universal Love and allow it to flow to my sexual organs and through my heart."

Okay, nice work!

The key to healing is to make peace with fear. If there is any fear, apprehension or hesitation when you hear the word sex, then this is an area to work with and heal. The best way to start is to talk about it. Do some breathwork around any area of your sexuality where you feel uncomfortable with the intention to heal. Beyond conservatism and rebellion arises the wisdom that comes from facing your fears. The only way to be skillful in life is to face the places inside that scare you. If you get complacent, don't worry, the Universe will push you towards new places in your life where fear hides.

After some conscious work with fear, you will begin to see it as a creative energy that has a strong magnetism for Grace. You will look forward to facing fear, from the lived experience that, on the other side of fear, is intimacy and connection. Fear is the gateway to expansion. Sexuality is the source of your creative power. When you mix sexual energy with Universal Love via the axis of the heart and kidneys anything is possible. Set your sights ever higher, breathe deeply, and trust the Universe to unfold a life that is deeply satiating and full of laughter and joy.

STEP INTO YOUR POWER

Life will present you with challenges. Some people may even feel threatened by your radiance. One reason I feel passionate about you taking up a regular life practice that will enhance Universal Love running through you, is for you to face such darkness with greater skill and poise. You can dillydally in the mundane world for so long. At some point, the desire to take a stand and do something awesome knocks on the door.

🪷 ANSWER THE CALL EXERCISE

- *In the middle of fear, doubt, and insecurity, will I answer the call?*

- *What am I waiting for? Why do I think I am not ready? Is that fear speaking or something else? What do I call that part of me?*

- *Am I trying to give my Light to people who don't want it? If so, move on!*

Share your beauty with those who are ready to receive it. You can spend a lifetime trying to save your family and friends. When they're ready, they will let you know. Everyone has his or her own pace on the path and it's not for you or me to know when the time has come. A higher sense of order and timing is at play. We only see what we need to see to bring the Light forward. Trust that the path will reveal itself. If you're waiting for a sign, a lottery ticket, or someone to hand you a dream on a silver platter, it's time to show the Universe that you're willing to invest energy in your dreams. It's okay to be afraid. Fear is a powerful energy that can be transformed into enthusiasm, which in turn attracts Grace.

If you're not expanding, you're stagnating. Stagnant fear is a recipe for physical disease. Move your body, breathe, and examine if you have a dream that is not fulfilled. The kidneys are the storehouse of dreams and aspirations yet realized. Allow yourself to remember an agreement you made with your self, long before you ever came into this body. There is something you are here to do; something you are here to offer. It has to do with love. You are the only human being who can offer it. If you hesitate for too long, Spirit will move that support to someone else, who is open and willing to bring more Light into the world. As long as you breathe, your dreams live within you. I believe in you. It takes discipline to rise above fear. There is a dimension of love and Light on the other side of hesitation ready to lift you up. Pierce through the initial layer of fear, call your guardian angels forth, and allow the Light to carry you onward!

Sequence of Separation Quick Guide

You've read through the Crux section of Born to Heal. Congratulations! What follows is a chart that summarizes the Sequence of Separation. It will walk you through how imbalances manifest throughout your systems, and specifically which organs are most affected. Reading from left to right, if the **spleen** is the organ system you resonate with the most, you'll likely have a tendency to **worry** or overthink. The next column to the right is the way you deceive yourself—in other words, how you ignore the voice of your heart. The spleen system does this by **ingratiating**. You put other people's needs and emotions above your own, to the detriment of your wellbeing. The next column explains the type of unworthiness that leads to how you deceive yourself. You ingratiate because deep down you don't feel worthy of giving and receiving **love in your relationships**.

Moving right, the next column provides the polarizing behaviors that arise when you are misaligned with your inner wisdom. In the case of the spleen, being overly **self sufficient or needy** arise. The column that follows shows the pathway through which you become present to your heart for your particular organ system. For the spleen, you learn to **value your self worth** by restoring the balance of resources in your relationships. This could pertain to money, energy, time, or respect—a gesture of acknowledgement.

Exchange is the skill that the spleen person cultivates, shown in the last column in the right of the chart.

ORGAN	ELEMENT & EMOTION	FORM OF DECEPTION AND THWARTED BEHAVIOR	UNWORTHINESS
LUNGS	METAL & SADNESS/GRIEF	Seeing only the downside/flaws e.g. Glass half empty behavior: snide	Of being embodied or feeling safe in your body
LIVER	WOOD & ANGER	The end justifies the means behavior: seething, passive+/aggressive	Of divine purpose/ destiny
SPLEEN	EARTH & WORRY	Ingratiation behavior: complaining, neediness	Of love in relation-ships with people
KIDNEY	WATER & FEAR	Withholding behavior: secretive	Of divine lineage/ bringing forward the highest from ancestors
HEART	FIRE & JOY/ ANXIETY	Exagerative flat out lie behavior: sarcastic teasing	Of Universal Love

IMBALANCED POLARITIES	PATHWAY TO PRESENCE	SKILLS AND VIRTUES THAT ARISE IN BALANCE
Materilistic/ascetic or vanity/self deprication	Graditude for what is	Graditude preserves innocense and purity like that of a diamond.
Beligerence/timidity or arrogance/false humility	Recognize the inherent goodness in all	Deep inner goodness fosters an equilibrium of flexibility and strength.
Self sufficient/needy or self indulgent/martyr	Restore the exchange to honor the value of those present	Exchange stemming from a deep value of self and others.
Rebelious/conservative	Honor the teachings of what is. Learn the lesson at hand	Wisdom from experience brings the ability to look deep into reality.
Controlling/chaotic or guarded/exessively vulnerble	The divine insight that comes from accepting what is	Intuition results from presence of heart Ceremony & ritual activate the heart.

Restoring the
Autonomy of the Heart

This series of questions are an in-depth approach to reconnect with the inner guidance of your heart. Once you've uncovered the principal organ(s) that need to be harmonized—through the Sequence of Separation Quick Guide—use the questions, virtues and affirmations here to heal the stuck energy, beliefs, or wounds that you're experiencing. On your smart phone or recording device record yourself answering these questions. Then listen to your answers as a way to reaffirm your healing.

LUNGS

What am I grateful for right now in this situation? How is this current situation really a blessing? What action can I take to reflect my gratitude?

Are my judgments creating clarity for love to flow or do they dismantle a sense of trust and safety within my relationships and me? Looking past judgment, where in my body do I feel wounded?

Feeling love from the earth flow up through your feet and move into the wound, say, "I am safe and I receive love and healing now." Feel that energy moving inside, bringing warmth and ease to your body.

Discernment of right from wrong is important to navigate the world, but when judgment is disconnected from the heart, it only causes more separation.

Gratitude *reasserts the sense of worthiness to be present, to be embodied, and to notice the preciousness of life.*

Affirmation *I see wounded feelings as an opening to receive love from the earth to transform my pain into a blessing for the world. I am grateful for this moment, this breath, this opportunity to embrace life. I choose to focus on the Light.*

LIVER

To what extent am I aware of the inner goodness in myself and in the present circumstance? Can I see everyone is trying their best, from what they know? Become aware of the inner goodness (first in self) and respond in a way to bring out the best in everyone. Identifying the goodness in the situation and people involved disarms the resistance of all involved.

If someone does not own their part in the situation, first acknowledge that everyone is doing the best they can with what they know. Then own your responsibility. Finally share with those involved what they are responsible for, e.g. "Susan, you are responsible for your feelings." Let the situation be awkward or uncomfortable if it needs to be. Don't try to make everyone feel good. Let them feel the weight of their responsibility. This allows them to be worthy. Worthiness and responsibility are interlinked virtues. It's not your job to secure everyone's emotion. You are giving someone the opportunity to claim his or her divine purpose. There is no greater gift. Whether they choose to embrace that or not is their choice.

Deep Inner Goodness *reasserts worthiness of my divine purpose.*

Affirmation *I know deep down in my core that I am a good person. Even when I make mistakes, I choose to love myself.*

SPLEEN

How is the exchange off in this current circumstance? What do I need to do or say to restore my self worth and that of those around me? What do I need to say to allow love and respect to flow through this current circumstance? Does money or time need to be exchanged for things to flow again? Do I need to apologize or forgive someone, maybe myself?

Honoring **Exchange** reestablishes worthiness of love in relationships.

Affirmation *I open to love in all my relationships. I pledge to serve others and ask for support to strengthen the feeling of Universal Family.*

KIDNEYS

What is the lesson the Universe is trying to teach me right now? Am I willing to learn it? How much longer do I want to resist learning the lesson? If I feel confused or "don't get it," ask, "What am I afraid of?" Therein lies the lesson.

Identify the lesson and then take action steps towards it. Notice how it feels in your body as Grace supports you. Where and what do you feel? Are there any external signs that mirror you are in the flow of the moment? e.g. nature, trees, birds, animals, auras, coincidences, songs on the radio?

*Identifying the lesson at hand brings **Wisdom** and reconnects me to worthiness of my divine lineage.*

Affirmation *I open to the highest wisdom from my sacred lineage. I will pass on the gifts of my ancestors to future generations.*

HEART

Am I willing to accept my present circumstances exactly as they are right now?

Am I willing to accept people in my life exactly as they are?

Go tell people in your life about your newfound acceptance. If another person is involved, communicate that you accept him or her with all the good and the bad. The heart declares, "There is nothing you can say or do to make me stop loving you." Remember to say this to yourself too.

Acceptance of the moment summons **Intuition** *and reasserts worthiness of Universal Love.*

Affirmation *Whatever is occurring in my present circumstance is what the Universe wants for me. When I accept life as it is, I communicate to the Universe that I'm willing to work with and learn the lesson at hand. As I cooperate with the present moment, I begin to experience flow; the seamless movement of life force manifesting itself in all its creative power.*

In this moment I open to Universal Love and I trust the inspiration that moves through my heart, even, and especially if I feel afraid.

Section Two

THE TOOLS

MEDITATION

You are God. Not the wise old man sitting on a cloud somewhere above. You are God in the sense that you are of the energy that created the Universe, which is the same energy that sustains your life right now. If you place your awareness in a particular way on the Creative Force within you, the Universe reveals itself more fully to the parts of you that believe you are just a person with an identity, opinions, views and preferences. In the process, you will increasingly experience the Divine within. That realization will become natural and self-reinforcing as you bathe in Divine Love.

Now before you think, *Oh brother, meditation! My mind can't stop thinking. I've tried to meditate and I can't.* Continue reading because the meditation that I teach is easy to learn and has nothing to do with stopping your mind from thinking. In fact, the opposite is true.

That somehow during meditation you are supposed to stop the mind, grab it in a muscular way, and force it into submissive thoughtlessness is a profound misconception. I tried to meditate this way for more than a decade. I mentally pounded at a mantra over and over, for hours at a time. Internally, I clenched my mind to clutch the Divine. I aimed an impassioned sense of devotion towards a great meditation master as a method to connect more deeply in meditation. Sometimes, though infrequently, these methods worked, and I found myself in the exquisite repose of deeper states of meditation. Mostly, however, they did not, though the practice of discipline, focus, and concentration did yield a certain benefit to the rest of my life. I did not experience deep meditation on a consistent basis because my methods were not precise.

The divinity that keeps you alive in a physical body heals, listens, soothes, challenges, coaxes, loves, and believes in you. Increasingly, you are reuniting with the experience of your innate wholeness and power. It is your destiny.

AM I READY EXERCISE

- *Do I want to accelerate the experience of reunion with the Universe?*
- *Do I want to learn the easeful way to navigate life?*
- *Am I ready to release any sense of unworthiness and fully open to my divinity?*

You have a choice in how you learn your life lessons. Life can be free of suffering or full of it. There will be difficulty and pain at times. That is the nature of life. To get out of your own way and allow the Universe to guide you is a matter of daily practice. I offer you such a practice.

In the absolute sense, you are already one with the Universe. In a relative sense, you are not. Both statements are true and valid. Just as you experience feelings and sensations of connection and separation on a daily basis with people in your life, the same is true about your connection with the Universe. To bring about the sustained experience of your Divinity into daily life requires some effort. Like anything worth your effort, the work starts with a regular practice. The most reliable path to that connection, validated by virtually every spiritual tradition, is meditation. The only effort required of you is to create a comfortable place to sit and make it there everyday.

Meditation allows Universal Love to infuse into the fibers of your mind and body. Meditation shows observable improvement in my ability to maintain an awareness of Universal Love in my daily life and healing work. I feel that awareness translate into my body and mind as physical strength, finesse, mental clarity, and a particular kind of sensitivity that allows me to respond more specifically in the moment. I know that the daily meditation practice I do works and that it benefits many people beyond myself.

Meditation does not belong to any one group or religion. No one has a particular right to it over another person or group of people. The Sacred Vortex of Love within you is equally available to all. When you are ready to streamline your efforts and reduce the need to suffer, when your desire for the easeful, graceful way has matured into authentic readiness, then the time has come to cultivate the Angel within you. Your training is meditation.

In a sense, everyone meditates. The desire to still the mind, to experience a bit of mental and physical respite, is a self-borne desire. The yearning for freedom from the confines of mental and emotional pain is automatic. It's part of your innate ability for life to move towards healing.

The various pathways to actualize freedom differ in efficiency. Alcohol, drugs, sugar, and the like bring peace and a sense of ease to the mind and body albeit temporarily. They can be pleasant and effective—if you do not become addicted—which is part of their nature. And they are forms of superficial meditation in that they still the turbulence of the mind, yet always leave a desire and need for more substance to satisfy the yearning of the mind. Substances never quite satisfy the deep longing for inner satisfaction, the kind of satisfaction that feeds your soul. After the chemically induced euphoria wears off, a residue of toxicity to various tissues of the body remains. In the wake of euphoria, the mind and body are confused, manic, irritable, achy, nauseous, phlegmy, stinky, and so forth. To stave off these adverse effects, one may desire more chemicals. The more you imbibe, the more substance you'll need to feel a sense of freedom, and the more toxic the body becomes.

We live complicated, busy lives, and the act of suppression has planted unresolved emotions in our bodies, like unpredictable land mines. People can be annoying and slow. Or pushy, judgmental, and worst of all, right! As one of my meditation teachers says, without alcohol we would all kill each other. We are still killing each other, but it seems alcohol tempers the stress of life enough to avoid complete annihilation of one another—at least so far.

Everyone finds a way to quell tensions in life. In a sense, wanting freedom is an addiction. You cannot extinguish this inherent desire. This deepest desire for freedom is why you are alive. Anxiety and depression are symptoms of starving the desire for freedom. The longing to know Universal Love must, and at some moment will be, fed. The freedom that you desire, that you cannot live without, is the desire to know the Universal Heart fully, to live a sustained experience of your Divinity. It's the most fundamental desire of all desires, and it is what each and every human being is here to fulfill. The freedom that you seek is inside you. The only way to satiate the inner hunger is to look within.

Authentic meditation is a pathway to fully quench the desire to know Universal Love. Meditation is a means to absolute fulfillment. There are many forms of meditation and spiritual practice. I offer people practices for every step of the journey. The work I am focused on in this chapter is for people who are ready to make a more serious commitment to their health and freedom. As a new father, I am reminded of the brevity of life. When my daughter Corazón was born, the timeline of my life came into clear view. There is no time to waste. The time will go by either way. You might as well construct a foundation that brings real stability, clarity and Love to the world.

If you feel called, answer the call. I am walking the path with a purpose and nothing will stop me, Grace willing. You can walk with me and we will experience the thrill of meditation together.

MEDITATION PURIFIES

Dr. Masaru Emoto introduced fantastic findings in his analysis of water molecules. He compared water molecules exposed to different emotional tones and observed changes in their crystalline geometric structure. Water exposed to negative thoughts showed a collapse in the hexagonal structure of the molecules. The molecules appeared malformed, jagged, and lacked symmetry. Water samples from places of prayer, exposed to uplifting thoughts, demonstrated elegant lines of symmetry, intricate weaves, and striking composition that were consistent. Dr. Emoto's findings show consistent geometrical patterns that most people would agree are beautiful.

Authentic meditation is the most powerful way to organize the body and mind in alignment with beauty. The crystalline structure of your body and mind is amplified, strengthened, and expanded to hold increased Universal Light through meditation. Meditation affects the mind and body as if you had spent time in the most sacred place in the world. The beauty that you are has to be preserved, cleansed, strengthened, and refined.

To sustain and expand the presence of Universal Love through you: meditate.

I believe for the world to evolve and perhaps even survive, we have to introduce a new habit of self-care. You regularly brush your teeth, comb your hair, and shower. What do you do regularly to give your soul a clean place to inhabit? Just as you take a shower to cleanse your physical body, meditation is a shower of pure consciousness that cleanses your energetic, emotional, and mental bodies. This cleansing practice increases mental acuity, emotional intelligence, groundedness, wholeness, lowers blood pressure, and so much more.

Consciousness is the phenomenon of being aware. Right now you are aware of the words on this page. Your awareness illuminates the meaning of this sentence. Wherever you focus your awareness, information flows to you. That awareness, when directed upon itself, has a cleansing effect. Cleansing your self through meditation makes your awareness clear and crisp, so as to navigate life with precision and elegance. Without regular inner cleansing and cultivation, you are left with the limitations of your mind and belief system.

Have you ever looked down at your hands, and had a sense of, "How did I get here, alive in this body? This is so weird!" Life is weird. Here you are, a beautiful elegant soul, living in a wonderful, finite, and bizarrely elegant and complex structure called the body. And then there's your mind. The only information you can glean from your intellect, alone, is a reference of your past experiences or someone else's. The past, recycled, can be useful, but it also becomes predictable—and even boring—after several renditions, so you may fail to value the lessons learned over time, or even fail to heed them altogether.

True originality, authenticity, and creativity only come from inner cultivation. When you fail to care for your inner world, your only options are imitation and emulation. True expression only comes from peering deeply into the heart of anything. As you peer into the depths of yourself, you gain the ability to see deeply into any subject or object towards which you focus your awareness. Meditation is the tool that enables you to access the deep exploration of everything.

MORE BEAUTY

A deep feeling inside of wanting something more gnaws at you. This insatiable feeling will never go away. You will always look for more improved, distinct variations whether it's a new car, a better wardrobe, or a different partner. Many traditions of meditation teach the relinquishment of the desire-for-more, which pushes against the innate desire for "more".

In my freshmen year of college, my buddies and I adventured on surf missions up and down the coast of Santa Barbara. Sometimes we spent hours in search of surf and missed the entire window to jump in the water. I remember my buddy Alex teased us, "You kooks! The grass is always greener. Let's go surf."

This desire for something more fulfilling or more exquisite is a beautiful desire. It comes from a place inside that knows there is truly something even more resplendent to be experienced than already experienced. When you direct the desire for more within, gradually the deep Heart reveals more of its vast and dramatic beauty, which permeates your exterior life more and more.

As you drink in the pure Light inside your Heart, you begin to satiate that deep hunger for more. You actually feed the desire with something more satisfying than desire itself. In this style of meditation, we use the mind's desire for more to take us naturally into deep meditation, rather that trying to suppress our desire for more by controlling our thoughts. Trying to control thoughts keeps our awareness on the surface, and is at best an exercise in concentration.

All desires are really desires for the Divine. When you taste your source, it doesn't matter where you surf. You'll always have a great time because you're with someone beautiful…You.

MEDITATE ON YOU

Meditation is a compassionate, loving, courageous encounter with self. A few weeks after my 2012 Breitenbush Spring meditation retreat, a participant new to meditation commented, "Every time I meditate I feel angrier and angrier." I replied, "You're meditating on yourself. You feel anger because there is anger inside. Meditation cleanses anger out of your being, and it's doing that automatically, without you trying to help it along."

Everything that you are comes to bear during meditation. You will face all of yourself as you sit and allow your awareness to move deeply inside. As the pathway to the full expression of your heart clears out, you may face sadness, dark, horrible thoughts, confusion, fatigue, worry, and so on. These states and experiences are all normal and necessary spaces to move through, as your awareness settles deeper and closer to its emanational, peaceful source. Whether or not you meditate, these deep cleansing experiences surface throughout life. Meditation gives you the clarity to allow them to, the grace to let them go and the access to love, which translates into healing. In many ways the work is never done. Meditation heightens the talents, skill and virtues necessary to navigate life, enjoy it, and help others on their journey.

I'm telling you this to reassure you that we all go through it. You are not alone or unique in experiencing those states. Your memories and fears are personal, and we all have them. And we all need to acknowledge and heal them to make more room for the experience of our divine Nature.

The more you try to shape, control, or add-to your meditation, the more you impede the deepening of the practice and stay on a surface level of awareness. As you release your self to the natural, inward-flowing current of meditation, the impulse towards more beauty increases. You don't have to do anything, because your mind naturally looks for beauty. The nature of your mind to seek out beauty carries you to the source of all beauty within you. Quite naturally, you move past the stress of the day, painful memories of the past, and worries of the future, and settle into a very profound space of stillness and equipoise that gives rise to the most sublime and wondrous experiences. Just as in your meditation, these experiences will flow out externally into your life.

Authentic meditation is not an escape from life: It is not an entry point into an imaginary reality you dream of, nor is it the placement of your awareness on some exotic fantasy. Meditation isn't an attempt to rid your self of anything. Meditation on the inner Light causes reality to melt into a profound state of silence and peace. Gradually, without willful effort, meditation naturally moves your awareness deeper and deeper into more subtle layers of reality.

Meditation allows you to accept, embrace, and imbibe reality exactly as it is both within and without. As you meditate, you continue a *downward deepening* into awareness, and gradually become more established in a clearer, more potent, pulsation of the upsurging nature of consciousness. In deep meditation, you stand face-to-face with the heartbeat of the Universe. Exposure to the Universal Heart heals. Meditation gradually exposes your entire being to the healing and transformative power of the Universe.

A marker of a truly effective meditation practice is that the conditions of your external life improve. You become a more effective communicator; your skill sets become more refined; and your intention becomes more potent as a result of the clarity of your awareness gained from meditation. As the subtlest limitations of how you see life come in to view your understanding transforms. These micro adjustments of awareness yield exponential power to exchange love and healing with others.

Once you awaken to your Divine nature, the remainder of the

work is a journey of refining your awareness to reflect the fullness of Consciousness. This expedition is unique for all of us. Meditation contains and sustains this process in a safe, effective and healthy way.

Judging Your Meditations

I often hear from meditators of other traditions say things like, "That was a terrible meditation. All I did was think the entire time." Some people view thinking as a sign that meditation is not working. I often hear students say, "I remember someone once taught me that meditation happens when the mind is quiet, without thoughts. I have a monkey mind, it just won't stop." Universal healing energy accessed by meditation cleanses and brings a state of clarity and rest to the mind and body. Thoughts during the practice are a sign that meditation is working and cleansing you. Thoughts are not a bad thing, though absence of thought is wonderful, too.

As the inward current of meditation draws you deeper within, the current of purification releases random thoughts, emotions, memories, and sensations that are part of the house-cleaning process. The more thoughts are released, the more potent the Universal Light shines through you. Meditation creates more room inside by cleansing and strengthening the energetic system to hold more Love and Light.

Meditation is an active and automatic healing event. The only effort you need to make is to get to your seat. The practice takes care of the rest. The most sublime, lovely, and deep experiences can be followed by the most chaotic, swirly meditations. The most important concept is to keep going and be steady, consistent. There are many distractions along the path of meditation. Do not be swayed or captivated by inner light shows, ethereal visions, celestial sounds, or intense emotional catharses. They are not essential or necessary to progress on the path. If they happen, enjoy them; but do not let visions or celestial light shows stop you from going deeper within. They are street signs along the path, not the goal.

Be cognizant of the temptation to recreate a previously enjoyable meditation experience. I spent many years of meditation conjuring up visions and emotions in an attempt to duplicate intense previous *spiritual* experiences. When this attempt to recreate a previously enjoyable experience began to feel stale, I realized I was simply *imagining* a spiritual experience, rather than actually *having* one. Just like the saying, "You cannot force the river," meditation is a strong yet subtle force. It responds to authenticity, not manipulation or desire.

The rigor of meditation is to accept your awareness as it is and as it changes. Sometimes awareness is utterly blissful. Other times, the awareness field seems boring or difficult. Agreeing to be right where you are can feel arduous. Like entering a dark room, at first you see nothing. As your vision adjusts, you can see the contours of many objects around you. Although nothing seems to be happening, your vision is adjusting to a new inner landscape. Stay with it. Meditation is a sobering submission to all that arises within you. It sobers you from your delusions and fantasies of how you think life is or ought to be and allows you to digest life as it is. Only by accepting the truth about anything can you evolve. Meditation permits authentic, and total, acceptance of your life.

Avoid judging your meditations. The mind has an opinion about everything. The spiritual energy you imbibe through consistent practice is subtle. Over time, you recognize the spiritual energy and your experience of it becomes very apparent, tangible, and exact. Judging your meditation prematurely overrides the subtlety of the practice, which soon emerges more prominently regardless. If you're too busy looking for the fireworks, you'll miss the door to Universal Love that's right in front of you.

Some of my students who have had expansive, explosive highs on narcotics have trouble with the initial stages of learning meditation. They want the high to be less subtle and more obvious, like their days of drug use. The *high* available through meditation is so far beyond anything that a chemical can touch! But you have to earn it.

Meditation is good for all of you. Amazingly, the sustained expansive state available through a regular meditation practice or living a life where the *high* never goes away does not take long to sustain with meditation. After a short time you will truly gain a heartfelt sense of freedom. After a year of practice, you will feel incredibly grounded and connected to your sense of self. After another year or two, you will feel unstoppable as you create, manifest, and serve a world that is in need of more Love. A great Rinpoche once said, "There are only two regrets on the path to freedom: never beginning and stopping too early." Stick with the practice. The fruits of your efforts come to pass quickly in the scheme of things.

Of all the practices I teach for mind, body, spirit, and wellness, meditation is the most important. There is no greater investment in your health and spiritual growth than deepening an authentic relationship with your heart through meditation. The meditation I teach makes you physically, mentally, and emotionally strong. It clears your head, so you can focus on what's really a priority for you. Meditation refines your body's awareness and puts you in touch with your intuition, so that you can make better choices. Meditation is a practical tool that brings you front-and-center with who you are and gently helps you release negative thoughts, beliefs, and behaviors that you don't need. As meditation streamlines your thoughts and feelings it helps you achieve your most personal life goals as efficiently and as smoothly as possible.

I've been meditating for over twenty years. It brings me home to my heart and re-prioritizes my thinking towards the highest good. Meditation keeps my ego in check and my heart in the driver's seat of my life. It keeps a clear signal between my heart and Universal guidance. Meditation helps me soften my heart, so I can be a better husband, father, brother, son, friend, and healer. My meditation practice is my lifeline. Meditation has given me so much, that I feel compelled to share it with you.

FOUR STATES OF CONSCIOUSNESS

Right here, right now, you are awake and aware of something; perhaps a random thought or the words in front you. When you dream, you become aware of images, feelings, sensations, and stories that are played out in your awareness. The dreaming mind is playful, and rarely linear. But it is also part of healing. After a night of deep sleep, a sensation arises in the morning, and you think, "Ah that was a great night's sleep. What a deep rest." Some part of you that is aware while you're asleep reports either the story of your dreams or the rejuvenation of a deep sleep, absent of dreams. This reporter of your life, the observer-witness, activates and empowers the previous three states of waking, dreaming, and deep sleep. This state of consciousness is known as the fourth state of consciousness. It is called the *Turiya* state in Sanskrit. Turiya animates your waking, your dreaming, and your deep sleep. Through meditation the Turiya state works synergistically through the other three states of consciousness to help heal you.

In waking consciousness, awareness outwardly explores and dances from one interest to the next in search of something pleasing, beautiful and inspiring. In the dream state, this outward-facing consciousness continues to operate, and animates worlds of desire, interest, and concern, though seemingly with less control than in the waking state. In deep sleep, a more profound rest of the mind occurs, where very little to no thought or dream activity takes place.

The Turiya state of consciousness holds an even deeper place in awareness. It is the most restful and restorative state to the health of body and mind. Meditation is the means to access this fourth state of consciousness, and permits the Turiya state to imbue itself more fully into the other three states of consciousness.

Within the last decade, scientist and healers have talked about the delta and theta brain waves that are incredibly healing for all ailments, especially trauma. These brain wave states are a fraction of the intensity that is emitted as you delve deeper into meditation. Meditation gradually takes you into more profound states of healing that scientists are still trying to grasp. Likely within the next twenty years, researchers will develop technology refined enough to measure some of the subtler and powerful energetic frequencies activated in deep meditation. Like all things I teach, I prefer to know directly the power of meditation, rather than wait for the proof that it works. If I wait for the proof to follow my heart, it will be too late. My heart is all the science I need.

The source of a river is pure, whereas further downstream debris and pollutants accumulate from passing through greater and greater terrain. In the same way, the source of the mind and body is pure, powerful, and rejuvenating. Beyond the pure source of the mind, layers of awareness get mixed with thoughts, feelings and memories that dampen, and dull your experience of life. This thickening of awareness creates confusion, doubt, worry, and problems that need fixing. Like the area of a river downstream, the mind gets congested, and the crisp purity of the water, dulled.

The mind loves a good problem. It's addicted to solving problems. Have you ever noticed how your mind moves from one problem to the next without pause? There is always an abundance of problems to occupy the mind. Underneath every complaint, and every problem, is a desire for improvement. When you sit and enter into a deeper flow of awareness, the mind releases the addiction of fixing problems as if something is broken and settles into an awareness of being whole. There are important things to do in the world. Through meditation, the background feeling of brokenness inside of you disappears and you feel stronger, more pure, and ready for whatever life offers or throws at you.

THE METHOD

Understanding anything from the intellect alone is incomplete. Experience fills in the gaps. Experience and knowledge, combined, allow for greater levels of understanding to coalesce. Belief in the known world alone with the senses is a life bereft of imagination and innovation. If belief reaches to only the outer confines of the physical, the known and perceived, the Universe will seem very small indeed. The nature of the mind is to expand. This innate curiosity of the mind is how you eventually come to know yourself fully. Meditation pushes the intellect's knowledge beyond the physical world into the metaphysical.

So far I've spoken about meditation in general terms. To reiterate, there are many forms and traditions of meditation. All of them have their place and purpose. Some are truly effective in bringing about the experience of connection with Universal Love, Spirit, God, or whatever you like to call the Divine. There are also meditation practices that are less effective in bringing you in contact with Universal Love.

Out of respect for my teachers and the tradition that I teach, I am not sharing the specifics about my meditation practice here in *Born to Heal*. I admit that I want to share everything with you, in part because I want you to taste the freedom within you, and because I have always been rebellious about following rules—especially ones that start with "Don't." But from my own past mistakes,

I know the value of honoring time-tested traditions, and I recognize that meditation is an experience that must initially be experienced firsthand between two people. This is not a ploy to have you seek me out to learn from me directly, although I welcome you whole-heartedly to attend one of my workshops or retreats.

Also, I must make an important distinction between two definite traditions of practice. I am being as careful as possible not to alienate anyone, but I feel compelled, from my own misconceptions and past experiences, to share some insight on the subject of meditation for renunciates (those that live in monasteries or ashrams) and meditation for householders (people who live in the world and have worldly responsibilities). These traditions are very different in intent and technique.

The meditation I practice and teach is for people who have jobs, kids, relationships, debt, hobbies, teams, volunteer work, school, and any combination of responsibilities in the world. I do not teach people how to become a monk and let go of the world. I once thought renouncing the world was the goal of spiritual practice for many years. Then I learned it was only *one* method to attain freedom, among other methods, many of which also work.

Meditation for householders is just as effective, if not more so, than renunciation style meditation because you must maintain both your meditation practice and your worldly responsibilities. You must make your daily life your selfless service, i.e., your means to see the Divine in all people.

The two schools of practice lead to the same goal yet take different paths. Each path is beautiful and efficacious. If you want to be a monk, you should be, but don't do a monk's practice and try to live in the world. Likewise, don't try to do a householder's meditation practice in an ashram. Mixing the practices will result in confusion. I'm speaking from direct experience of which I mentioned earlier in this book.

The major difference between the two styles of practice is that renunciate practices heighten the desire to repudiate the world, whereas householder practices make you more efficient at serving the world only in the ways that bring about the highest benefit to all. Both the renunciate and householder contribute to the world by raising the vibration of the Universe through spiritual practice. The householder serves the world through sustained spiritual practice, which includes physically responding to the surface needs of society with precision and skill. This is achieved by living compassionately and courageously.

The renunciate releases all attachments and lives for the Divine alone. Often retreating to the sanctuary of an ashram or monastery, the renunciate releases all sense of individual identity. The householder's ashram is his or her home. Over time, the body and mind of both the renunciate and householder become very refined and sensitive to the external world. As the renunciate renounces all aspects of individual identity, interacting with the surface world becomes increasingly challenging. The external world is also challenging for the householder who becomes like a Jedi knight, orienting herself to the flow of Light that seeks to illumine dark places in the world. The renunciate becomes a warrior of the inner planes of consciousness and transforms darkness through deep and profound inner work. The householder delicately balances inner and outer spiritual work and straddles the razor's edge of societal reality with the Absolute reality of expansiveness consciousness.

Both paths are profound. Both are effective. And at some point they do merge onto the same path. If you live in the world, have a job and a relationship and practice a renunciate mantra, you will lose touch with the mundane sense of attachment and suffering of others, which will make you less skilled in relating to them. This happens because renunciate-style meditation causes your identity to disengage completely from itself to become wholly identified with the Divine. The householder method retains some aspect of the identity in order to be able to relate skillfully to the external world and the suffering of others.

I am not commenting on what makes a practice renunciate or householder here. If you are interested in learning more, I am happy to speak with you directly. Again these topics, as well as the specifics regarding how to practice, are something I teach in person to people who are truly ready to carry the Light forward into the world. Meditation is the highest commitment to positivity, increasing beauty and healing to life. It is the most beautiful experience of falling in love with everything that you are. And like all great relationships, it has its ups and downs, all the while gaining a deeper trust and commitment to your self.

Meditation teaches you to face your fear and be with it. Sometimes fear goes away. Sometimes fear remains, and you learn to use it creatively. Meditation is for warriors. To have a steady meditation practice, you have to be clear that the only way to make life work—not simply be happy, but make life functional—is to be consistently connected to Universal Love. And, yes, there are other ways to retain a connection.

I know meditation works because I've practiced it for over twenty years. When I go into meditation I drink in Light, and my state of connectedness rarely fluctuates when I'm out living my life. My practice shows me my limitations. I've gained compassion for my self and others as a result. Compassion is a magnet for Grace, and Grace makes life flow. Grace does not discriminate; it is equally available to all people. Meditation is a means to Grace.

Meditation itself is not a religious practice associated with a belief in anything. In fact, meditation brings about an experience of the Divine that frees you from the restrictions of belief and connects you with the source from which belief arises. At the core of every major religion is this pure experience of the Divine.

You can believe in anything you want and walk into meditation through any door of religion, identity, social class, profession, etc. The tradition you come from will only be enhanced and made more vibrant by your experience of God through your personal practice of meditation. Approach meditation with an open heart and a sincere desire to have the Divine Light penetrate and guide you.

We support each other on the spiritual path, and we walk the path individually. In the space of deep meditation, we meet united as an eternal spiritual family. Keep meditating. Every sit builds strength. It can be hard to notice the progress daily. Over time you will look back some months or a year and say, "I'm a new person, stronger, steadier, and solid like a rock." Though meditation is a journey we make individually in the deep space of the Heart, we walk together as One. If you feel lonely, meet me there. I would be honored to share meditation with you or help you find a practice that works for you.

So much Love ... Luke

BREATHWORK

When I was a kid, my dad told me "God is so intelligent. When He created humans, He gave them breath—such a simple way back: The way to God, right under your nose." The breath is so simple, yet so profound in its capacity to regulate consciousness.

> *Breathe deeply with the strong intention to heal, forgive, open, and connect with Spirit. With a clear and pure feeling in your heart say, "I ask for healing." Now breathe and let it in.*

Behind all of the work that I offer is the intention for you to experience the power of your heart. Breathwork is one way I do that.

In my healing work, I use the breath to heal pieces of the past that keep people from living fully in the present. This powerful tool allows you to let go of thinking part of the mind, and open to the wisdom of the heart's guidance.

I use a three-part breathing technique called *pranayama* yoga that I learned from my mentor, friend, and outstanding healer, David Elliott. You can learn more about David's work at www.davidelliott.com.

During a typical healing session, we talk about problems and issues that limit your experience of joy and love. As I listen to what you're saying, I use my intuition to tune into the places in your body that are stuck and disconnected from Spirit. After fifteen to twenty minutes of sharing, you lay face up on a massage table, and I demonstrate the three-part breath, done all through the mouth. Mouth breathing connects you with the energetic body, the chakra, and meridian systems. Nose breathing connects you with the thinking part of the brain. Soon you feel energy moving through your body. A little light-headedness during the first few minutes of breathing is normal. As you let go of the intellectual part of the brain, you begin to feel the energy of your body and your heart. The light-headedness fades away, and you find a comfortable rhythm with the breath and the energy flow in your body. As the energetic system begins to vibrate people often feel their hands tingling, along with other areas of the body. The breath massages places in the physical body that store energetic and physical tension. As the breath releases these blocks, I help you identify and release them using acupuncture, touch, affirmations, essential oils, music, and other tools.

As people let go of old, sometimes ancient, thoughts, feelings, beliefs, and memories, the physical body relaxes and opens to a greater flow of energy. As a result of the free-flowing energy in the body, you gain clarity, centeredness, and a renewed sense of purpose and direction. The breath reverberates subtly at first, and then gently opens the body. Then, as the energy begins to culminate, a choice point arises. You can choose to hang on to familiar patterns of sadness, anger, worry, and fear or you can choose to let go of them, and open to a deep sense of peace and love connected to your Divine essence. In just one session—as the physical crux of an issue dissolves—people often experience the freedom that was absent in years of other treatments.

The intention of the work is to connect you with the power and virtues of the heart: unconditional Love, abundant energy, forgiveness, acceptance, compassion, a profound sense of connectedness, and wholeness. This practice is an access point to living with a sense of fulfillment and joy. As the breath opens and releases layers of stagnant energy, I hold space for the you to go deeper into the experience, to move past resistance, and trust the innate wisdom, insight, and love that heals. When we open and accept the parts of ourselves that we've kept hidden, love arises and healing occurs. When we get down to it, love is what we're all here to experience and share. The breath has the power to open us to immeasurable Love.

At my Healer Studies courses you can learn to take others through the breathwork experience. As you learn how energy moves through your body, you gain the ability to hold space for others to heal. I love witnessing people experience the honor of guiding someone else into the space of the heart. To learn more about Healer Studies see the appendix at the end of the book.

HOME PRACTICE

Breathwork can be a daily practice. If you have a lot of suppressed emotions living in your body, I recommend that you do this practice daily as a powerful and effective tool for you to cleanse. You will feel more open to love and creativity after you've cleared your energetic system of stagnant energy. As a daily practice, breathe seven-to-ten minutes of the active three-part breathing, followed by five-to-seven minutes of normal regular breathing. When you feel that you're able to maintain the spiritual flow of energy through your body, do the breathwork once a week to cleanse your energetic field.

As a weekly practice, find a comfortable place to lie down where you won't be disturbed. Cue up about twenty minutes of re-laxing or evocative music to help you get in touch with your emotions. Set a timer or pick a song on a playlist to signal you to shift out of the three-part breathing. Do the active three-part breathing for seven-to-fifteen minutes depending on how much time you have and how deep you want to go—the longer you breathe the deeper you will go.

- Cover your eyes with an eye pillow or a towel to help bring your awareness inside.
- Breathe all through your mouth.

- The inhalation consists of two parts. First inhale half way full and fill the low belly—the area where we suppress our emotions. Then inhale and fill the high chest—the area where we feel our emotions. Exhale and release all the air from your lungs and abdomen. Continue.

- Inhale and fill the low belly and the high chest. Exhale completely. Release all the air out of your lungs. Keep the breath flowing and continuous.

- You will feel more open and energized several moments into the three part breathing as your body's energy begins to flow.

- When it's time to shift out of the three-part breathing, take five long breaths in through your nose and out through your mouth.

- Then, find a more normal breathing rhythm as you allow your body and spirit to go deep into a restorative state. This is an important part of the meditation for your body, mind, and spirit to assimilate the experience. Take your time and rest for another five-to-ten minutes.

Make sure you feel grounded before you become active again. Eat a piece of fruit and drink some water to help you ground.

I have produced two guided breathwork meditation albums called Heart Cleanse and Universal Vision. Many of my clients use them as a regular spiritual practice. Allow me to guide you through the breathwork by downloading breath instructions and the Lite Heart Cleanse from my Heart Cleanse album at luke-adlerhealing.com/products

Therapeutic Clinical Dialogue

The issues are in the tissues. In the Sequence of Separation, the Universe grabs your attention with a powerful thought, and if you choose not to face that thought, you move the energetic imprint of that thought into unconsciousness, which generates stagnation, inflammation, and eventually disease if left alone. To prevent this, sharing and acting on your inner guidance is essential.

One of the tools I use to help release unconscious tension in the body is called Therapeutic Clinical Dialogue (TCD). Here I need to draw a distinction between venting, bitching, and complaining (VBC), and sharing with the intention to release unconscious tension (TCD). Venting, bitching, and complaining are unconscious ways to share about what sucks in life. When people do this with me in the treatment room, and I allow it, I can feel and see people's unconsciousness vomit upon my energetic system. My visions gets blurry; my energy level plummets; and I begin to dislike my job. I will act to stop VBC and help people shift into TCD to create healing. Most people connect socially through their wounds, so much so that venting, bitching, and complaining has become socially acceptable ways to develop relationships. Though it might be fun to complain about your boss or partner with a co-worker or friend, it actually reinforces a negative limited point of view about your life, which further engrains a bio-neurological pattern for your life to be like your complaint. We reinforce the energetic patterns we are supporting with our words. We may have an unconscious desire for things not to change, or may be making it harder for ourselves to shift the very patterns we claim to want to alter.

Therapeutic Clinical Dialogue is different from VBC because you share the exact same content of a complaint, but with the deeply conscious intention to let it go. Both the intention and the follow-up open physical, mental, and emotional spaces for new possibilities in your life to arise.

When I stimulate an acupoint on a patient, the unconsciousness is right there in the tissue in form of physical sensation like pain or numbness. I press on the point and encourage people to openly share thoughts, memories, or emotions. I remind them that we are not trying to fix, understand or change anything. We simply want to explore the mind and body with the intention to release tension. Therapeutic Clinical Dialogue hands the healing over to the innate intelligence of the body, which knows a lot more about healing than the intellect alone. This is a powerful method that allows the patient and practitioner to collaborate, and to stretch their collective intuitions, as well as utilize all personal and professional skills at hand. Often a storehouse of emotion and suppressed memory releases inside of the powerful intention to heal, as a patient spontaneously shares using therapeutic clinical dialogue.

✿ VENTING BITCHING COMPLAINING EXERCISE

- *Do I have a tendency to vent, bitch, and complain unconsciously?*

- *Do I have an addiction to complaining?*

- *Who modeled this for me?*

- *What is the benefit for me to continue to complain?*

- *Who do I make responsible for what I complain about?*

- *How are the people I complain about like me?*

- *How does my body feel when I complain?*

- *Do I have a tendency towards headaches, abdominal, or back pain?*

- *If I let go of my story related to my complaint, who becomes responsible for my happiness?*

- *What belief blocks me from sharing my issue with the intention to let it go?*

Often the unconscious weight of blaming someone for your pain keeps you from taking responsibility for your pain and perpetuates the cycle of complaint. If you have a complaint, there is something you haven't done or said that needs to be addressed. If you choose not to address it, then own that and be willing to let your complaint go. Holding a grudge is not letting go. To let go, compassion needs to flow through the situation.

Susan's Complaint

Recently, I worked with Susan, a new patient who suffered from pain and numbness in her left hip, thigh, leg, and foot. She shared with me details about the onset and progression of her ailment. It seemed to come from out of the blue and worsened progressively with time. She had an X-ray and MRI that showed a minor disk herniation in her lower back, along with a partial tear in a small muscle that aids in hip articulation. She'd already consulted with an orthopedic surgeon, physical therapist, chiropractor, and massage therapist. Surgery was not indicated, and she refused to take pain medication. As she relayed her journey to me, she became emotional about the loss of her social life, which revolved around her swimming team which she could no longer join for workouts and competitions.

After performing several exams, I relayed to her information about her physiology and structural health. I then spoke with her about doing some emotional work around the loss of her main social outlet. Susan's neck and face suddenly turned red and she began to weep, overcome by sadness. She exclaimed, "My physical pain seems even worse, and now I'm depressed because I can't be social." We spoke a bit more as her emotions began to settle. I offered, "Perhaps when, and if, you are ready, we could work to separate the emotional pain from the physical pain." She seemed confused, believing that her physical pain was the cause of her emotional pain.

This is a sticky point for many people because the tendency is to think you feel a certain way because of your circumstances. I offer that you can feel however you want regardless of your circumstances. How you feel about your circumstances is your choice regardless of the favorability of your circumstances. Circumstances are subjective, and so is happiness.

I suggested to Susan that it would be useful to acknowledge her emotions and feel them with the intention of letting them go, rather than continuing to work so hard to compartmentalize them. I shared with her my thought that to release the emotion would help her physical body heal faster. Susan nodded in agreement, and said, "It makes sense." After a few more sessions, she agreed that she has a habit of, "Throwing the baby out with bath water," meaning that if a few things didn't *work, then she believed that nothing will. Susan's attitude towards pain improved with each visit. Her chronic pain also decreased. Still, I can sense some reluctance on her part to truly believe that she can get better. However, she feels safer acknowledging her feelings. We use therapeutic breath with acupuncture and electro-muscle stimulation to help her let go of fear that she will never be able to live the life she had before her injury. The more she opens up, the lighter she feels, and her body continues to improve.*

Awareness placed on an area of stagnation in your body increases blood flow, and thus, healing. If a patient is blocked or resistant to trusting their intuition, I'll incorporate therapeutic breath to move blood throughout the area of stagnation.

❁ THERAPEUTIC BREATHING

This breath exercise is a little different from the pranayama breathwork I talked about in the previous section. A therapeutic breath is a long, deep, full inhalation through the nose and down into the lower belly.

- *Bring the inhalation from the lower belly all the way up the high chest to the throat, and exhale through the mouth. Breathe this way continually without resting in between the inhalation and exhalation.*

- *On the inhalation, gather and breathe through all tissues that feel tight, stagnant, and constricted.*

- *On the exhalation, have the intention to completely release tension in the blocked areas of your body.*

- *Continue to breathe like this for two to five minutes,
  or until you feel that you've released the issue.*

These exercises are far from "one and done" techniques. We are assembling a toolkit for you, one that I hope you will utilize often enough that you'll know what to reach for when you need it. There's the old saying, "To a man with a hammer, the whole world's a nail." I want your toolkit to be full of much more useful techniques than hammering your way through life.

Nutrition and Cleansing

Food is delicious. I love to eat good food and really enjoy the distinct flavors, textures, tastes, and temperatures in a meal. Like food, the body comes from the earth and is eventually transformed by and back into the earth. In all the modalities of healing, from East to West, how you nourish yourself is believed to be fundamental to your healing. You can receive the best health care in the world, but if your diet is filled with toxins that create free radical stress, any treatment is, at best, only temporarily life sustaining.

One of the primary keys to longevity and quality of life is nourishment; not only in the foods you choose, but in the intention behind how you prepare food and how you eat it. Even if you indulge in a hamburger and fries, if they are prepared with love, and if you enjoy each bite with gratitude to the earth that provides you with nutrients to fuel your body, you will digest the meal well.

Just as you are dependent on the earth for everything in the physical world, so are you dependent on the spleen and stomach to digest and assimilate nutrients in order to provide structure and context to live. The spleen and stomach represent the earth element within the body. As I shared in the Spleen chapter, what makes this organ system unique is that, unlike the lungs that operate involuntarily and without awareness, the spleen and stomach require a degree of consciousness to function. It's an act of volition you contribute to every time you take in food. The quality of your consciousness profoundly impacts your state of health with regard to how, what, and where you eat. Therefore, in order to really heal, you have to come into a balanced relationship with food. How you nourish yourself with food is reflective of your mood and relationship to yourself. How you eat is just as—if not more—important than what you eat. Of course, fresh and in-season, locally grown, organics are better than imported processed foods.

🪷 NOURISHMENT EXERCISE

- *Do I love myself?*
- *Do I respect myself?*
- *How do I show myself love?*
- *How do I show my body love?*

Emotional eating, binge eating, orthorexia—the obsession with clean eating—are several examples of imbalanced expressions around self-nourishment. Self-love and self-nourishment go hand and hand. How and what you eat reflect this relationship. You practice self-love with the thoughts you think and the words you create, all fueled by the foods you eat.

I've worked with nutrition for more than a decade and found it accelerates the healing of seeming unrelated symptoms, like back and neck pain, for example. This chapter presents various cleanses I've researched and prescribed to my self and my patients. The best times of the year to cleanse are around the spring equinox, as Nature prepares for new life and the fall equinox, as Nature begins to turn Her energy within to restore. The body naturally follows this same cycle as you emerge from the hibernation of the winter in early spring and prepare to store your energy for winter in the early fall. Nutrition and cleansing are essential for vibrancy of cellular life, longevity of the body, and aid in the blossoming of the Spirit.

This chapter ended up being a book unto itself. Rather than include it as part of the *Born to Heal* text, I've made it available as a free PDF download on my website. Go to lukeadlerhealing.com and log on to the resources page. Use password: (healing) to access the full chapter on Nutrition and Cleansing.

The chapter on lukeadlerhealing.com includes coaching on nutrition and various cleanses that I use in my practice. Here is what it contains:

- Quick Nutrition Coaching
- The Big Green Delicious Smoothie
- The Sinister 7 + 1 Inflammatory and Metabolic Slowing Foods
- Cleansing
- The Luke Adler Healing Soul Food Cleanse
- Master Cleanse
- The Luke Adler Healing Cleanse
- Luke's Juice Cleanse
- Coffee and Saline Enemas
- Metabolic Cleansing
- Building Immunity, the Chinese Medical Perspective
- Luke Adler Healing Snacks and Quick Eats
- Final Thoughts on Cleansing

If you have no experience cleansing, professional guidance is essential to help you interpret your body's needs and the changing needs you will experience as you start a cleanse. My staff and I are available to guide you through any of the cleanses. Please call my office at (541) 465-9642 if you would like to schedule a consultation, or if you have any questions or comments. You can feel better and enjoy your life more. My team and I are more than happy to help.

Essential Oils

In graduate school, I studied essential oil therapy with David Crow, author of *In Search of the Medicine Buddha* and founder of Floracopeia essential oils. The medicinal properties and the aromas of the pure plant oils mesmerized me. Five years later, during my residency in the jungles of central India, I caught a wafting aroma of the Ylang Ylang flower in bloom during the early morning hours. The voluptuous, candy-like aroma had the exact characteristics as the Ylang Ylang oil I smelled in David's class. That evening, night blooming Jasmine found my olfactory bulb for the first time. The intoxicating, sultry, aphrodisiac liquefied my nervous system, and drew me into a euphoric state. I learned later that king cobras burrow under Jasmine bushes. I'm glad I had somewhere to go that evening and didn't linger.

Before I worked with essential oils, I thought they were simply nice aromas to smell. After years of study, personal use, and prescribing them to patients, I have found their benefits to be comprehensive across the spectrum of maladies, and specifically effective for pain, anxiety, and depressive conditions. Ample research on essential oils continues pertaining to their antibiotic, antimicrobial, antifungal, and analgesic effects.

- Lavender has been shown to be sedating, calming to the nervous system, and aids with sleep rhythms.
- Studies on Ylang Ylang and Jasmine show increased mental clarity and faster decision-making times.
- Used as a chest rub, Cedar is beneficial for the respiratory system with symptoms of cough, bronchitis, asthma, colds, and congestion. Trees are the hairs of the earth, and, as such, Cedar oil from the cedar tree is great for

dandruff or mild eczema when applied directly to the scalp or skin.

Essential oils are unique, not only as a pleasurable treatment, but in their mechanisms of action via the brain and endocrine system.

Why do essential oils work so well? Smell is primitive, in that it bypasses the executive function of the prefrontal cortex or the thinking mind. Olfactory neurons or nerves located at the top of the nasal canal connect to the olfactory bulb between and behind the eyebrows. The olfactory bulb is approximately the size of a kidney bean, and covered with over ten million nerve cells. This is the only place in the body where the central nervous system is exposed to the external environment. From the olfactory bulb, the aroma moves on as an electrical impulse to the hypothalamus. When the hypothalamus interprets a pleasurable scent, the entire nervous system settles into a parasympathetic response. The parasympathetic nervous system governs rest, digestion, and tissue repair. This all occurs in less than a few seconds. Scent circumvents the thinking part of the brain and allows instant relief from pain, anxiety, depression, and many more conditions.

Some things you might not know about scent:

- The sense of smell is ten thousand times more sensitive than the sense of taste.
- The sense of taste is primarily the sense of smell.
- There are only four primary flavors: bitter, sweet, sour, salty; everything else is smell.
- When people lose their sense of smell, they lose their appetite for life.
- Anosmia (absence of smell) is frequently accompanied by depression.
- We smell differently according to our moods.

- Women's sense of smell increases and decreases according to hormonal rhythms.
- A male butterfly can smell a female six miles away.

The science of essential oils utilizes biochemical and neurological pathways to thwart pathogens, bacteria, pain, and psycho-emotional imbalances. The ability to look at life objectively separates humans from other sentient beings. This faculty is at times a hindrance, as pain increases due to obsessive, repetitive thinking. Pain, whether emotional or physical, is compounded by added commentary, opinions, and thinking about the pain itself. Essential oils have the power to cut-through this cognitive function of the brain, thereby alleviating the added layers of mental stress, strain, and pain quickly.

Essential oils are the life-blood of a plant. They have a strong affinity for your constitutional essence. Oils are powerful medicine. Less than a drop of oil on the right energetic point can have tremendous effects on the physiology. Within the oils, potent biochemical constituents hold tremendous health benefits that are still unknown. The best way to understand and reap the benefits of the oils is to try them out. I encourage you to use the blends that you really like and really dislike. The ones you don't like will help heal the places within your self that store latent pathological factors. The oils powerfully and gently help you integrate the moments of life that have been put on the back burner to be dealt with "someday."

To learn specific energetic actions, work with a practitioner well versed in essential oil therapy. One method of application is as follows: Take a toothpick and barely dip it into the essential oil of your choice. Then gently apply the tip of the toothpick with the oil on it to the desired acupoint. This method of treatment harnesses the life force of the plant and sends a powerful neurological message to the body. Another method of treatment is to apply multiple drops of the oils onto your chakras or other energetic points. This method effects the skin and tendino-muscular regions of the body. It also strongly resonates with the chakras. I mostly use my seven chakra blends with this latter method.

Below is a description of the actions and indications for my custom blends. In addition to using them for physical signs and symptoms, I include an emotional and energetic explanation for use with the chakra system. Scent has strong emotional triggers. The blends used with the chakra system soothe and clear away psychic and emotional stress, especially when there is a mix of emotions and thoughts that create a state of confusion. Following each description of the blends, I include a description of relevant excess and deficient emotional pathologies.

All of the oils work adaptogenically, which means whether a condition is hyper- or hypo-functioning, the blend will bring the system towards homeostasis. Be gentle with yourself. Have fun with the oils. Respect them, and they will reveal more to you.

Sacred Roots is a blend of Fir, Spruce, Cedar, and other hardwood essential oils energetically used for grounding by forming a connection to the earth and clearing the first chakra. Use this blend for bronchitis, sinusitis, and flu as they are signs of feeling ungrounded, and reflect the lungs' inability to smoothly grasp the energy of the root chakra. Apply a few drops directly on muscle aches, sites of rheumatism, and bruises. Apply this oil to the soles of the feet to stabilize and clear first chakra energetics. The first chakra is located at the base of the spine in the vicinity of the sacrum and pubic bone. This chakra is associated with the earth, survival, and desire to be in the physical world. Having this chakra out of balance in an excess state can lead to feeling overly possessive (with an excessive need to ground, or hold on); when deficient, one can feel homeless, ungrounded, or victimized. Use

Sacred Roots to ground negative energy so you can see the divine in others. This blend rectifies the Qi, which helps you feel clear enough to let go.

Sexual Freedom is a blend of South African Peppermint, Atlas Cedar, Cinnamon, Fennel, and other refined essential oils. Make this blend a part of your first aid kit, as it eases shock, dizziness, and general weakness. As a chest rub, this oil is a powerful expectorant for acute congestion accompanying the cold or flu. Sexual Freedom is used for clearing stagnant, crystallized, or dormant energy in the hips and pelvis. Use this oil to heal past sexual trauma and to access full creativity for healthy sexual expression. Apply a few drops of Sexual Freedom a few inches below the belly button, parallel to the upper hip-bones or anterior superior iliac spine. The second chakra, located just below the umbilicus, is associated with polarity, pleasure, and desire for emotional and sexual expression. When the second chakra displays an excess imbalance, one can experience manipulative and controlling behavior and when deficient, energies of co-dependency, martyrdom, or submissive behavior are present.

Harmonize is an organic blend of Coriander, Chamomile, Ginger, Oregano, and other essential oils that aid in the digestive process. Use this blend topically to stimulate and strengthen digestion. You can ingest this blend orally to aid in digestion. Add 1 drop of oil to at least 8 ounces of water for a digestive elixir. Harmonize energetically helps you redefine the tendency to digest the pain of others in exchange for what you perceive to be love. Apply Harmonize to the third chakra, located in the region of the solar plexus, just below the sternum. This chakra is associated with digestive fire, individual willpower, self-esteem, and vitality. Having your third chakra out of balance in excess leads to egotism and self-absorption; when deficient, it is associated with poor self-worth or feeling disliked.

Surrender a blend of South African Clary Sage, Geranium, and other essential oils. Use this blend topically for wound healing, as an antiseptic and an anti-inflammatory rub. Surrender is used to aid in digestive issues, as well as issues of control and exerting your will upon others or vice versa. Apply Surrender to the third chakra, located in the region of the solar plexus, just below the sternum. The third chakra is associated with fire, individual willpower, self-esteem, and vitality. This chakra out of balance in excess leads to egotism and self-absorption, and when deficient, it is associated with poor self-worth or feeling disliked.

Awakened Heart is an organic blend of several varieties of Rose, Dawn blooming Jasmine, Neroli, and other exotic essential oils. Use this blend to increase mental clarity and lift the spirit. This is a superior blend to address any emotional pathology, i.e., severe mood swings, bipolar disorder, borderline personality disorder, and others. Apply this blend undiluted on shingles to ease viral load. Awakened Heart is used to open the Heart chakra and facilitate the energy of Divine Love. Place Awakened Heart on the center of the chest to soothe the Heart chakra. The fourth chakra, positioned on the sternum and even with the fifth rib, is associated with air, equilibrium, love, and openheartedness. One presents an excess imbalance with inappropriate manic emotional expression and poor emotional boundaries; in deficiency, one can feel dull, withdrawn, and forsaken, accompanied by the inability to feel emotions.

Crystal Voice is an organic blend of *Eucalyptus globulus*, Atlas Cedar, Juniper, and other essential oils. Use this blend to soothe nervous exhaustion, adrenal overdrive, worry, chronic fatigue and shock. Massage a few drops on the chest for high blood pressure, palpitations, and anxiety. Apply Crystal Voice to clear lung and throat pathologies, such as sore throat, plum pit Qi syndrome, and swollen glands. Apply this oil to the fifth chakra, situated in the neck region. The throat chakra governs sound, vibration, communication, and the desire to speak and hear the truth. An imbalance in excess presents as controlling or judgmental behavior; when deficient, one exhibits a lack of faith and the inability to creatively express oneself.

Sacred Fire is a blend of Ecuadorian Palo Santo, Clary Sage, and Cedar—three sacred plants used both ceremonially and in daily living to clear stagnant and negative energy. Indigenous cultures from the Americas have used these sacred plants for thousands of years to sanctify and prepare space for communion with Spirit. In oil form, these plants are much stronger than when burned as incense. Apply this blend sparingly on the sixth chakra, found slightly above the eyebrow region on the midline of the forehead. This chakra governs the mind, representing light, luminosity, intuition, and self-reflection. In excess, an imbalance of this chakra can make one appear overly intellectual or overly analytical; when deficient, one can experience unclear or deluded thoughts.

Illumination is an organic blend of *Boswellia carterii* Frankincense, Bulgarian Lavender, Geranium, and several other essential oils. Use as a mouthwash for gingivitis. Add a drop of Illumination to three ounces of water for use as a mouthwash. This blend is great to transform grumpiness, negative moods and low self-esteem. Illumination is used on the crown chakra to open a connection to Spirit and communion with a higher sense of being and knowledge. Apply Illumination on the seventh chakra at the crown of the head, the highest point on the body. This chakra is the doorway to receive the bliss of pure consciousness and allows for the recognition and desire to know oneself and the Universe. In excess imbalance, one can be seen as an egomaniac, and when deficient, one can feel no spiritual inspiration.

Blessings is an organic blend of Bosnian Blue Chamomile, Damascus Rose, and Neroli. Add a few drops in a bath to ease tension from a rough day. The varietal of chamomile in Blessings contains azulene, an organic compound with a deep-blue crystal structure that has powerful anti-inflammatory properties. Use Blessings to offer and receive grace and goodwill to and from the universe. Blessings is the holy water of essential oil blends. Use it to bless yourself and others. Apply to any chakra with a loving intention.

Heart Melter is an organic blend of Himalayan Cinnamon, Sweet Orange, Cedar, Basil, and Rosemary. Use this oil when you notice the walls of your heart begin to close, and you sense a loss of receptivity with Spirit. This blend melts the heart and opens you to the flow of love and wisdom. You can also use Blessings for someone whose heart has hardened over or does not seem to have an open heart. My wife inspired this oil, because she has the ability to soften my stubbornness and help me to see the bigger picture. When I smell it, I think of her.

Akrodha is an organic blend of Citrus oils and Peppermint. Lemon excites pleasure circuits in the brain and stops acute and chronic pain quickly. Peppermint blocks substance P, a neuropeptide that transmits pain signals from sensory nerves to the central nervous system. This blend quells emotional outbursts, eases depression, and strengthens the immune system. *Akrodha* is a Sanskrit word that means freedom from anger. Use Akrodha to help see what is hidden beneath the smokescreen of anger in order to transform it into love and connection. Akrodha is ingestible. Add 1 drop of oil to 8 ounces of water for a refreshing beverage that will calm your nerves and refresh your spirit. You can also apply a drop to the area around your liver to move stagnant emotion through your system.

Ancestors is an organic blend of *Tagetes* Marigold, Jatamansi, Valerian, and Lavender. In eastern traditions, Marigold is a traditional flower used to honor the highest virtues of ancestors.

Jatamansi, or Spikenard, is one of the oils used in the days after Passover that Mary Magdalene rubbed on the head and feet of Jesus. Along with Valerian and Lavender, this blend evokes ancient memories of those who came before us that paved the way for our arrival. Ancestors Blend activates deep feelings of gratitude and sanctity for the work and attainments of our ancestors. It heals pain and suffering from the past, so that you can be free to create an inspired future. Use this blend in times of loss, transition, and celebration, in order to connect with the strength and gifts of your lineage. Apply a drop of Ancestors to your pillow for a night of deep sleep.

Essential Oil Mists

While studying with shamans in Mexico and South America, I learned the *limpieza* or *cleansing* ritual. Traditionally shamans use Agua de Florida to cleanse the energetic body, which is an essential oil blended with liquid. During the *limpieza* the shaman holds a small amount of Agua de Florida in his or her mouth and sprays it over the client or space for cleansing. It's a beautiful, powerful, and ancient ritual.

I've eliminated the mouth spray element by putting my alchemical blend in mister bottles. Hold the intention to cleanse whatever or whoever you're working on as you liberally douse the area with the spray that calls to you. The essential oil sprays cleanse the energetic field just like the *limpieza* ritual. The fine mist calms the subtle body quickly. Sometimes after a long day at work, I'll bathe my self in the Illumination spray all over my head neck and face. Instantly, I can feel the stagnant and out-of-balance energies I've encountered dissipate from my subtle system. Essential oil sprays take the residue of the day off you, leaving the energetic body cleansed and refreshed.

Neuroplasticity, a Brain-Body View of Healing

The Sequence of Separation is rooted in the brain-body connection. Neuroplasticity is an area of science that explains how the hardwiring of the brain (actually, more like "soft" wiring) can change, and thus the body can change if we choose to learn to see life in a new way. Neuroplasticity teaches us that the Sequence of Separation is learned and can be unlearned. The power to heal is a choice you make with every thought and word you create.

The brain and body are inherently neutral. They don't, by nature, have a preference for good, bad, right, wrong, sweet, sour, salty, and so on. It's a curious phenomenon. Preferences are learned. Just as you can learn to be healthy, you can learn to be unhealthy. In this way, the brain and body serve our choices. I use the phrase "brain and body" as a unit because they are one and the same. What occurs in the brain affects the body and vice versa. Humans are unique because we have a higher brain function to choose how we respond to life, our survival response or strategic response.

The field of neuroplasticity has profound implications for health and consciousness. For many decades, the held belief in science was that after passing through critical stages of development in early childhood, the brain remains unchanged. Scientists believed (and some still do) that the brain is structurally fixed and remains that way throughout life. The old adage goes, "You can't teach an old dog new tricks." But now we're finding it is wrong. As early as the 1950s, researchers challenged this notion with studies that showed that the brain did change throughout life. Throughout the 1970s and into the last two decades, research has extensively shown that the brain can and does change throughout your entire lifetime.

Neuroplasticity is the anatomical and physiological changes in the brain that occur from new learning. Every cell in the body is connected to the brain for input and output. The brain body loop passes information and directions electrically via the central nervous system thirty times per second over an entire lifetime. Think about that staggering speed and amount of information for a moment. Our bodies and brains are one and the same. Hundreds of studies and real life cases demonstrate that the brain indeed changes throughout life. What you think, say, and do matters, and has a profound impact on strengthening neurological patterns in your brain and body.

The ancient scientists of consciousness knew that the brain and the body were one. They called this notion *prakriti*—the union of the mind and body. Thus, illness in the mind is reflected in the body and vice versa. This phenomenon is taken deeper by a distinction Buddhists call imprints. In Hinduism the same idea is called *samskara*—the karmic trace of past actions imprinted on the subtle system. Samskara impacts your experience of the world, like a filter that skews the quality of your vision. Neuroplasticity is the scientific explanation that describes these ancient understandings on a cellular level.

Everything you've ever thought, said, and done has left a trace of itself in your brain body and subtle system. I have fond memories of sledding in the mountains of Idyllwild and Mt. Baldy in southern California as a kid. My brother and I built massive jumps. Then we bombed our plastic saucer sleds down the track, launched into the air, and laughed our heads off as we crashed into the slushy snow below. As the day went on, our tracks deepened, we created a direct line that slung us, bull's-eye, onto the snowy ramp below.

Likewise, the more you think, say, or do something, the stronger the neuron or nerve pathway develops in the brain and body. In the brain, that pathway is called a neuron. In the body it is called a nerve. When you become really good at something, you don't have to think about it. It just happens automatically. This occurs because the amount of neuron connections in the brain increases, and sends information faster than conscious thought. Through repetition, a skill that you used to have to think about becomes effortless and automatic due to strong neural connections. You can fully trust your brain to do whatever you tell it to do through regular practice.

The neutrality of the brain and body means that innately you have freedom of choice to create the reality you want. All of us come into the world and learn a reality taught to us by our guardians. As life goes on, many people discover there are elements of their inherited reality that serve them and others elements that do not. This is where neutrality is important. Just because you see your mother's annoying tendency show up in you doesn't mean you're doomed to become your mother or pass it along to your kid: Neuroplasticity proves that you can teach an old dog new tricks. You have to want to change, and you have to work at it—and work harder, the more entrenched the neuro memory and belief system is in you.

The first step is to recognize a habit you want to change. Bring consciousness in to it. Breathe and acknowledge the tendency. Then make a new choice. Over and over. This is one of the principles of neuroplasticity. To wire a neuron you must first fire it: *Fire to wire; wire to fire.*

What you focus on will bear results over time. This is guaranteed. Whatever you work to shift in your life, keep it up. You will succeed with enough repetition. When you reach the point of frustration, you are close to breaking the old habit and close to creating a new one. Frustration is like the combustion point of an engine. At the greatest point of stress, everything is about to start working. Stay with your commitment to change. When you get frustrated, you are close to a new reality.

Don't give up. When you give up, you lose your abilities. This is the next principle of neuroplasticity. *Use it or lose it.* If you do not fire a network of neurons, they become weakened and thereby recruited for other tasks. Therefore, stick with it. Especially when you feel squeamish inside; the discomfort you feel is an indicator that you're breaking old pathways and laying down new ones. Change is often a gritty and grueling process. Many people give up on new undertakings as soon as it gets hard. The irony is that when things become more difficult, you are actively rewiring your brain, and making progress that is more permanent. It's supposed to be hard.

Yes, you can do it. Stick, Baby! Don't Give Up. Never give up on the people you love, which, if you haven't figured it out yet, includes you.

The next principle of neuroplasticity is: In order to make a new neuron, you have to break an existing one. It's called: *Make it to break it, and break it to make it.* If you break an old habit, don't dwell on what a bad habit it was and what a bad person you were. Rather, focus on the change, and what a great job you are doing. As the cutting-edge clinician and researcher of neuroplasticity, Dr. Moskowitz, says:

> 66 *Most of us don't realize it, but we are actually training our brains every time we learn a new skill, such as reading, typing, singing a song, learning a dance, or riding a bike. It is*

through repetition, practice, creativity, and improvement that we master any activity. This happens through electrical and chemical signals in our cells creating pathways in our brains that allow us to perform these tasks. We are literally changing the anatomy of our brains. By being aware of this process we can consciously utilize it to our benefit. 🎗 🎗

A recent discovery in neuroplasticity is that the brain becomes most plastic or changeable during an intense experience. Research shows the most powerful positive emotion you can experience that changes your brain and body is Love. When you love something, your brain releases a plethora of hormones and neurotransmitters that calm the nervous system, balance the endocrine system, and boost the immune system, among others. So I say, let's take all that love and point it back to its source. When you love yourself, your whole being shines with health and vitality.

You have energy to exchange love with the world. Neuroplasticity is the technology behind self-love. The power to choose love in the midst of negativity and pain is yours. Self-love works. Try it. Let me know how it goes.

Section Three

NAMASTE

To the Light in you, I bow.

You Are Love

You are Love.

You are born to Love.

You were born to heal any part of you that is gripped by the illusion that you are not Love and not here to exchange Love.

Make no mistake, you were born to heal the corrosive energy that makes you believe, feel, and sense that you are anything other than the most Supreme, Intelligent, Magnificent, Ever-Wonderful Love that surges, pulsates, and expands as the throb of the Universal Heart. This is who you are and why you here.

At your core and at your soul level, you know who you are and why you here. Now, what is the unique way for you to express your Essence in this lifetime? Formulas and philosophies are helpful at the outset of an undertaking. They help stabilize the mind's quandary of "What's happening to me?" as new realms of consciousness burst forward from a previously unawakened state. But no formula or philosophy that you adopt or follow will ultimately fulfill your Divine destiny. The only way to align with your Divine Essence is to know It directly and allow It to guide you spontaneously moment by moment. Said simply, Live from your heart. To live from the Presence of your Divine Heart is to be of the highest service to humanity and the planet. From that Presence, real and lasting change organically matures.

Living from your heart is a process of refinement that requires dedication, discipline and Grace. It is not a simple declaration such as, "I am Divine and I choose to live that." To serve others from the space of the Universal Heart is a commitment to go within, to steep in the inner Light and purify that, which obscures the luminosity of your True Nature. It is a journey you are already undertaking.

You will be supported through life's challenges the more consciously you allow Grace to support you, especially in the moments when you feel afraid. The great traverse across the landscape of consciousness requires courage, fortitude, and Grace. The one who makes this journey in an accelerated fashion learns to cooperate with the impulses of the Universe and most efficaciously extract the nectar, joy, and bliss from life.

You are born into bliss. Love is the medium that facilitates the burgeoning forth of Love in all things sentient and non-sentient. Go forth into the unknown, and discover the powerful companion of Grace all around you!

Born to Heal

You are born to heal. At the highest level of evolution the awareness arises: *I am the creator of my life. Every nuance of my circumstance is my creation.* If that is true, then what is it that I am born to heal? You are born to heal any idea that is in opposition to the above realization. Your mind might be saying, *Luke, You're nuts! I didn't choose my family. I didn't choose this body or these diseases. I didn't choose this circumstance. You're really out there buddy!* I may be, but I'm not putting on an act. What I'm sharing here is my life, my work. And I've seen these teachings and practices transform people's lives.

Popular spirituality teaches us that in any given moment you have two choices, either resist what is arising or surrender to it; choose it, and give yourself to whatever is in front of you. In a sense, this teaching instructs you to practice the highest level of awareness. The irony is that the deepest part of you already knows that you are the creator of your life. The dis-ease is the game of choosing life as it is and then resisting it, back and forth, to-and-fro, again and again, as circumstances change, which they always do.

Evolution is the growing sobriety of the notion that not only did you choose your life, you are creating it. And as you sober up to the reality that you are indeed the creator, you assume the power—and albeit, perhaps the initial terror—of consciously creating your life. The creative impulse that arises into thought and transforms into word and action is the very seed of reality birthing. You are the creator who is healing the sense of separation from your primordial creative self. You are already free. You are simply playing the game of being small, stuck, and holding on to a finite level of responsibility because it feels safer, more familiar, than a reality that is continually expanding.

Anything you want is within your grasp. Though life is not necessarily about acquiring *things* with your creative power, things can make the journey more enjoyable—to an extent. Ultimately, all anyone really wants is Love. Love is the deepest of all desires. And it is a very pure one. Life is about helping others realize the game they are playing. Loving yourself through your resistance to what is, is the shortcut to freedom. To paraphrase Marianne Williamson, our deepest fear is not death; it is moving into the unknown recesses of ourselves to behold how powerful we are. That power can make this planet a utopia and it can be done without the game of hurting one another. It is time to take up your power and use it to awaken all beings into a culture founded in the highest virtues of who we are. This is the work. This is the healing we are born to do.

LORD OF HEROES

The one who makes the great traverse across the vast ocean of consciousness in all its facets of luminosity—from twilight to darkness—emerges, stripped down as an essential, refined, utterly clarified vessel of Grace. That one is the Lord of Heroes. To consciously engage with healing, to take up the responsibility to examine your mortality, to choose life in all its beauty and vulnerability; to reach through great challenges, adversity, and against all odds, requires the heart of a lion. The world calls on each of us to be courageous beyond our fears; to move into the unknown and on the other side, find a strength we didn't know was there.

Each organ system embodies a Heart-centered virtue. The heart is the intuitive Truth receptor. The lungs embolden gratitude for the preciousness of life. The liver opens up to deep abiding goodness in all beings. The spleen gives you the ability to truly value yourself and offer your love in an honorable dignified exchange with others. The kidneys provide the will power to face the darkness in life and emerge ever wiser and lighter.

No matter how grim the outer circumstances of life seem, you always have choice to further engrain a limited point of view or bring forward the Light of the Heart and see what good can come from it. You can create positive patterns and habits for healing and freedom for yourself and the world.

Ultimately, healing is a matter of choice. It is a great challenge to choose Love when the negative addictive patterns of diminishment whisper, "I'm not worth it. What do I know anyway?" You can make huge gains in your capacity to hold Universal Love when you choose Love, especially when dark or doubting tendencies of the mind flare up.

Whether you are aware that you are on a path of growth and evolution or not, Universal Love continues to serve up life lessons to help you grow and open your heart. At some point on your journey you will wonder, "There must be an easier way to navigate through life. Do I have to get my butt kicked so hard in order to grow?" The answer of course is No. There is a way to learn and grow that is smooth and efficacious. Like anything, it requires some regular attention and practice. Every negative and limiting habit can be replaced with a life-enhancing, love-affirming one that gradually feels more easy, effortless, and automatic. Humans are teachable creatures. Healing initially requires some effort. Later, it feels more like taking a shower or brushing your teeth.

Growing the luminous fire of the Cosmic Heart within you is possible, probable, and sequential. Just as there is a sequence to the occlusion of the Light of your heart, there is a sequence to ignite the inner fire of Supreme Love. My job is to let you know that it's possible to heal, and so I offer to help you accomplish the healing you commit to. In fact, healing is pretty fun, once you partner with the Universe.

I offer my friendship and my service as a trail guide on your journey. When you are sad, I will practice gratitude with you. When you forget your value, I will point out your worth. When you fail, I will encourage you to get up and try again. When you are afraid, I will remind you of your wisdom. When you feel all alone, I will show you the door to your heart. Ultimately this great traverse is a solo journey, a hero's journey if you will. The strength and skills needed are waiting inside you to be developed. I will support you and accompany you where, when, and how I can. There will be leaps that you will make alone, but I will cheer you on as you jump, and welcome you when you land.

You are more soul than you are body. Take care of your body as much as you need to in order to fulfill your curriculum, but do not be obsessed with your physical health. You are here to learn your lessons and evolve. Just as all forms in Nature have a growth and decay cycle, the body will decline. Follow your heart. Love your heart. Care for your heart. It will lead you well if you let It, and that guidance and learning will transcend your body's role as a teacher.

There are aspects of life that are unexplainable, tragedies that defy reason and go against all the magnificence, beauty, and dignity of life. At some point, life demands a warrior spirit. Life requires you to summon the courage and strength to face the most awful and horrific. The Light is for healing. The Light is not for you to hide out and escape life's pains. The Light is a refuge that rejuvenates you. Universal Love exists to uplift the people and places that are enshrouded in depression. Healing requires massive courage. Healing calls on you to be a leader, to wield the power of Universal Love into the world.

You are born to heal and share your Light with all. I implore you to take up meditation, breathwork, and any other practices that serve the burgeoning of your Spirit. The practices will strengthen and protect you. They will embolden the Divine Light within you as an authoritative guide and source of Grace. The practices will open an unlimited resource of healing for you to share with others.

Wherever you are on the path of healing and awakening is the perfect place. Every time you choose to think, speak, and take actions that are life affirming, you increase the flow of Universal Love through you. You are the Lord of Heroes, the one who vibrates Universal Light into the world.

Thank you for choosing to further open and trust Love. You make a difference every time you do. I love you when you soar. I love you when you fall. No matter what you say or do, my Love will never stop flowing towards you. I see your Light and the dwindling of insecurity. I choose to focus on that Light and am eager to watch it grow.

My whole heart full of Cosmic Love to you...Luke

THE ARGUMENT OF NATURE

Follow Nature.

As long as the sun shines, the rain falls, and the world spins, you will heal, physically, mentally, emotionally, and spiritually.

The pace of nature is elegant. The night-blooming jasmine emits her intoxicating fragrance hours after dusk. The desert rose curls centripetally inwards as the moon rises, with the peaking of the sun, the desert rose uncoils white spindles of fleshy petals reaching towards the sun's rays.

The timing of Nature is exquisite.

Gradual, steady, Nature displays her power, beauty and force with rhythmic bursts. The ocean tide steadily rises and subsides, undulating with the exact calculation of the magnetism of the moon.

We can count on Nature because She is true to Her Self. She honors her pace.

I notice the opposite phenomenon in myself at times and in our world. Rushing to work, high stepping from patient to patient, scarfing down lunch with minimal enjoyment. The pace of Nature is forgotten, and my energy, inspiration, and enjoyment, wane. How do I become steady, consistent, and strong? Watch the old growth Douglas fir. Year after year, from the heartwood, concentric circles overlay themselves upon one another. Five hundred years later, the great-grandfather tree wraps itself in strength. I can learn a lot from Nature.

How do you shift from dis-ease to ease … with lasting improvement? Do it like Nature.

I can't argue with Nature. Nature is steady. Disconnection from Nature is always at the source of disease, and in order to correct it, we must reconnect to our source—to Nature.

We forget we are Nature too. Like plants and animals, we are born of natural elements and stardust. We come from Nature, and we will return to Nature.

How do you heal the afflictions of worldly life? Connect with the Nature in you. I'm not talking necessarily about forests, flowers, and water here—although they are allies, to be certain. What I'm getting at is forming a connection to your Natural rhythms. Not the rhythms of work life, home life, or evening traffic. I'm talking about your own inner rhythm. Your innate, elemental, intuitive, soul rhythm. The rhythm that is at the very core of you and that is intrinsically connected with the One.

Nature freely and spontaneously seeks to express through you. Where do you block, impede, go unconscious, and on automatic to your Nature? Do you know what I'm referring to? Nature is always making a ploy to remind you to sync up with Her.

Are you in sync with that pulsation?

Healing happens when we align with the undulating surge of life force. We are not meant to operate at one hundred percent output all of the time. The life wave rises powerfully forth and surges to its crest towards heaven; gently, the life wave coalesces back to its source. The intercostal muscles contract and draw the ribs in all direction. The lungs fill with life-giving oxygen. Exhale, and the ribs retract. On and on, Nature shows its awesome power. When we are not careful with nature, She reminds us with illness.

How can we more fully attune to Nature? This is our constant inquiry.

Healing. You can disagree with science, religion, politics, and so on, but Nature... Nature is its own authority. And you are Nature.

THE VISION

In the midst of this marvelous journey, family is most important. I have a vision of all men, women, and children, regardless of belief systems, economic status, or ethnic background, living together as family. We respect each other, and the felt presence of Love flows from heart to heart unimpeded. We have passionate arguments, infused with anger, sadness, and fear, supported by a foundation of love and admiration. There is no war, bombs, killing, abuse, or crime. We work as family to rear our children and heal wounds of the past. As we look into one another's eyes, we see the Light of ourselves reflected back. Gratitude for all life and creation is the value that grows all our institutions. We know that we are connected, and our future is interdependent.

We live sustainably with the earth. Clean water and air is abundant to all. Community oriented transportation fueled by renewable clean fuels are the norm. No one starves from hunger. People own how food is produced, not corporations. Most food is organic. People eat food grown in the regions in which they live and in the seasons of their lives.

Massive creativity, collaboration, and expression abound. A new rule orders commerce. Capitalism, socialism, or communism no longer govern trade. The best aspects of each, and a new value system, has emerged out of heart-centered values that naturally inspire people to develop and bring forward their unique skills and contributions for the betterment of all.

This reality is here now, moving into the foreground of life. People like you and me see the Universal Family emerging. There is great work to do. Each one of us is needed.

Wherever you are, I am thinking of you with Love in my heart.

I can feel Grace moving between us and out through the Universe. I am happy now as I watch this brilliant and luminous Light intensify, and I know it won't be long until the vision of the Universal family is fully realized. The full power and freedom of Universal Love can be known by each one of us. No particular group of people, race, religion or ethnicity has more of a right to this knowledge. Universal Love belongs to all.

Love is Free! Love Rules!

Love is You! Love is Me!

We are One!

We are One with Spirit!

Appendix I

Healer Studies

Healer Studies is another way you can put into action the exercises and teachings from this book. Everyone is a healer. Everyone heals. Your presence is healing. The capacity for your healing presence can increase. You don't have to be a professional healer to take Healer Studies. All you need is the desire to help other's heal. By healing yourself, your ability to hold space for different types of stagnant energy increases, and you will be able to help people just by being with them. If you want to make healing work a profession or part of a profession, then Healer Studies will support that too.

Healer Studies teaches you to develop a relationship with your inner healer as you learn to facilitate healing sessions for others. You discover practices and tools to serve the world with the intention to raise the vibration of Universal Love. You'll understand how to create environments for others to experience a connection with the Universe. Healer Studies is for anyone who feels called to bring more depth and inspiration into his or her professional and personal life and have more fun with the people you love.

Holding a healing space is a high honor. The healer heals by looking at his or her own reflection with every interaction. By being vulnerable, the healer inspires vulnerability, which acts as a bridge for Grace to heal. Healing is innate. It's always happening. The Universe impels each of us deeper into our Essence. By feeling into the pulls and nudges of the Universe through your body and life, you learn to cooperate with Universal guidance. You heal the sense of wounded separation from Love. Healing is the evolving and deepening realization that you are whole, complete, and perfect, exactly as you are right now. There is nothing to fix or change, only this moment to embrace and unconditionally love.

The breath is the first part of your being effected during stress or trauma. You hold your breath, or breathe shallowly or rapidly when something catches you by surprise. If you don't make time to process the stressor, you store the imprint of the event in your physical tissues. The breath is a powerful modulator to get people out of their habitual ways of running energy and become aware of the stagnant patterns that limit their experience of Universal Love. In the same way that the breath facilitates prolonging illness, in Training, we use the breath to free up the moments of past pain and stress, be it emotional or physical.

The first course in the Healer Studies series is called Nourishing the Healer, and it consists of five modules that can be taken in any order. The focus of this series is the interrelationship of the spiritual, energetic, and physiological functions of the five major organs of the body as dictated by the Taoist healing tradition: the heart, lungs, liver, spleen, and kidneys. After completing any one class, you will be able to offer healing sessions to others. Upon completion of the entire series, you will receive a Healer Studies Certification in Nourishing the Healer.

Nourishing the Healer

Enter the Field of the Heart is the first module of Nourishing the Healer. Focused on the heart system, this class examines what it means to hold space. Whatever shows up in any arena of your life is what you hold space for. This part of the class explores ways to make room for the Universe to move through all aspects of your life. The class continues with how to create layers of sacred space, pulling from your own lineage traditions, and teaching you prayers and ceremony to acknowledge the presence of the Universe in your life and work. You will work in partners and learn the initial stages of how to facilitate healing for others through the breathwork meditation. Throughout the Healer Studies Series, you will learn tools and methods to create a safe, potent space for others to have an experience of their Divinity. A major component of all the Healer Studies Classes is self cultivation. I will revisit seated meditation throughout the course as the principle way for you to cultivate the presence of Universal Love through your being. Enter the Field of the Heart delves into developing your intuition. The course will help you refine your subtle sense capacities to hear, feel, sense, see, and know deeper layers of truth in your life.

The Power of Embodiment is the second level of Nourishing the Healer Series focused on the lungs. This class delves into the power of skillfully speaking your truth especially in the relationships that are the most challenging. This class continues the emphasis on self-cultivation with the practices of seated meditation, and layers in more practice with breathwork facilitation. Energetically the lungs provide the sense of your spirit being embodied. You will learn methods to track aspects of your spirit that have left (and leave your body under trauma and duress) and learn to reintegrate these aspects in a way that feels safe and whole. A major component of all the Healer Studies Classes is self-cultivation. We dive deeper into seated meditation throughout the course as the principle way for you to cultivate the presence of Universal Love through your being. The Power of Embodiment looks at how and when to transform the energy of control into letting go and forgiveness as powerful frequencies for healing.

Open to Your Divine Purpose is the third module of the Nourishing the Healer Series, which is focused on the liver. What is your divine purpose? What has the Universe intended for you to offer this lifetime? This course examines how to align with your

Divine purpose. What does it feel like when you are aligned with the Universe? What does it feel like when you are not aligned with the Universe? Open to Your Divine purpose looks at your relationship to anger and how to use anger as a powerful ally to align with your purpose and actualize your dreams. This class asks, "How do you find flow and ease in the midst of stress, fatigue and challenge?" We'll cover more subtleties of seated meditation throughout the course as the principal way for you to cultivate the presence of Universal Love through your being. As you facilitate breathwork, you will support your class partners to connect with any pieces of the past or future that feel fragmented, in order to bring healing and wholeness to the present moment.

Embrace Universal Community is the fourth module of Nourishing the Healer, and is focused on the spleen. The spleen teaches us how to relate to others and to give and receive love and respect in relationships. In this course, you will learn how to facilitate breathwork in groups and lead healing work in community. A major component of all the Healer Studies Classes is self cultivation. We'll revisit seated meditation throughout the course as the principle way for you to cultivate the presence of Universal Love through your being. Embrace Universal Community looks into the tendency to ingratiate, and examines the archetype of the wounded healer, who gives without refueling his or her own cup. You will learn to connect with the energy of the Earth as a powerful ally for nourishing yourself and others.

Facing the Darkness, the Warrior Within is the fifth module of Nourishing the Healer, and it is focused on the kidneys. The kidneys are said to be the container for your life lessons. Ultimately, spiritual practices are designed for you to build the strength needed to face the darkest parts of yourself. In Facing the Darkness, the Warrior Within, you will learn to work with your darkest fears, as well as sexual energy, and what the Buddhist tradition calls the Rakshasic energies–possession of dark forces. As you gain skill in working with your own dark side, you will be able to support others through these most difficult spaces to heal. You will work with the breath to guide others into and through some of these spaces and help connect the darkness to the light.

Appendix II

The Roaring Silence of the Heart Meditation Retreats

Seated meditation is a practice that focuses on easing the deep accretions from past suppression. I've designed the Roaring Silence of the Heart Meditation Retreat to be a comprehensive introduction and immersion into the practice of meditation, perfect for a new comer, and equally potent for the seasoned practitioner. You will thoroughly learn how to meditate correctly to bring forward the experience of enlightenment.

In a short period of time, with regular practice, you will witness your progress on the path that will translate into you being more effective in your career, relationships, finances, and so on. This is also a practice for people who want to develop their spiritual lives and who want to be effective in the real world. I love these retreats. I've watched some of the most stuck people transform as a result of meditation. To truly learn to meditate and be able to replicate the experience of deep meditation on your own, coming to one of these retreats is essential. I whole-heartedly encourage you to join me for an ecstatic experience of healing, insight, and love.

Luke Adler

Appendix III

Universal Warrior of Compassion Meditation Training

The power of healing that occurs in your presence is in proportion to the quality of space you hold for the Universe to move through you. Real transformation, or lasting healing, occurs because people experience a new possibility for their lives. Something new cannot be something recycled, rebranded, or reformatted from something in the past. To speak plainly, something new has to come from God. To bring true inspiration forward, first go within.

The intention of the Universal Warrior of Compassion Meditation Training is to prepare you to practice healing work in the world, whether it be professional or more informally. Learn to establish a regular practice that feeds your work to uplift the planet. To offer service over time, your mind, body, and spirit must be tended to. You need a practice that cleanses and releases the psychic accumulations of interacting with the external world. You need a practice that strengthens your central nervous system to hold increasing potencies of Universal Light. You need a practice that you can dive into and be rejuvenated, refreshed and ready for the next task, a practice that transforms you into a Universal Warrior of Compassion. Wield the full power of the Light through you and hold a space where others can come and experience of their own inner Light.

ACKNOWLEDGEMENTS

My first teachers were my parents, and they continue to push the ceiling on creativity, transformation, and healing. Dad, without you, I would likely be unexpressed, afraid to follow my dreams, and clueless about how to make an impact in the world. It is all the more difficult to be a sensitive, spiritual man while being effective in the world we live in. Thank you for accepting me as I am and working with me to be a warrior with my love and vision. Mom, without you, my heart would be cold. I might be in prison and certainly not have the capacity to know the deep love of the Universe. You continually have pointed me back towards the great Self. You've taught me how to drink from the well of immortality until I had tasted so much that nothing could tear me away from it. Mom and Dad, you are at the source of everything I do. You imbue all of my actions with power, love, and Grace. As I chose you to be my parents, I thank you for choosing me to be your son, a gift I will never be able to repay, but will always strive for in everything I think, feel, say, and do. I love you.

A special thank you to Dr. Yvonne Farrell for sparking my love of Chinese medicine and introducing me to the profound esoteric principles of this powerful tradition. Thank you for teaching me to value myself as a healer and a teacher; for showing me your vulnerability; and for teaching me that it is okay to receive love, and that it is, in fact, essential, to heal. Lastly, thank you for being my editor for the soundness of theory presented in this book and for encouraging me to write from my heart. I miss you. I love you, and I always treasure the opportunity to be in your presence.

Early in my career, I longed for a way to do deeper work, to provide a space for people to experience the power of love. For this, I thank David Elliott. When I met you, I knew I had found the tools and the mentorship I was looking for. I voraciously ate up as much as I could handle, and you assured me that the Universe would teach me all I needed to know and more. You were right. This book would have never happened without your encouragement to share my gifts, deliver my message, and stretch my heart as wide open as possible. You are a profound healer and teacher. I hear you in the hummingbirds, hawks, and osprey. Thank you for showing me that Love is always speaking to me if I'm willing to listen. I look forward to seeing you soon. Love and respect...Luke

Writing a book is an intimidating process, especially when the time comes to think about how to make it camera ready and deliver it to the world. Gali Kronenburg, you are truly a gifted editor. You appeared in my life exactly at the right time to bring this book to the next level. You helped me distinguish my voice and my audience and encouraged me to keep writing with ease and breez-i-ness. Thank you for your friendship on this path. I look forward to working with you on the next one.

Finishing this book was at times daunting, at times overwhelming, and at other times, thrilling. Helen Rosenau, you are an angel sent to encourage me to finish my bell lap. You are an outstanding editor. Thank you for loving this book and helping me "put it out there." You are a dear friend, a great writer, and a companion on this mysterious journey. I love you, and so look forward to working with you soon.

To my copy editor Jean Kang, and my friends Justin Overdevest, Josh Manders, Sarah Adler, and Paula Taylor, thank you for being the last eyes on the book. As I came into my bell lap, it was hard to trust that I could catch the final edits. Thank you for bringing *Born to Heal* as close to a smooth read as possible. Love and Gratitude to each of you.

To my wife Emily: marriage is a gift that you give me everyday with every kiss, touch, and kind word you share. I know I am a lucky man. You are my life partner, and equally important, my spiritual partner. Thank you for picking up the slack in our household to enable me the time and energy to write this book. I know you work hard as a mom, a therapist, and a teacher. You are a wonderful wife. I cherish you. I adore you. I am here for you. I will walk into the scary places with you and breathe deeply with your hand in mine. You and Sona Bear are the most important part of my life, and I pledge to always show you that in my actions and in the texture of our love.

To my beloved Guru. From the days I first laid eyes on you as a young teenager to becoming a man whose mission it is to share the Love you first awakened within me, the greatest debt I have to repay is to you. I have searched for thousands of years for your beautiful face, and in this lifetime, I saw the face that ended my search. Through your Grace, my sense of unworthiness, fear, shame, guilt, and rage dissolved into an ocean of Cosmic Love. You sow the seeds of all flowers. You are the Queen of the moon. You are the primordial sound of Om. You are the prayer and the one being prayed to. You are the heart and the pulsation. You are Shiva. You are my beloved. Nothing in this world exists without you. Thank you for being the pen that writes and the paper I write upon. May this book add to the momentum of ascension for the planet! May it be infused with your Divine power and beauty! May it carry the weight of the this sacred lineage! May it honor you to be my Guru! Thank you, Divine Goddess, for showing me the true purpose of life and giving me a way to share that with others. Wherever my mind goes, may your essence be there. Wherever I bow my head, may your lotus feet be there! Koti Koti Pranam Maha Devi SGMKJ!

Lastly to Juliette Mulgrew, Melinda Wheeler, and Shea Ford, who produced events, products, retreats, trainings, purchased herbs, supplements, planted gardens, harvested herbs, wrote formulas, booked flights, watched the baby, managed the schedule, cared for patients, and all the other one hundred details it took to manage a practice that continues to burst at the seams, from the bottom of my heart and the depths of my soul, THANK YOU SO MUCH. Together, we have supported thousands of people to heal the common cold, infertility, the effects of chemotherapy, radical surgery, and radiation, joint pain, depression, anxiety, and so much more. We have held hands for the final breaths of a life and for the first breaths of a life. Ultimately, we've helped connect people more deeply into their hearts and the things that matter most to them. You have each held the lineage of the Divine Sequence Goddess. Without your expertise, precision, kindness, and ability to find a way, none of this would be possible. You are my charioteers. I love each one of you. You are each extraordinary healers in your own right. I am so excited to watch you impact this world through your careers and your amazing hearts. Just as you have helped make my dreams come true, I will always be here for your dreams. Love... Luke

Bibliography

Anderson, Richard. *Cleanse and Purify Thyself*, Medford, OR: Christobe Publishing, 1987.

Beinfield, Harriet, and Efrem Korngold. *Between Heaven and Earth*. New York: Random House Publishing Group, 1992.

Bennett, Peter and Stephen Barrie. *7-Day Detox Miracle*. New York: Three Rivers Press, 2001.

Bryant, Edwin F. *The Yoga Sutras of Patanjali*. New York: North Point Press, 2009.

Carson, David and Jamie Sams. *Medicine Cards*. New York: St. Martins Press, 1988.

De Angelis, Barbara. *Soul Shifts*. United States: Hay House, 2015.

Doidge, Norman. *The Brain that Changes Itself*. New York: Penguin Group, 2007.

Elliott, David. *The Reluctant Healer*. Los Angeles: Hawk Press, 2005.

Elliott, David. *Healing*. Los Angeles: Hawk Press, 2010

Farrell, Yvonne. "Treating Suffering and Non-responders." Lecture presented at LA Herbs and Acupuncture, Los Angeles, July 14, 2014.

Philip B. Kurland and Ralph Lerner, eds., *The Founders' Constitution* (Chicago: University of Chicago Press, 1987), accessed February 28, 2010, *http://press-pubs.uchicago.edu/founders/*.

Fruehauf, Heiner. "All Disease Comes From the Heart." *Jade Institute*, accessed April 26, 2013, *https://www.jadeinstitute.com/jade/disease-comes-from-the-heart.php*

Gerson, Charlotte. "Gerson Insititute" *Scientific basis of Coffee Enemas*, accessed August 12, 2013, *http://gerson.org/pdfs/How_Coffee_Enemas_Work.pdf*

Jarrett, Lonny. *Nourishing Destiny*. Stockbridge: Spirit Path Press, 2001.

Jacob, Jeffrey H. *The Acupuncturists Clinical Handbook*. New York: Integrative Wellness Inc, 2003.

Kendall, Donald E. *Dao of Chinese Medicine*. New York: Oxford University Press, 2002.

Lewis, Randine. *The Fertile Soul,* New York: Atria Books, 2007.

Lewis, Randine. *The Infertility Cure*, New York: Little Brown and Company, 2004.

Lewis, Randine. "9 Heart Pains." *The Fertile Soul, http://thefertile-soul.com/infertility_cure/?p=443.*

Liangyue, Deng et al. *Chinese Acupuncture and Moxibustion*. Beijing: Foreign Languages Press, 1987.

Maciocia, Giovanni. *The Foundations of Chinese Medicine*. China: Churchill Livingstone, 1989.

Manné, Joy. *Conscious Breathing*. Berkeley: North Atlantic Books, 2004.

Moskowits, Michael. "Changing the Brain in Pain." *Bay Area Pain Medical Associates, http://www.bayareapainmedical.com/page1/page18/files/brain-training-newsletter.pdf*

Pomroy, Haylie. *The Fast Metabolism Diet*. New York: Crown Publishing, 2013.

Perlmutter, David. *Brain Maker*. New York: Little Brown and Company, 2015

Williamson, Marianne. *A Return to Love*. New York: Harper Collins, 1992.

Yuen, Jeffrey. "Essential Oils and Shen." Lecture presented at the Hilton Garden Inn, Marina Del Ray, CA, June 23, 2007.

Yuen, Jeffrey. "Male Infertility." Lecture presented at the Hilton, Financial District, San Francisco. June 21, 2014.

Yuen, Jeffrey. "Personality Through the Pulse." Lecture presented at the Hilton Garden Inn, Emeryville, CA. June 4, 2013.

To Learn More

For more healing resources visit www.lukeadlerhealing.com.

Check out the events page for upcoming Healer Studies events, Meditation Retreats, and other offerings at Luke Adler Healing.

See the Products page for the latest guided meditations. Some are free, and others available for purchase.

Sign into the resources page with the password: "healing" to find healing resources to support your journey. Visit regularly for inspiration and opportunities to connect with like-hearted souls.

Hope to see you soon.

with love,

Luke Adler

Made in the USA
San Bernardino, CA
12 May 2016